Becoming an
Architect

W9-CEL-735

M.

You are the best. Thanks for making fit position easy. Do keep in touch as you find what.

Yours [signature] 5/08

Other Titles in the Series

BECOMING A GRAPHIC DESIGNER, 3RD EDITION
Steven D. Heller and Teresa Fernandes

BECOMING A PRODUCT DESIGNER
Bruce Hannah

BECOMING AN INTERIOR DESIGNER
Christine Piotrowski, ASID, IIDA

Also from Wiley

THE SURVIVAL GUIDE TO ARCHITECTURAL INTERNSHIP AND CAREER DEVELOPMENT
Grace H. Kim, AIA

For this and other books for emerging architects, visit www.wiley.com/go/youngarchitect.

A GUIDE TO CAREERS IN DESIGN

Becoming an
Architect

Lee W. Waldrep, Ph.D.

WILEY

JOHN WILEY & SONS, INC.

This book is printed on acid-free paper. ♾

Copyright © 2006 by John Wiley & Sons, Inc., Hoboken New Jersey. All rights reserved.

Published simultaneously in Canada

No part of this publication may be reproduced, stored in a retrieval system, or transmitted in any form or by any means, electronic, mechanical, photocopying, recording, scanning, or otherwise, except as permitted under Section 107 or 108 of the 1976 United States Copyright Act, without either the prior written permission of the Publisher, or authorization through payment of the appropriate per-copy fee to the Copyright Clearance Center, 222 Rosewood Drive, Danvers, MA 01923, (978) 750-8400, fax (978) 646-8600, or on the web at www.copyright.com. Requests to the Publisher for permission should be addressed to the Permissions Department, John Wiley & Sons, Inc., 111 River Street, Hoboken, NJ 07030, (201) 748-6011, fax (201) 748-6008, e-mail: http:// www.wiley.com/go/ permission.

Limit of Liability/Disclaimer of Warranty: While the publisher and the author have used their best efforts in preparing this book, they make no representations or warranties with respect to the accuracy or completeness of the contents of this book and specifically disclaim any implied warranties of merchantability or fitness for a particular purpose. No warranty may be created or extended by sales representatives or written sales materials. The advice and strategies contained herein may not be suitable for your situation. You should consult with a professional where appropriate. Neither the publisher nor the author shall be liable for any loss of profit or any other commercial damages, including but not limited to special, incidental, consequential, or other damages.

For general information about our other products and services, please contact our Customer Care Department within the United States at (800) 762-2974, outside the United States at (317) 572-3993 or fax (317) 572-4002.

Wiley also publishes its books in a variety of electronic formats. Some content that appears in print may not be available in electronic books. For more information about Wiley products, visit our web site at www.wiley.com.

Library of Congress Cataloging-in-Publication Data:

Waldrep, Lee W.
  Becoming an architect : a guide to careers in design / Lee W. Waldrep.
    p. cm.
  Includes bibliographical references and index.
  ISBN-13: 978-0-471-70954-1
  ISBN-10: 0-471-70954-9 (pbk.)
  1. Architecture — Vocational guidance. I. Title.
  NA1995.W35 2006
  720.23—dc22
              2005034526

Printed in the United States of America

10 9 8 7 6 5 4 3 2 1

To Cassidy, Karli, Anslie,
and my loving wife, Sherry

Contents

Foreword   xi

Preface   xiii

Acknowledgments   xv

Chapter **One**

The Definition of an Architect   1

What Do Architects Do?   2

Why Architecture?   4

Is Architecture for You?   4

QUESTION — What Is Architecture?   5

Profile of the Profession   31

    Diversity   32

QUESTION — What Are the Most
Important Skills an Architect Needs
to Be Successful?   33

Chapter **Two**

The Education of an Architect   69

Preparation: Pre–High School   70

    Toys   70

    Books   70

    Activities   70

    *Selected Books on Architecture for
Children*   71

    Resources   71

Preparation: High School   72

    Academic Coursework   72

    Exploration   73

    Visits   74

    Summers   74

    After-school Programs   75

QUESTION — What Advice Would You
Provide to Someone Who Wants to Be
an Architect?   76

Routes to an Accredited Degree   94

    Bachelor of Architecture (B.Arch.)   94

    Pre-professional Bachelor of Science (B.S.)
      and Master of Architecture (M.Arch.)   94

    Undergraduate Degrees (B.A./B.S.)
      in Fields Other than Architecture
      and Master of Architecture (M.Arch.)   95

    Doctor of Architecture (D.Arch.)   96

    Post-professional Degrees   96

Decision-making Process   96

You   97

Institution   98

Architecture Program   99

Resources   102

    Promotional Materials, Videos,
      Catalogs, and Websites   102

    Guide to Architecture Schools   102

    New England Career Day in
      Architecture   102

    Campus Visits   102

    Admissions Counselor/Administrator   103

    Students, Faculty, Alumni, and
      Architects   103

    NAAB Architecture Program Report
      (APR)/Visiting Team Report (VTR)   103

    Ranking of Architecture Programs   103

Application Process   104

    Application   104

    Personal Statement   104

    Test Scores   105

    Transcripts   105

    Portfolio   106

    Recommendations   106

You Are an Architecture Student   117

    NAAB Student Performance Criteria   117

    Courses   121

    Architecture Electives: A Sample   123

Academic Enrichment   124

    Independent Study   124

    Minors/Certificates   124

    Double Major/Degrees/Dual Degrees   124

    Off-campus Programs (Semester
      Abroad/Exchange Program)   125

    Lecture Series   126

    Community Service   126

    Mentoring   126

    Student Organizations   126

Conclusion   127

Chapter *Three*

**The Experience of an
Architect   157**

Gaining Experience as a Student   158

    Shadow   158

    Volunteer   158

    Research with Faculty   158

    Externship   159

    Internship   159

    Cooperative Education   159

    Career-related Experience
      (Part-time/Summer)   161

    Full-time Positions   161

QUESTION—What Do You Look
for in Hiring a New Designer?   162

A.R.C.H.I.T.E.C.T   190

    Assessment   190

    Research   190

    Connections   190

    Help   190

    Interim Positions   191

    Tools   191

    Experience   192

    Commitment   192

    Transition   192

Moving toward Licensure   193

    Intern Development
      Program (IDP)   194

      Intern Development Program (IDP)
        Training Areas   195

    Architect Registration
      Examination (ARE)   196

    NCARB Certification   197

Chapter **Four**

The Careers of an Architect   223

Career Designing   224

Assessing   224

Values   224

Interests   225

Skills   225

Exploring   226

Decision-making   227

Planning   229

Career Paths   230

The Careers of an Architect   232

Chapter **Five**

The Future of the Architecture Profession   261

QUESTION: What Do You See as the Future for the Architecture Profession?   262

Appendix **A**

The Resources of an Architect   271

Collateral Organizations   271

Architecture-related Associations   272

Associations — Related Careers   274

Architectural History   274

Construction   274

Design — Graphic, Industrial, Furniture, Lighting   275

Planning/Landscape Architecture   276

Technical/Engineering   276

Interior Design   277

Historic Preservation   278

Institutions Dedicated to Architecture   278

Community Service   279

Recommended Reading   280

Websites   283

Appendix **B**

NAAB/CACB-Accredited Architecture Programs in the United States and Canada   285

Appendix **C**

Career Profiles   293

Index   297

Foreword

THIS BOOK IS A COMPREHENSIVE guide to the sometimes mysterious process of becoming and being an architect. It is an important and appropriate resource for anyone considering architecture as a career, including high school students, college undergraduates, and individuals considering architecture as a second career.

The author, Lee W. Waldrep, Ph.D., has wisely included within these pages the voices of many architects and emerging professionals. Through their experiences the reader is exposed to the diversity of paths to becoming an architect and the variety of career paths that exist as destinations. The passion, candor, and sincerity of these forty-nine voices make the book particularly believable and engaging. Despite their range of experience, these architects speak with surprising consistency of the key characteristics of charting a successful career in architecture.

The process of becoming an architect often starts early in an individual's life and continues until the end. This is because architecture, the mother of the arts, is a discipline that cannot be completely known.

There is always more to learn, as the associated materials, methods, delivery systems, technology, and legal and risk frameworks are constantly evolving. There is always more to know, as the context and constituents of the processes and products of architecture are different with every project. There is always more to accomplish, as architects gain credibility, influence, and value in contributing their knowledge and passion to the good of society, resulting a more commodious, sustainable, and delightful world.

This book recognizes the breadth and depth of architects' responsibilities and possibilities. It recognizes that architects are uniquely placed by virtue of their education and experience to understand and mitigate the complex predicaments of the twenty-first century. This book is a fundamental beginning to a life of accomplishment as an architect.

KATE SCHWENNSEN, FAIA
2006 National President of
The American Institute of Architects
Associate Dean and Associate Professor
in the College of Design at Iowa State
University

Preface

IN SECOND GRADE, my ambition was to become a clown. Only later did I realize I wanted to become an architect. One of my older brothers first pursued architecture in college (he later switched to music). A ninth-grade drafting class was my first formal introduction to what I thought was the profession. At the same time, I had the opportunity to meet with an architect in my hometown. In high school, I interned in an architect's office, drafting and making models. All of these experiences helped me decide to pursue architecture in college.

After six years of college, two degrees at two universities, a year as national vice president of the American Institute of Architecture Students (AIAS), and three months working in a firm, I decided architecture was not a good fit for me. However, from my experiences in architecture, I realized I wanted to help others in their pursuit of becoming an architect. Thus, the idea for this book is over twenty years in development.

Becoming an Architect will help you navigate the process of becoming an architect. Its purpose is to provide you an outline of the educational process: an accredited professional degree in architecture, the experience or internship component, and the Architect Registration Exam (ARE). Further, it helps you launch your professional career in architecture.

The first chapter, "The Definition of an Architect," introduces the professional's basic duties and tasks. After reading this chapter, you will be better able to decide if you are suited to become an architect. The chapter outlines the basic skills, characteristics, attitudes, motivations, and aptitudes of architects. Finally, it provides a profile of the architecture profession.

The second chapter, "The Education of an Architect," outlines the education necessary to becoming an architect. It emphasizes that the education of an architect is lifelong and does not end with the receipt of a formal degree.

The first of the chapter's three parts focuses on preparation — the courses you can take and the activities you can pursue to prepare for an architectural education.

The second part provides insight into selecting an appropriate program in architecture. It delineates the three routes to graduation with a professional degree program. Further, it outlines the attributes — individual, institution, and academic unit — to consider when selecting a program. It also lists resources to seek when making this crucial decision.

The third part of the chapter describes the typical architecture curriculum as outlined by the criteria and conditions set forth by the National Architectural Accrediting Board (NAAB), the body that accredits degree programs in architecture.

As training is a required element of becoming an architect, the third chapter, "The Experience of an Architect," concentrates on gaining experience. First, it discusses strategies to gaining experience while in school through part-time, summer, or cooperative education opportunities. It outlines programs at various universities that expose students to the real world of architecture. An additional portion uses the acronym A.R.C.H.I.T.E.C.T. in support of the search for positions that provide useful experience.

The chapter also provides a basic overview of the Intern Development Program (IDP), a required program in almost all fifty states for documenting your experience for licensure. It outlines the training requirements, the advisory system, and the recordkeeping system. Further, the chapter briefly introduces the requirements and process of applying to take the ARE.

The fourth chapter, "The Careers of an Architect," outlines the career designing process (assessing, exploring, decision-making, and planning) and the careers available to graduates of an architectural education — both traditional and nontraditional.

Finally, the fifth chapter provides insight on the future of the architectural profession as those profiled throughout the book answer the question, "What do you see as the future for the architecture profession?"

Career profiles of architecture students, interns, educators, and practitioners appear throughout the book and are a wonderful resource for personal stories. Some profiles highlight the traditional path of an architect within a private architecture firm, while others describe related settings in which an architect might work — corporations, government agencies, and education and research. A series of pointed questions related to the profession, and the responses of those individuals profiled, are also distributed throughout.

The first of three appendixes lists resources for further information. Note especially the first five associations listed: The American Institute of Architects (AIA), American Institute of Architecture Students (AIAS), Association of Collegiate Schools of Architecture (ACSA), National Architectural Accrediting Board (NAAB), and National Council of Architectural Registration Boards (NCARB). Also included are career-related associations and other useful resources, including websites, and a list of recommended reading.

The second appendix lists institutions offering NAAB/CACB-accredited programs. The third includes those students, interns, and professionals profiled in the book.

As you will soon discover, becoming an architect is a satisfying and worthwhile endeavor. Enjoy the process of becoming and being an architect, as it will provide a long and meaningful career path for your life.

LEE W. WALDREP, Ph.D.

March 2006

Acknowledgments

WHEN I COMPLETED my doctoral degree in 1993, I stated that authoring my dissertation was the closest I would ever come to designing an architectural project. This statement remains true, but in terms of work, authoring this book far exceeds my dissertation. I still may never design a residence or a skyscraper, but I hope this book helps future architects design their careers.

Foremost, I would like to acknowledge the support of my family — Sherry, my wife, and my triplet daughters, Cassidy, Karli, and Anslie. Without their willingness to let me escape from family obligations, I would not have completed this project. I promise to be home every Saturday morning from now on.

As well, I wish to express my appreciation to the students, interns, educators, and architects profiled throughout this book, many of whom I have known throughout my career (see Appendix C). Without exception, all were more than willing participants to this project and are as much the authors of this book as I am. Thanks are also due to Brian P. Kelly, director of the Architecture Program of the School of Architecture, Planning, and Preservation at the University of Maryland, along with its faculty, staff, and students, who again supported and encouraged me.

Special kudos to the following individuals: Jenny Castronuovo, who more than assisted me with the collection of images for the book; Margaret Deleeuw and Shawna Grant, who provided insight as the manuscript was being written; Michal Seltzer, for mocking up the cover for daily inspiration; and Suzanna Wight, AIA, for referring me to many of the individuals profiled in the book. Also, I wish to express my appreciation to Dr. Kathryn Anthony, a special friend who knows all too well the struggles and joys of authoring a book. My appreciation is also extended to Grace H. Kim, AIA, a friend who recommended to Wiley that I would be a good author for this project. She was also instrumental in providing images.

Last, I wish to express my appreciation to John Czarnecki, my editor at John Wiley & Sons, for contacting me about the idea for the book and guiding me throughout the process. My thanks also to the others with whom I worked at Wiley.

Jubilee Family Resource Center, Chicago. Architect: Ross Barney + Jankowski.
Photographer: Steve Hall, Hedrich Blessing.

Chapter One

The Definition of an Architect

He looked at the granite. To be cut, he thought, and made into walls. He looked at a tree. To be split and made into rafters. He looked at a streak of rust on the stone and thought of iron ore under the ground. To be melted and to emerge as girders against the sky. These rocks, he thought, are here for me; waiting for the drill, the dynamite and my voice; waiting to be split, ripped, pounded, reborn, waiting for the shape of my hands will give to them.

AYN RAND, *THE FOUNTAINHEAD*[1]

After reading the preceding text from *The Fountainhead* by Ayn Rand, what are your thoughts and feelings? Can you relate with the main character, Howard Roark, in this passage? Are you overcome with the possibilities of creating with the materials around you?

Do you want to be an architect? Do you wish to study architecture? If your answer is yes to any of these questions, this book is for you.

What is the definition of an architect? *The American Heritage Dictionary*[2] defines *architect* as:

1. One who designs and supervises the construction of buildings or other structures.

är-kĭ-tĕkt, n. [MF architecte, fr. L architectus, fr. Gk architekton master builder, fr. Archi- + tekton builder]

Of course, this definition simply scratches the surface. Becoming and being an architect is much more. It is not the intent of this book to provide a complete overview of architecture or a full career profile; here, however, is a brief introduction to what architects do.

What Do Architects Do?

People need places in which to live, work, play, learn, worship, meet, govern, shop, eat — private and public spaces, indoors and out; rooms, buildings, and complexes; neighborhoods and towns, suburbs and cities. Architects, professionals trained in the art and science of building design and licensed

An Architect at Work.

Parthenon, Athens, Greece. Photographer: R. Lindley Vann.

to protect public health, safety, and welfare, transform these needs into concepts and then develop the concepts into building images that can be constructed by others.

In designing buildings, architects communicate between and assist those who have needs — clients, users, the public as a whole — and those who will make the spaces that satisfy those needs — builders and contractors, plumbers and painters, carpenters, and air conditioning mechanics.

Whether the project is a room or a city, a new building or the renovation of an old one, architects provide the professional services — ideas and insights, design and technical knowledge, drawings and specifications, administration, coordination, and informed decision making — whereby an extraordinary range of functional, aesthetic, technological economic, human, environmental, and safety factors is melded into a coherent and appropriate solution for the problems at hand.

This is what architects are, conceivers of buildings. What they do is to design, that is, supply concrete images for a new structure so that it can be put up. The primary task of the architect, then as now, is to communicate what proposed buildings should be and look like.... The architect's role is that of mediator between the client or patron, that is, the person who decides to build, and the work force with its overseers, which we might collectively refer to as the builder.

— Spiro Kostof[3]

Why Architecture?

Why do you desire to become an architect? Have you been building with Legos since you were two? Did a counselor suggest it to you because of a strong interest and skill in mathematics and art? Or are there other reasons? Aspiring architects cite love of drawing, creating, and designing, desire to make a difference in the community, aptitude for mathematics and science, or a connection to a family member in the profession. Whatever your reason, are you suited to become an architect?

Architect Working.

Is Architecture for You?

How do you know if the pursuit of architecture is right for you? Those within the profession suggest that if you are creative or artistic and good in mathematics and science, you may have what it takes to be a successful architect. However, Dana Cuff, author of *Architecture: The Story of Practice*, suggests it takes more:

There are two qualities that neither employers nor educators can instill and without which, it is assumed, one cannot become a "good" architect: dedication and talent.

— DANA CUFF[4]

Because of the breadth of skills and talents necessary to be an architect, you may be able to find your niche within the profession regardless. It takes three attributes to

be a successful architecture student — intelligence, creativity, and dedication — and you need any two of the three. Also, your education will develop your knowledge base and design talents.

Unfortunately, there is no magic test to determine if becoming an architect is for you. Perhaps, the most effective way to determine if you should consider becoming an architect is to experience the profession firsthand. Ask lots of questions and recognize that many related career fields might also work for you.

For the architect must, on the one hand, be a person who is fascinated by how things work and how he can make them work, not in the sense of inventing or repairing machinery, but rather in the organization of time-space elements to produce the desired results; on the other hand, he must have an above average feeling for aesthetics and quite some ability at drawing, painting, and the visual arts in general.

— EUGENE RASKIN[5]

What Is Architecture?

Architecture is the built environment, and what architects do is design the environment.

> Carol Ross Barney, FAIA
> Principal, Ross Barney + Jankowski, Inc.

Architecture is the physical and spirtual transformation of chaos into order, darkness into light, and space into place.

> Nathan Kipnis, AIA
> Principal, Nathan Kipnis Architects, Inc.

As a creative science, architecture is the marriage of art and science.

> Lisa Van Veen, Associate AIA
> Architectural Designer, Design Forward

Architecture is a dream fulfilled. Designing and creating the built environment is an opportunity to express not only hopes and dreams but also the hopes and dreams of our entire society and culture. Architecture is foremost an artistic expression. The result is an environment that provides fulfillment, blessing, and peace, the things that compose the dreams of all peoples.

> Jack Kremers, AIA
> Professor, Judson College

To me, architecture is anything that can be designed — a chair, a light fixture, a website, a logo, a building, or a city.

> William Carpenter, Ph.D., FAIA
> Associate Professor, Southern Polytechnic State University
> President, Lightroom

Here is a socially responsive definition of architecture: the making of safe, healthful, sustainable places for human use and inhabitation.

> W. Cecil Steward, FAIA, APA
> Dean Emeritus, University of Nebraska — Lincoln
> President/CEO, Josyln Castle Institute for Sustainable Communities

Architecture is an attempt to consciously control the built environment through the balanced application of art and science. Those of us who practice architecture orchestrate economics, politics, art, and technology exclusively to create objects that impact the physical world we inhabit.

> W. Stephen Saunders, AIA
> Principal, Eckenhoff Saunders Architects

Architecture is the design and construction of forms to create space.

> Margaret DeLeeuw
> Graduate, University of Maryland

Architecture is the result of all that is conceived, planned, and created by an architect. It involves taking leadership in the process of working with a client, societal, or business challenge, identifying and defining the specific problems and opportunities for that challenge, and then synthesizing them into the most basic components and developing solution alternatives. Architecture is the result of using this process under the direction of a technically knowledgeable professional.

> Randy Tharp, RA
> Senior Vice President, A. Epstein and Sons International, Inc.

Architecture is the built environments that shape the daily lives of people.

> Grace Kim, AIA
> Principal, Schemata Workshop, Inc.

Architecture is the special place, the extraordinary space that enriches our lives.

> Dianne Blair Black, AIA
> Vice President, RTKL Associates, Inc.

Architecture is the forming of space and program into an aesthetic system.

> Doug Garofalo, FAIA
> Professor, University of Illinois at Chicago
> President, Garofalo Architects

Architecture is a collaborative process, the result of which is a building, a series of buildings, or interventions in the landscape that enrich the environment.

> **Lynsey Gemmell**
> **Architect II, Holabird & Root**

Architecture is construction that embraces the aesthetic, symbolic, tectonic, and cultural characteristic that best describe a particular place, people, and epoch.

> **Robert M. Beckley, FAIA**
> **Professor and Dean Emeritus, University of Michigan**

Architecture is the shelter for human existence. The process of architecture is the blend of art and science.

> **Patricia Saldana Natke, AIA**
> **Principal and President, Urban Works, Ltd.**

Architecture is the art of designing buildings and spaces within a given set of parameters. Those parameters may include the programmatic needs of the project, the client's budget, building code regulations, and the inherent properties of the materials being used. Great architecture finds the best

solution to a design problem by using both creativity and practicality. Part sculpture, part environmental psychology, part construction technology, architecture is the combination of many separate forces into a harmonic whole.

> **Carolyn Jones, AIA**
> **Associate Principal, Callison Architecture, Inc.**

Architecture is a blend of art and science for the creation of spaces and places that elevate the human spirit.

> **Kathyrn Anthony, Ph.D.**
> **Professor, University of Illinois at Urbana-Champaign**

Architecture is the synthesis of art and science utilized to develop a solution to a challenge in the built environment.

> **Elizabeth Kalin**
> **Architectural Intern, Studio Gang Architecture**

Architecture is creating an environment within a site that composes space and creates an interesting, functional space for the user.

> **Brad Zuger**
> **Student, University of Nebraska — Lincoln**

New York City — View from Empire State Building. Photographer: Michael R. Mariano, AIA.

More than a building, architecture is beauty and function in form.

> **Christopher J. Gribbs,** Associate AIA
> Senior Director, The American Institute of Architects

Architecture is everything. It is the house in which one lives; it is the office in which one works. Architecture is the hospital in which one watches loved ones die or recover. It is the church in which people marry the people they love. Architecture is the movie theater where you had your first date. Architecture is the room you grew up in, on that quiet street in the country. It is the apartment building you lived in with your first college roommate. It is the playground where you first encountered the merry-go-round.

Architecture is in every memory you will ever have, because it is everything and everywhere. One might dare to ask, "What is *not* architecture?" At its purest, architecture is the form that follows the function.

> **Ahkilah Johnson**
> Senior Analyst, Cherokee Northeast, LLC

Architecture is, formally, the design of our built environment. Informally, it is everything else.

> **Monica Pascatore,** LEED
> Freelance Designer, P Inc.

Architecture is that form of building and place-making that elevates and illuminates the meaning of being human.

> **Joseph Bilello, Ph.D.,** AIA
> Dean, Ball State University

Architecture is the thoughtful and expert integration of aesthetics, function, and usability in buildings and facilities.

> **Lois Thibault,** RA
> Coordinator of Research, U.S. Architectural and Transportation Barriers Compliance Board (Access Board)

Architecture is the art and science of planning and designing structures and environments to house the activities of humans.

> **H. Alan Brangman,** AIA
> University Architect, Georgetown University

Grounded by a broad understanding, architecture is the conscious shaping of the mental and physical forces and relations within a specific environment to sustain and celebrate life. When entering an exemplary piece of architecture, our senses are heightened, we slow, pause, and upon reflection we are fundamentally changed.

> **Max Underwood,** AIA
> Professor, Arizona State University
> Architect and Principal, Underwood + Crisp

Architecture is the design of the built environment through the programming of needs, three-dimensional design, and the application of appropriate building technologies.

> **Eric Taylor,** Associate AIA
> Photographer, Taylor Design & Photography, Inc.

Architecture is the art of building. Simply put, architecture is those buildings or places that inspire us. Architecture is also about the act of place-making, or making one feel comfortable. Architecture is not a slave to fads or trends. It is timeless and ages gracefully. God created a beautiful earth. Man has been charged with the stewardship of the earth. Good architecture enhances God's creation.

> **Edward Shannon,** AIA
> Assistant Professor, Judson College

Architecture is the creation of habitable space where social interactions and individual functions can take place.

> **Michelle Hunter**
> Lead Designer, Garage Takeover, Discovery Channel

Interior, Johnson Wax Building, Racine, Wisconsin. Architect: Frank Lloyd Wright. Photographer: R. Lindley Vann.

Architecture is about the creative process of making and involves the many disciplines of craft and design. It touches all of us, informing and shaping the experiences of our lives in rich and meaningful ways. We cannot underestimate the human experience as part of the designed world we live in.

> **Barbi Crisp**
> **Principal, Underwood + Crisp**

Architecture is problem solving at its highest level. It is the provision of the space, the light, the shelter, and the inspiration to allow a human to grow, create, and prosper.

> **Katherine S. Proctor,** FCSI, CDT, AIA
> **Director of Facilities, Jewelry Television**

Exterior, Johnson Wax Building, Racine, Wisconsin. Architect: Frank Lloyd Wright. Photographer: R. Lindley Vann.

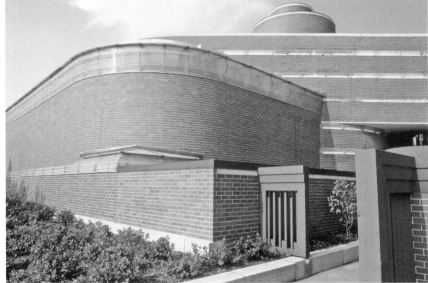

Architecture is the result of the configuration and enclosure of space, primarily for human habitation. Good architecture is that which accomplishes this result while incorporating elements of design that favorably appeal to all of the human senses and satisfies all of the needs for which the design was created.

> **Gaines Hall,** FAIA
> **Vice President, Kirkegaard & Associates**

Architecture is the combination of art and science to design spaces, whether enclosed or open to the elements, for the protection, use, and enjoyment of others.

> **F. Michael Ayles,** AIA
> **Director of Operations, Antinozzi Associates**

Architecture is the conceptual, cultural, and physical manifestation of space and time. We, as a culture, will be measured by our creativity or lack thereof, and architecture is one of the lasting measures of culture and civilization.

> **Roy Abernathy,** AIA
> **President, Jova/Daniels/Busby**

Architecture is the creation of place. Place is defined by the inherent qualities of our environment that are necessary for our individual and social well-being. More specifically, people, as the inhabitants of architecture, must feel a sense of belonging, not isolation — identity, not ambiguity.

> **Joseph Nickol**
> **Graduate, University of Notre Dame**

Beyond buildings, architecture is about the relationships between materials and among things more than it is about the things themselves. As such, architecture is primarily about prepositions: above, below, between, within, among, through, under, etc. This is partly why Renaissance painters made such good architects, but it is also what I think the contemporary painter/architect Sam Mockbee was talking about when he said, "Architecture has to be about more than just architecture." Being based on relationships, architecture is also fundamentally about human interaction.

> **Casius Pealer, J.D.**
> **Associate, Reno & Cavanaugh, PLLC**
> **Co-founder, ARCHVoices**

Architecture is the design and building of instruments for living at the scale of a building and, at other times, the scale of a doorstop or letter opener.

> **Richard A. Eribes, Ph.D.,** AIA
> **Professor and Dean Emeritus, University of Arizona**

From my perspective, the process of creating architecture is puzzle-solving on a majestic scale. This translates into the critical thinking and problem-solving aspects of the profession that architecture programs are so good at teaching and that our clients rely on us for as we help them accomplish their goals.

The architecture project/puzzle contains an infinite number of variables. Some are static; some are dynamic. The attributes of some are known and universally understood; for others, the attributes are unique to the person investigating them or experiencing them. The puzzle is constantly evolving, and no one has control over it! Most interesting of all, the result of the architecture project/puzzle is never complete, and no one ever sees it the same as someone else or even experiences it themselves in the same way.

> **Kathryn T. Prigmore,** FAIA
> **Project Manager, HDR Architecture, Inc.**

Architecture is the process of creating useful, efficient, and attractive structures.

> **David Groff**
> **Intern Architect, Dalgliesh, Gilpin, and Paxton Architects**

Stonehenge, England.
Photographer: Karl
DuPuy.

Architecture is the shaping of environments, real or imagined, that affect the way people think, feel, act, or respond to their surroundings. In this context, architecture can be both a noun and a verb; in other words, it can be the painting itself, or the act of painting.

Architecture appeals to the senses. It can comfort us or intimidate us. It can make us feel welcome and home, or alone and cold. Architecture can be as much about the intended desires of the designer's imagination or the unintended consequences delivered when architecture is not considered more fully in its proper context. Real or imagined, the environment we live, work, and play in is directly influenced by the architecture that surrounds us. In essence, architecture is humanity.

Shannon Kraus, AIA
Associate Architect, HKS

The development of architecture is as much a design process as it is a simulation of inhabitable space(s) and building vocabularies. I will go as far to say that architecture is not architecture unless it was developed by means of an analytical process.

Thomas Fowler IV
Associate Professor and Associate Head, California Polytechnic State University — San Luis Obispo

Sustainable Place-Making

W. CECIL STEWARD, FAIA, APA

Dean Emeritus
University of Nebraska — Lincoln

President/CEO, Joslyn Castle Institute for Sustainable
Communities
Omaha and Lincoln, Nebraska

Why and how did you become an architect?

As a freshman in high school, I became acquainted with a teaching mentor who helped me discover a fascination and a modest talent for drawing, design, and the craft of making structures from pieces of material and technologies. In college, I had a mentor who awakened me to the breadth and human/community connections of the profession. This same mentor, who was an academic descendent of Walter Gropius, guided me into a personal set of standards and principles by which to distinguish excellence from the common, and the means to evaluate the context for architecture.

Why and how did you choose which school to attend for your architecture degree? What degree(s) do you possess?

In 1952, from my home in Pampa, Texas, my choices were limited to the three accredited public institutions in the state of Texas due to limited family financial resources. After a thorough investigation of each, I determined that the all-male military environment of Texas A&M University would best suit my financial needs and interests. I graduated in 1957 with the five-year bachelor of architecture.

Thanks to scholarships and outside financial aid, I accepted an invitation to three months of study at the École des Beaux-Arts in Fontainbleau, France, between my fourth and fifth years. I received a certificate in architecture and planning, but, more importantly, I received my first bit of education in an unending quest to know and understand cultures and places foreign to my own native experiences.

After completing my postgraduate obligation of three years active duty in the military service, I felt a deep need to reconnect myself to the professional world and elected to apply to graduate school. I received the master of science in architecture with a major emphasis in architecture for educational facilities in 1961 from Columbia University in New York. In 1991, I was awarded the honorary doctorate in humane letters (Hon. DHL) from Drury College, Springfield, Missouri, for contributions to the profession.

What has been your greatest challenge as an architect/faculty?

My greatest challenge as a twenty-nine-year-old faculty member in 1963 was to practice what I taught and to teach what I practiced — with integrity, passion, and the highest of standards for both the academic and professional outcomes. A second part of the challenge was to find new mediations or paradigms to celebrate through architecture.

What were your primary responsibilities as dean? Why did you choose this career? What are you doing now?

The principal reason I moved from practice into full-time education was to maximize the opportunity to continue learning through teaching while concurrently learning and experimenting through secondary roles in practice. The principal reason I sought the dean's position in 1973 at age thirty-nine was to be able to influence the innovations in both education and practice that I believed were becoming necessary for a more influential profession.

My principal responsibility as dean had four parts:

First, I felt accountable to every class of students at the University of Nebraska (1973–2000) to assess their distinctive needs and expectations, as they may have differed from the preceding class, and to aggregate the culture of the school across the disciplines (architecture, planning, and interior design), the age groups, and the cultural backgrounds of the student body.

Second, in keeping with the mission of the University of Nebraska, I felt obliged to create and manage a significant public service and creation-of-new-knowledge profile for the college.

Third, I advocated for the faculty and their needs and desires, both as individuals and collectively, with the university administration, state government, the public, and the professional bodies. This effort was central to the quality of classroom and life experiences for the students.

Fourth, I worked to steadily enhance and increase the value of a degree from the University of Nebraska for each alumnus.

In 1996, with assistance from the University of Nebraska, I formed a nonprofit organization in Omaha and named it the Joslyn Castle Institute for Sustainable Communities (JCI). Today, I serve, pro bono, as its president and CEO.

In 1991, you served as the sixty-eighth president of The American Institute of Architects (AIA), the first career educator to have been elected. Can you provide details of that professional experience?
In the late 1970s and mid-1980s, I served on a number of profession-wide committees and boards with both professional and educational missions. Through these experiences and networks of educators and professionals I gained a broad understanding of the missions and relationships of the national organizations that establish and oversee the policies and standards for the education and practice of architecture in the United States.

By the mid-1980s, I had determined that the board of directors of the AIA was the body politic through which the greatest change in both education and practice might occur. Accordingly, I initiated efforts to be elected to the AIA board for a three-year term in 1988, as one of the two directors representing the Central States Region. In the meantime, I was a member of the board of directors of the Association of Collegiate Schools of Architecture (ACSA) and was appointed through the ACSA to the National Architectural Accrediting Board (NAAB); I was elected NAAB president in 1989.

By the end of my AIA board term in 1990, I was more convinced than ever that an architect who happened to be a career educator had as much right to and opportunity for leadership in the profession's largest organization as had the previous sixty-seven presidents from practice backgrounds, and that it might be possible, and useful, to bring certain educational and collaborative strategies to the table of policy discussions about the future of the profession.

I campaigned for first vice president/president-elect and was elected to the position for service during the two-year period of 1991–1992. In retrospect, the years of service through the AIA committee structure, the regional engagement, and the national board and presidency positions were the most gratifying and productive experiences of my professional life.

Optimism abounds. The first female career educator in the position, Professor Kate Schwennsen, FAIA of Iowa State University, will serve as the 2005 AIA first vice president/president-elect and 2006 Institute president.

Reflecting on your professional career in architecture, was it a good career choice? Would you do it again if given the opportunity?

During my fifty-plus years of education for practice, practice for education, education for learning, and continuing education, I have never experienced a single day when I wondered whether I would have been happier in another career, another job, or among other people. The opportunities and the support that have accrued to my path — for engagement, for creativity, for discovery, for learning, for trial and error — have been nothing short of fortuitous and miraculous. I hope I have not squandered much of the opportunity, and, especially, I hope I have not shunned or disappointed the support that has been so generously offered, by so many, to my efforts.

Who, or what experiences, have been a major influence on your career?

I am always mindful that no accomplishment is made in today's world without the preceding work, sacrifices, and contributions of others. It is a truism that we all drink from wells we did not personally dig. I owe everything to my associates, friends, colleagues, and family.

Mentors have been especially influential in my career development and in my career choices. One in particular, professor and former dean of the College of Architecture and Environmental Design at Texas A&M University, Edward J. Romieniec, FAIA, gave me the confidence as a student to reach for more than I thought I could, to have larger visions as a faculty member and junior administrator than I thought worthy of my place and background, to strive to always learn through teaching, and to value the community context for all architecture. These values continue to guide my work for education and practice in sustainable place making.

Daring to Lead

SHANNON KRAUS, AIA
Associate Architect
HKS Architects
Dallas

Hadassah Medical Center Bed Tower, Jerusalem, Israel. Architect: HKS.

Why and how did you become an architect?
I became an architect simply because it was a lifelong goal. A life's goal achieved. A passion delivered. I set my mind on architecture when I was in fourth grade, when the only class I had true interest in was art; my mother had the vision to open my mind to architecture as an occupation that would fit my interests.

I was able to express myself through art and imagination — through the pictures I drew, the models I built, and the forts I enlisted the neighborhood kids to help construct. Becoming an architect simply felt right.

However, in the end, I became an architect to make a difference. While I pursued architecture because that is where I could express myself, I find that what I enjoy most about this amazing profession is the ability to work with diverse groups of people to solve complex problems so that others can fulfill their dreams — thus making a difference by turning vision to reality.

From my first day on campus at Southern Illinois University to gaining registration as an architect in the state of Texas, my journey took approximately twelve years — four years of undergraduate work, one year as American Institute of Architecture Students (AIAS) vice president, three years in graduate school for the MBA and Master of Architecture, and four years of internship at RTKL, finished concurrently with nine exams spread over eighteen months.

Why and how did you choose which school to attend for your architecture degree? What degree(s) do you possess?
Coming out of McArthur High School in the central Illinois town of Decatur, with the ambition to pursue architecture, I found myself at a small but terrific undergraduate program at Southern Illinois University (SIU) at Carbondale. I ended up there primarily due to economics and a lack of information. The school had a four-year architecture program, and it was less expensive than any other school in the area. I did not know that it was less expensive because the architecture program was not accredited. In the end, this turned out to be a blessing — SIU was one of the best, if not luckiest, decisions I made.

Through SIU, I learned the art of architecture. I learned to think, draw, paint, sketch, and resolve complex variables into rational solutions. While not known for design, the school was heavily based in the fundamentals, including learning how buildings go together — more so than most schools cover. My education at SIU provided me with the best foundation for becoming an architect I could have asked for.

For graduate school, I chose the University of Illinois at Urbana-Champaign. Having just completed my term as national vice president of the AIAS, a full-time position in Washington, D.C., following my undergraduate studies, I came to realize that business skills are the single biggest thing missing in the amazingly rich and diverse education that architecture provides. Thus, I applied to universities where I could also go to business school — a decision that ultimately led to my acceptance into the schools of architecture and business at the University of Illinois, where I graduated summa cum laude with a master of business administra-

Hadassah Medical Center Bed Tower, Jerusalem, Israel. Architect: HKS. Artist: Michael Lungren.

tion (MBA) and a master of architecture (M.Arch.). The MBA equipped me to think holistically about business and refined my communications skills; the M.Arch. filled in the gaps with a curriculum focused on design and design theory.

I believe the profession does not have an adequate guidance system for assisting students interested in architecture. I say this because in many ways your choice of school goes a long way toward determining the type of professional you become.

What has been your greatest challenge as an architect?

My greatest challenge as an architect is one of my current projects for Hadassah in Jerusalem, Israel. Not only is it a challenging project in terms of health care planning, it is also is a challenging design problem due to the numerous site variables (it is located at the top of a mountain in Ein Karem, overlooking the birth site of John the Baptist), the diverse culture, and the rich context. Our goal is to provide a modern, state-of-the-art facility that can respond to the needs of the region while embracing the historical significance of the surrounding area. Like most projects, this is a collaborative effort where we draw from the combined strength of the design team and our consultants to deliver a project that exceeds the client's needs.

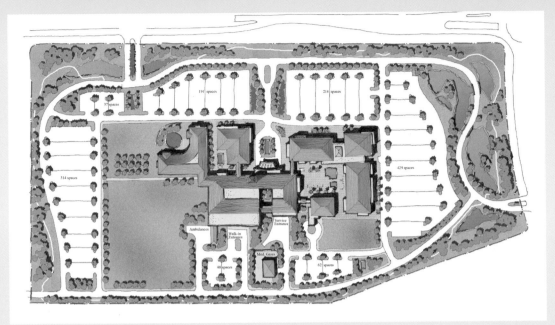

Viera Health Park, Viera, Florida. Architect: HKS.

Why did you pursue two graduate degrees — master of architecture and master of business administration — during your graduate studies?
I believe that an architect is a generalist. Architectural education is comprehensive and provides the foundation suitable for many careers; however, business seemed to be the one missing ingredient.

As AIAS national vice president, I quickly came to realize that architecture is a business and that I had much more to learn, so I decided to round out my education by earning an MBA in addition to the M.Arch. After speaking with others, I knew that was the right time to pursue the MBA, as I had no guarantee that such an opportunity would be available later in life.

Ultimately, I felt the MBA would help me simply by providing additional tools for me to draw on. However, in addition to business skills, the MBA conferred many benefits I did not anticipate. My program helped me hone my communication skills, problem-solving ability, and leadership skills. In many ways, the business degree was not as much about accounting or finance as it was about maximizing resources and leadership.

As an incoming vice president of the AIA in 2005, what are your goals?
My role will be to facilitate the continued growth and development of the AIA's transformation into a knowledge-based organization. My goal as vice president is simply to make a difference — to have a positive impact, no matter how small, on the evolution of the institute. I hope that others as passionate about the profession as I am will be similarly encouraged to get engaged and get involved.

How has your involvement with the ATA assisted you in your professional career?

I owe much of my growth and professional development to my experiences in the AIA and AIAS. During my ten years of active involvement, I have had the opportunity to plan and lead numerous committees and convention seminars, organize speakers, lead workshops, author articles, and network with many incredible people who I otherwise would not have known. In many ways, my involvement has supplemented my career by providing a way to gain experience and pursue interests where my work does not always allow. For interns, I can say there is no better way to enhance your growth than by being involved in a professional organization.

While organizations have their critics — and I have, at times, been among them — we can effect change in them only by getting involved. In fact, the ability to change the profession lies in the hands of people who choose to be involved. For me, being involved is not only an extension of my job but also a professional obligation. Whether you join AIA, AIAS, or a community organization like Habitat, you should become involved whenever or however you can.

What are your primary responsibilities and duties?

My primary role as an architect is that of health care designer and planner. My projects range from domestic to international and vary in scope from small additions to multimillion-dollar master plans and green field replacement facilities. I often work directly with clients on the front end of projects through programming, utilization, master planning, and design.

My recent projects include the programming and master planning for Viera Health Park in Florida, master plan validation and concept design for a new bed tower in Jerusalem, health care medical planning for a new hospital addition in Stoke, England, and a multimillion-dollar phased replacement master plan for Parkland Hospital in Dallas. In all of these projects, my goal is to understand the clients' needs, listen to their dreams, and work with them to identify innovative solutions they can implement on time and on budget.

What is the most satisfying part of your job?

The most satisfying thing is knowing that architecture is not just a job but also a career. I say this because I am pursuing something I love and look forward to. I enjoy the firm I work for and the people I work with. I love exceeding client expectations with innovative solutions and accurate results. I love that I cannot do this on my own; we can meet or exceed client expectations only by means of a team effort to bring clarity to the building process and put the client first.

What is the most important quality or skill of a health care designer?

Patience, communication, and knowledge are the most important skills a designer in health care — or any area, for that matter — must have. As a programmer and designer in health care, I work directly with clients, physicians, nurses, equipment specialists, contractors, builders, project managers, and business leaders. In each case, I must know enough of the subject matter being programmed to communicate in the language of each user I meet. Most issues and challenges are the result of poor communication, so the patience to work through misconceptions and differences of opinions is key to resolving problems as I develop a program or a project design solution. I learned about health care facilities through trial and error on the job rather than in school. Architects in this field must be "heads-up" in the office and seek every opportunity to participate in meetings or go on tours.

Who has been a major influence on your career?

I have had many great influences on my career, but none greater than my parents and my wife. While I have benefited from many great mentors and try to learn from everyone around me, my parents helped shape me into the man I am today, teaching me to believe I can do anything I put my mind to. My wife helps keep me focused, motivated, and on track; she has an even-keeled perspective that brings with it humility and grace. Without a doubt, I am blessed to have them as positive influences in my life. I would not be where I am today if not for them.

What has been your most rewarding endeavor as a professional?

Without hesitation, I can say my most rewarding professional job was the planning, design, and construction of a clubhouse for a Make-a-Wish child named Giovanna. At the age of thirteen, Giovanna, who was challenged with a potentially life-threatening illness, was given the opportunity by the Make-a-Wish Foundation of North Texas to have one of her wishes come true. Her wish was to have a clubhouse — a place she could have as her own and a place she could have friends over for a slumber party.

The result was a 400-square-foot clubhouse with a loft, fire pole, and screen porch, inspired by Giovanna's own vision. Interns designed the project with Giovanna as the client. She was given schematic designs, models, and material boards. Knowing we were able to utilize our design skills to make her vision — her wish — a reality was enormously rewarding.

Architecture as a New Media

WILLIAM J. CARPENTER, PH.D., FAIA

Professor
School of Architecture, Civil Engineering Technology and Construction
Southern Polytechnic State University
Marietta, Georgia

President, Lightroom
Decatur, Georgia

Why and how did you become an architect?
I became an architect because of a teacher I had in sixth grade; his name was Robert Fisher. I was his first student to go to architecture school, and I could not have done it without him. He invented classes for me, such as eco-tecture, that emphasized sustainable design before it was in vogue. He collected donations from many of the businesses in our town to create a scholarship for me that he gave me at high school graduation.

Why and how did you choose which school to attend for your architecture degree? What degree(s) do you possess?
B.Arch., M.Arch., and Ph.D. in architecture. I went to Mississippi State for my undergraduate studies because I asked Richard Meier at a career day what school he would attend, and he said he had just returned from there and something interesting was happening there. At seventeen, I packed my bags and arrived from New York. He was so right—I

The Breen Residence, Atlanta. Architect: William Carpenter. Photographer: Kevin Bryd.

Decatur Arts Festival Poster Design, Decatur, Georgia. Graphic Designers: Kevin and Aaron Byrd.

was able to study with Samuel Mockbee, Christopher Risher, and Merrill Elam.

I chose Virginia Tech for graduate studies because of its emphasis on urbanism and tectonics. No school in the world offers a better balance of these pedagogical intents — of course, I *am* an alumnus. Jaan Holt and Gregory Hunt were amazing professors and left an indelible imprint on me.

For my doctorate, I wanted to go to England. There I was able to study with Professor Thomas Muir before he retired. I studied at the University of Central England at Birmingham Polytechnic, which is one of the oldest programs in the United Kingdom. Muir, Alan Green, and Denys Hinton gave me an appreciation for Europe, how to live, and where to find the best pubs. I have never met anyone with a deeper commitment to architectural education and learning.

What has been your greatest challenge as an architect?

The greatest challenge I have is balancing my time. I have two wonderful daughters and want to be an integral part of their lives. I have amazing students to teach, and I work for great clients on architectural commissions. I have been blessed. The biggest challenge is getting all of it done well.

Lightcatcher, Decatur, Georgia. Architect: William Carpenter. Photographer: Kevin Bryd.

How does your work as a faculty member inform your architectural practice, and vice versa?

My students constantly inspire me and help me see things in new ways. I always invite them to my studio and to see new projects. I try to be involved in their lives during and after school. They are why I teach, and I owe them a lot.

What are your primary responsibilities and duties as an architect and a faculty member?

I am president of Lightroom, an architecture and new media firm in Decatur, Georgia. One of my former students, Kevin Byrd, is now my colleague and business partner. He was one of my best students, and now we work together. I am also director of the evening professional program in architecture, where I teach the thesis studio, which I enjoy very much. I like teaching at the fifth-year level.

Pursuit of Design Excellence

CAROL ROSS BARNEY, FAIA

Founder and President
Ross Barney + Jankowski, Inc.
Chicago

Why and how did you become an architect?
I thought, growing up, that I would be an artist, an illustrator or a painter most likely, but I always felt an obligation to help improve the world and society. When I was in high school, it occurred to me that I could do those things as an architect. I went to my guidance counselor at my Catholic, all-girls school and told her I wanted to be an architect. To her credit, Sister Catherine Patrick did not even flinch or tell me architecture was only for boys; instead, she cheerfully looked up architecture schools.

Why and how did you choose which school to attend for your architecture degree? What degree(s) do you possess?
I was fortunate that my state university, the University of Illinois at Urbana-Champaign (UIUC), had and still has a distinguished school of architecture. I applied to other schools, but UIUC fitted me best. I earned a bachelor of architecture in 1971.

Barrington Area Library Addition, Barrington, Illinois. Architect: Ross Barney + Jankowski. Photographer: Steve Hall, Hedrich Blessing.

What has been your greatest challenge as an architect/principal?
Finding work.

What are your primary responsibilities and duties?
Finding work.

What is the least satisfying part of your job?
Not finding work.

One of your responsibilities is for the design excellence of all projects undertaken by the firm. How do you accomplish design excellence?
Projects are excellent when the solutions embody the senses of inquiry, innovation, and optimism. Design is a search for answers, multiple answers that can be distilled into a single holistic entity. My job is simple; first, I need to make sure we are considering the true question and not being distracted by noise and fashion; analysis, or programming, is key at this stage. Second, I need to make sure that a diverse and expansive set of possible solutions is considered. Never, or at least rarely, should you build your first idea.

To accomplish this, my studio is pretty free-flowing. People who work with us do not need a lot of structure, are not too concerned about the ownership of ideas, and definitely are not happy on the sidelines.

Little Village Academy, Chicago. Architect: Ross Barney + Jankowski. Photographer: Steve Hall, Hedrich Blessing.

Clearly, you are successful, given the numerous awards your have received. How do you feel when one of your projects is so recognized?
Outside of making us feel great, awards are important because they represent the evaluation of your peers, the people who know how difficult it is to design good buildings. Another important aspect of award programs is educating the public about the quality of their environment — helping people imagine a better world. That being said, we have never had winning design awards as a project goal.

Oklahoma City Federal Building, Oklahoma City, Oklahoma. Architect: Ross Barney + Jankowski. Photographer: Steve Hall, Hedrich Blessing.

One of your recent commissions is the new United States Federal Campus in Oklahoma City. Given the charged circumstances, how did you approach the design of this project?

Oklahoma City was a watershed for me, at the same time strengthening and renewing my basic ideas about design. Many concerned stakeholders were involved, from survivors of the Murrah Building bombing to the U.S. Congress. We were developing new security design standards as we worked. Finally, I had not worked outside of Illinois before.

So we started the design process with an intense research phase, something I may have short-circuited in the past because I was at home in Chicago working for people with life experiences like my own. We learned as much as we could about Oklahoma history, geology, and culture, and that information served as a starting point for our design discussions. The approach worked so well that we have made research the first phase of nearly every project we do, especially the Chicago projects. We have even extended the practice of thorough investigation through the entire design process. The process is revealing, even inspiring, especially with respect to material investigations.

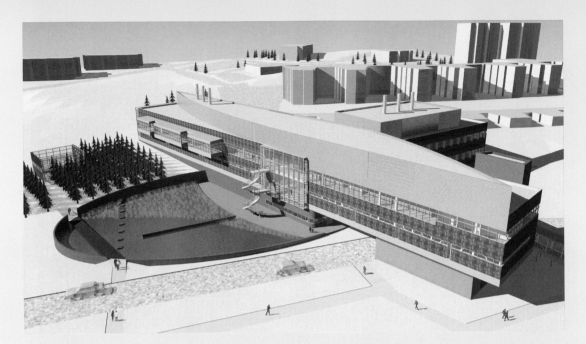

James Swenson Science
Building, University of
Minnesota — Duluth.
Architect: Ross Barney +
Jankowski. Rendering: Ross
Barney + Jankowski, Inc.

**Following graduation, you served as a Peace Corps volunteer in Costa Rica.
Can you describe this experience and how it contributed to your professional
career?**

My job in el Cuerpo de Paz was for the National Parks of Costa Rica. In 1971, the
Costa Rican government had just established the ecological reserves for which the
country is renowned. I was part of a multidisciplinary team of scientists and
designers that did the initial planning for the park system. The projects I worked
on included the restoration of a historic ranch house, designing worker housing
on a volcano, and assessing visitor impact on a fragile reef environment. This was
my first experience working on a truly multidisciplinary team. The experience
made me aware of the fragile balance in nature and provided me with a value system for the sustainability of built environments.

Who or what experience has been a major influence on your career?

I was fortunate to find two architects in the early part of my career who have
been my mentors. John Holabird Jr., for whom I worked at Holabird and Root, my
first real job after my Peace Corps service, gave me confidence in my own architectural skills as well as an appreciation for the timelessness of architecture. I
think our bond was due, in part, to his being a fourth-generation architect in his
family firm and the father of seven daughters.

At about the same time, I met Natalie de Blois, who was with Skidmore, Owings
and Merrill (SOM) and later a professor of architecture at the University of Texas.
We have been friends ever since. She is my confidante and role model. I see her
often and still seek her counsel.

A Teacher's View

THOMAS FOWLER IV
Associate Professor and Associate Head
California Polytechnic State University — San Luis Obispo

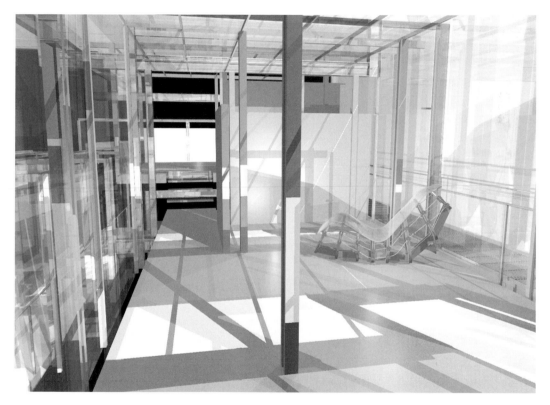

Immersive View of Housing Project by Deric Mizokami in Third-year Design Studio at California Polytechnic State University — San Luis Obispo. Faculty: Thomas Fowler IV.

Why and how did you become an architect?

My primary motivation for pursuing architecture began at a very young age with a desire to understand how everything worked. I took things apart and sometimes got them back together. At the time, I did not know of another profession that would give me a global sense of how things worked and allow me to document discoveries I made through drawings. I had naïve but romantic notions of what architects did. These notions were the vehicle that propelled me into going to school to learn about architecture.

Why and how did you choose which school to attend for your architecture degree? What degree(s) do you possess?
I possess a B.Arch. from New York Institute of Technology at Old Westbury and an M.Arch. from Cornell University. I chose my undergraduate institution based on what I could afford to pay, the location, and admission. I selected the graduate program because it offered an opportunity to work as an administrator and do graduate work at the same time. I pursued graduate work to learn additional design theory and to explore the possibilities of teaching.

What is the greatest challenge facing the future of the profession?
The greatest challenge is the lack of accessible and visible role models in the profession and in the academic environment for aspiring ethnic minority and women students. I was fortunate to have a cousin practicing architecture in New York City who allowed me to work in his office from high school on through my undergraduate studies. This was the component of my education that actually kept me in school, as I was challenged to see the relevance of my schooling to the practice of architecture. For all students, a link to a role model is always helpful when things get tough to sort out.

From my undergraduate years and beyond, I have always been fortunate to find role models to keep me on track and to expose me to opportunities I would not have known about otherwise. I think it is important to have a strong sense of your destination but also to be flexible about the path to this goal. Ultimately, you should stay agile in your ability to modify your goals with respect to experiences acquired on your path of learning.

Solar Decathlon House by Hugo Martinez in Third-year Design Studio at California Polytechnic State University — San Luis Obispo. Faculty: Thomas Fowler IV.

How does your work as a faculty member inform your architectural practice, and vice versa?
Being constantly surrounded by bright minds — always a diverse range of individuals able to collectively generate a range of ways of seeing a problem — is a valuable learning experience for the teacher. Teachers learn at an accelerated rate from their students. Students always challenge the conventions of how things go to together.

I am an academic whose practice of architecture is embedded in working with students in the design and construction of building mockups and prototypical structures. This form of practice has helped me acquire small-scale examples of the intimate process of design and construction. The academic involved in practice always has a voice in the back of his or her mind asking the question, "How can I capture this process and explain it to students so they can learn from it?"

What are your primary responsibilities and duties as an architect and as a faculty member?

I think some practitioners want to see faculty as practicing architects first and as academicians second, as this seems a logical way to ensure that students will learn the skills they need to become architects. From my experience, being a practitioner first does *not* ensure this; success depends more on teaching strategies that provide students with the tools for understanding these connections.

Practitioners must understand that they play an important role in the education of architects too. Some feel students need to deal with more complex design issues in school, but I think issues must be simplified so students can develop ideas beyond the planning stages of a project into constructible architectural vocabularies. Acceptable levels of design development are lacking in many studios, as students spend too much time thinking about complexities.

How does teaching architecture differ from practicing it?

What a teacher does is a mystery to those who do not teach. I think universities must work to decode what academics do. I often hear that the role of an architecture professor is to teach students the skills to build buildings, but I think the role of an architecture professor is far greater. Teaching is a modeling of future citizens who will make great contributions to society as upstanding citizens in addition to having the knowledge needed to create architecture. Good teaching is where both the student and teacher learn from the interaction. This is why people are attracted to teaching — because it provides a continuous learning mechanism.

You have been a member of more than one of the national boards of the collateral organizations. What has that involvement meant for your career?

People often think that individuals who volunteer with associations have limited interest in the broader issues that affect the profession — that is, design. I have the opposite view: Active involvement with the collaterals gives a broader view and appreciation for the profession. Navigating association work is the ultimate design problem for consensus, as you must move through a bureaucracy. I served as national president of the AIAS in 1984–1985 and as secretary for the ACSA in 2004–2006. Association work allows you to establish a macro view of the profession through networks that, over time, disperse and expand.

Tobacco Barn Collage, Horry County, South Carolina. Architect: Thomas Fowler IV.

Accessible Architecture

SCOTT WINDLEY

Accessibility Specialist
U.S. Architectural and Transportation Barriers Compliance
Board (Access Board)
Washington, D.C.

What has been your greatest challenge as an architect?
Getting other architects to recognize the need for their work to account for persons with disabilities; getting them to realize that accessible design is the right thing to do.

You work for the United States Architectural and Transportation Barriers Compliance Board, more commonly known as the Access Board, as an accessibility specialist. What are your primary responsibilities and duties?
I answer calls from architects, designers, and others who are trying to implement the guidelines of the Americans with Disabilities Act (ADA). I also write some of those guidelines. And I travel around the country training on the guidelines.

You have cerebral palsy, a birth condition, and have used a wheelchair since you were five years old. What impact has this disability had on your career as an architect?
It has caused me to be more aware of accessibility. I think some instructors assumed I would not be able to be an architect. I suppose I have proven that assumption wrong.

What would you say to people with a disability who desire to become an architect?
Be prepared to work hard, and don't take no for an answer!

What are the most and least satisfying parts of your career as an architect?
Dealing with architects who are unwilling to make their building accessible and who try to find loopholes to use to avoid it.

Who or what experience has been a major influence on your career?
Two people come to mind: my high school drafting instructor, who always challenged and pushed me to do my best, and my friend and boss from 1995 to 1997, Ron Mace, who was the biggest person in the universal design movement.

Profile of the Profession

According to the Bureau of Labor Statistics, U.S. Department of Labor,[6] 113,200 architects were practicing in the United States in 2002, the last year for which statistics are available. Employment projections for the occupation of architect are expected to grow by 19,500 (17 percent) between 2002 and 2012. The employment of architects is projected to grow about as fast as the average for all occupations through 2012, and additional job openings will stem from the need to replace architects who retire, transfer to new occupations, or leave the labor force permanently for other reasons. Growth in construction, particularly of nonresidential structures such as office buildings, shopping centers, schools, and health care facilities, is expected to spur employment.

With this projected growth of the profession, should you consider architecture? Before you answer, consider the following. According to the National Architectural Accrediting Board (NAAB),[7] 38,599 students were studying architecture in the pre-professional (15,822) and professional (22,777) degree programs in the United States during the 2003–2004 academic year. Further, 8,139 students graduated from the degree programs in the same year, 5,422 with the NAAB-accredited degree. If you assume that the number of graduates with the accredited degree remains the same for 2002–2012, the projected time frame, 54,220 individuals with an accredited

degree may be competing for the 19,500 openings. Clearly, based on employment projections, the competition for architectural positions will be keen over the next decade. Take solace, though, because graduates with an architectural education can enter many career fields other than architecture.

In its 2004 survey of registered architects, the National Council of Architectural Registration Boards[8] (NCARB) reports 101,179 architects living in the fifty-five reporting jurisdictions, including all fifty states, the District of Columbia, Guam, the Northern Mariana Islands, Puerto Rico, and the Virgin Islands. This total is an approximate 4 percent increase from the 1999 survey, the year the annual survey began.

According to the Bureau of Labor Statistics, U.S. Department of Labor,[9] the 2002 median annual earnings of wage and salary architects were $56,620. The middle 50 percent earned between $44,030 and $74,460. The lowest 10 percent earned less than $36,280, and the highest 10 percent earned more than $92,350. Salaries fluctuate depending on the region of the country, the amount of experience an individual has, or even the type of employer.

While the AIA[10] does not represent the entire profession, its membership does constitute a majority. As such, it is worth reporting their facts and figures. Of the nearly 75,000 members of the AIA, 80 percent (60,000) are licensed architects. The remaining are associate or allied members. Of all AIA architect members, 83 percent practice in architecture firms, 8 percent practice in the commercial/industrial/institutional sector, 3 percent practice in government, while the remaining practice in design firms, universities or schools, contractors or builder firms, and engineering firms.

DIVERSITY

What is diversity, and why is it important? The following answer is from *Designing for Diversity*, by Kathryn Anthony, Ph.D.:

Diversity is a set of human traits that have an impact on individuals' values, opportunities, and perceptions of self and others at work. At minimum, it includes six core dimensions: age, ethnicity, gender, mental or physical abilities, race, and sexual orientation.[11]

In the context of the architectural profession, diversity is extremely important because for many years, the profession has been known as a white man's profession. This label is no longer appropriate, as the profession is beginning to make strides, but consider the representation of women and individuals of color. Again, the AIA is the most reliable source for estimates.

According to the AIA, 10 percent (about 7,500) of full members are women, and 8 percent (about 6,000) are individuals of color. Within the schools, the numbers are dramatically better. According to NAAB, the percent of female students pursuing architecture is 41 percent, or approximately 16,200. Twenty-eight percent of students, or about 11,000, are individuals of color.

What Are the Most Important Skills an Architect Needs to Be Successful?

Hands down, the most important skill is problem solving, with the ability to see the not obvious solution. Being able to think in three dimensions is a close second.

> **Carol Ross Barney, FAIA**
> **Principal, Ross Barney + Jankowski, Inc.**

To be successful, you must be able to adapt to your surroundings. You must be a good communicator and, more importantly, a good listener. You must be open to taking risks and looking at things in a different way.

> **H. Alan Brangman, AIA**
> **University Architect, Georgetown University**

To be successful professionally and personally as an architect, passion, the courage to create, the ability to listen, communication, collaborative spirit, and perseverance are all essential.

> **Dianne Blair Black, AIA**
> **Vice President, RTKL Associates, Inc.**

Architects must have the following skills (the order depends on the individual): (a) excellent communication skills (e.g., writing, speaking, and traditional and digital drawing ability); (b) tolerance for ambiguity; (c) agility; (d) an analytical mind; (e) attention to both the macro and the micro; (f) humility; and (g) graphical diagramming.

> **Thomas Fowler IV**
> **Associate Professor and Associate Head**
> **California Polytechnic State University — San Luis Obispo**

The most important skill an architect can acquire is communication. Computers, technology, materials, and styles will all change, but written, spoken, and graphic communication will always be required to successfully compete in architecture.

> **Roy Abernathy, AIA**
> **President, Jova/Daniels/Busby**

Learning to communicate both visually and verbally is critical. Design work must be able to speak for itself, with no verbal explanation. In addition, however, architects must learn effective oral communication skills. They must practice their presentations over and over again, and they must learn from their mistakes. They also must learn how to be attentive listeners, as understanding the needs of clients and users is critical to a successful practice with repeat clients.

> **Kathryn Anthony, Ph.D.**
> **Professor, University of Illinois at Urbana-Champaign**

Communication is the most important skill. An architect must be able to communicate with clients differently than with contractors. An architect must be able to present in front of a twelve-person board of directors or a married couple. An architect must create written proposals and reports in the morning, then must turn around and create a massing diagram sketch or stair detail later in the day. An architect must be able to explain a technical aspect of a project in a project meeting just as well as attempt to convince a client of an aesthetic idea in a design.

> **F. Michael Ayles, AIA**
> **Director of Operations, Antinozzi Associates**

Every architect must have two attributes. First is the ability to deal with ambiguous problems. Architectural problems, while often complex, cannot, for the most part, be reduced to a single optimized answer. Typically, architectural problems have many possible solutions. The answer often lies not in finding the *right* solution but in finding the *best* solution. Le Corbusier, one of the twentieth century's greatest architects, described finding architectural solutions "as a patient search."

The second attribute is curiosity. Architecture is not a static profession. What you learn in a formal education is just the beginning. To be a successful architect, especially in this age of rapid change, you must acquire new knowledge and skills nearly every day. To do this, you need insatiable curiosity that drives you to know more and to continue a process of lifelong learning.

Notice I have talked about attributes rather than skills. I believe these personal attributes are more important than learned skills. I do not mean to skip the skills issue. The necessary skills are basic — reading, writing, and arithmetic in all their current manifestations — plus communication skills, leadership skills, cognitive skills, and — I think the most important skill of all — the skill to imagine unbuilt worlds.

Robert M. Beckley, FAIA
Professor and Dean Emeritus, University of Michigan

Self-knowledge. Exercise your capacity for self-learning as soon as you can — understand how deeply you want to be an architect and reflect on it throughout your decision making. For some, the want is a passion or obsession; for others, it is a curiosity that grows over time. These people require alternate paths.

Travel. Observe and talk to people. Travel may be the greatest teacher.

Don't worry about failure. Follow the maxim of IBM's Thomas Watson Jr.: "Want to succeed faster? Accelerate your rate of failure!" Have the courage to take that risk!

Joseph Bilello, Ph.D., AIA
Dean, Ball State University

The most important skill is listening. I find that too many architects do not listen well; it takes practice.

William Carpenter, Ph.D., FAIA
Associate Professor, Southern Polytechnic State University
President, Lightroom

To observe and to listen, and translate the information gained into a meaningful medium that can be understood by clients. Architecture is not about you and what you want; it is about your clients and working as a team to achieve their goals. You can educate them, which is critical, but you must step back from your own ego-based agenda and serve them. This does not mean the design is compromised; it just means you know and honor the constraints.

Barbara Crisp
Principal, Underwood + Crisp

Cosmonaut Museum, Moscow, Russia. Photographer: Ted Shelton, AIA.

Architecture requires imagination, compassion, and the capacity to lead. Imagination is the unmistakable tool of the designer. Compassion serves any architect well in understanding the fears, concerns, and hopes of those for whom they design. Leadership carries architects beyond the expectations of a drafting room or a construction site to the dreams of a visionary.

> **Jacob Day**
> **President (2004–2005), American Institute of Architecture Students**

The two most important skills for success in architecture are critical thinking and problem solving. I used to think creativity was the most vital skill for an architect to possess; however, I have come to realize that creativity alone does not produce substance. A rational thinker who knows architectural history and has a strong design process will make good architecture.

> **Margaret DeLeeuw**
> **Graduate, University of Maryland**

Passion, persistence, and three-dimensional spatial skills.

> **Richard A. Eribes, Ph.D.,** AIA
> **Professor and Dean Emeritus, University of Arizona**

A creative sensibility, the ability to solve complex issues without precedents to follow, and a commitment to the discipline.

> **Doug Garofalo,** FAIA
> **Professor, University of Illinois at Chicago**
> **President, Garofalo Architects, Inc.**

Good communication skills. Architecture is a collaborative process and requires that architects be good team players as well as leaders.

> **Lynsey Gemmell**
> **Architect II, Holabird & Root**

Drawing is the most important skill; the second is the ability to research and understand history. One more vital skill, especially today, is the ability to work in a team. Nearly all buildings are complex machines, and no one person can do it all. In summary, you must be a well-rounded, competent individual.

> **Christopher Glapinski**
> **Student, University of Miami**

Be both patient and persistent. Often the work of the architect is a series of compromises.

> **Christopher J. Gribbs,**
> ASSOCIATE AIA
> **Senior Director, American Institute of Architects**

An architect must be open-minded and able to constantly evaluate and reevaluate every decision. Also — this isn't really a skill — an architect must realize you don't need to reinvent the wheel with every design; they don't teach you this in school. So many beautiful and efficient structures already exist; we need not create something unique every day. We can be creative, but we must learn from the past and try to make it better.

> **David Groff**
> **Intern Architect, Dalgliesh, Gilpin, and Paxton Architects**

A parallel and equal emphasis on communication abilities — oral, written, and graphic — is essential to being a successful architect, regardless of talent.

> **Gaines Hall,** FAIA
> **Vice President, Kirkegaard & Associates**

Patience, diligence — because architectural education is so rigorous, diligence is a must — attention to detail, and passion. I know I still want to be an architect because my passion for creating is undiminished.

> **Michelle Hunter**
> **Lead Designer, Garage Takeover, Discovery Channel**

Sensitivity. Architects must understand what the environment and the end user need and want. Architects cannot properly respond to the needs of the end user if they are not sensitive to the need. The need may be structural, environmental, aesthetic, climatic, religious, or a combination of these elements — or others.

> **Ahkilah Johnson**
> **Senior Analyst, Cherokee Northeast, LLC**

Collaboration, teamwork, and people skills are probably the most important and most undervalued skills an architect needs in today's professional practice. But perhaps most importantly, the ability to work collaboratively with clients, to lead them through the project process, can make the difference between a good project and a great one.

> **Carolyn Jones,** AIA
> **Associate Principal, Callison Architecture, Inc.**

Having a good eye is one of the most important attributes of a successful architect, but "a good eye" is difficult to describe in words. It affects your projects, your presentations to clients, your marketing efforts to obtain new projects — everything.

Being good with your hands is important, especially in building models but also to get a tactile feel for materials and how they are put together in the field.

Strong writing is also important for architects. Writing is critical to obtaining jobs or awards, preparing contracts, and developing complete and accurate specifications for a particular project.

Enjoying the social aspects and challenges of working with people is very important. Every real-world project involves teamwork. Often, multiple consultants are involved, sometimes multiple clients, always many people who do not always naturally communicate well with each other! It is always the architect's job to keep the lines of communication open via drawings, meetings, conference calls, and so on.

> **Elizabeth Kalin**
> **Architectural Intern, Studio Gang Architecture**

Chicago Townhomes, Chicago. Photographer: Isabelle Gournay.

Leadership is the most important skill an architect can possess. As the client's advocate and the head of the consultant team, the architect must maintain an overview of the project and provide consistent guidance to ensure its success as well as the long-lasting relationships developed during its course. A great leader is a skilled at listening, showing empathy, and creating a vision.

> **Grace Kim**, AIA
> **Principal, Schemata Workshop, Inc.**

I have found that people who like to solve puzzles can do well in architecture. Getting a building designed and through construction takes a tremendous amount of patience and keeping your eye on the big picture. The design of the building, in my opinion, is the easy part. Turning that design into something the owner approves, figuring out the detailing, coming in on budget, getting approved by the local community, and working within applicable building and zoning codes requires tremendous focus.

Playing psychiatrist to clients is another critical quality. Balancing various client representatives' demands, whether for a couple or a board of directors, requires listening carefully to them and coming up with solutions that satisfy all of their important criteria. They may have other agendas in getting design solutions to go their way, so I find I have to handle their requests carefully.

Excellent design skills are a given to being an architectural designer. However, being an architect does not necessarily mean being a great designer. Few people involved in the profession of architecture are designers. Many are office managers, specification writers, marketing personnel, architectural critics who write for newspapers or magazines, people who work at banks and for developers to review projects, and so on.

> **Nathan Kipnis**, AIA
> **Principal, Nathan Kipnis Architects, Inc.**

The most important skills are communication, imagination, communication, problem solving, and communication. Architects must have the imagination to dream up the vision of clients, the communication skills to articulate that vision so the client can understand it, and the ability to resolve complex variables in order to make that vision a reality. The fundamentals of math, science, and art are relevant, but they are tools that support imagination, communication, and problem solving.

> **Shannon Kraus**, AIA
> **Associate Architect, HKS**

An architect must be intelligent but more so, he or she must be wise or possess a great deal of common sense. A strong moral code is important in order to balance all of the issues that must be addressed. Further, an architect must be able to see or imagine big ideas, to create concepts that tie everything together. An architect deals with a great amount of information and criteria.

An architect does not have to be a great artist as far as drawing is concerned, but he or she must be able to document and communicate three-dimensional and spatial ideas. I have observed many good architects whose drawing skills are not great. Anyone can learn the technique of sketching. Computer drafting skills are essential today for new graduates. The architect must be able to use the computer for communications, presentation, and research as well as drafting.

The architect must be able to work with and to enjoy working with people, including clients and coworkers. Clients are the reason to practice architecture. An architect must be able to understand and decipher their needs and goals. The program that emerges is the basis of the concepts and architecture that result.

An architect must be able to understand and communicate with consultants and experts in a variety of disciplines. Architecture is far too broad today for one individual to comprehend and be expert in all its aspects. It is a team effort. Leadership calls for the concept of service and the recognition of others' expertise and insights. This can be a humbling role. At the same time, the architect must understand the place of all the systems and interests that combine to make an architectural product.

The architect must be a leader in bringing science to the built environment. The vital interest of our society and world in conservation and stewardship of our natural resources will only increase. The architect is the natural leader in this effort.

Jack Kremers, AIA
Professor, Judson College

Communication is the most important of all skills. Without the ability to communicate orally, in writing, and through graphics, one probably cannot be a successful architect. Through communications one interacts with clients, the com-

munity, and the people with whom one learns and works. Though an architect may have outstanding strengths in one area of communication, few are successful without being professionally competent in all three.

Clark Llewellyn, AIA
Director, Montana State University

Architecture requires the most diverse training of any professional field. To be successful architects, we must understand a wide spectrum of knowledge. We must combine a profound appreciation of tradition and history with an artful eye. As creators of human environments, we must understand society at both the macro and micro levels. We must also balance our progressive desire to incorporate the latest technologies, materials, and design trends with constraint and adherence to what is tried and true.

Joseph Nickol
Graduate, University of Notre Dame

A positive attitude — anything is possible! In addition, architects need the ability to communicate well, to convey their ideas, and to acknowledge the ideas of others.

Monica Pascatore
Freelance Designer, P Inc.

Architects must have the ability to be creative (which includes the creative use of precedents). They must be able to think at different scales (simultaneously). They must have the ability to inspire confidence (which is conveyed largely by listening). They must have the ability to communicate ideas (either orally or in writing, as well as through drawing). Finally, they must have the ability to be able to tell good stories.

Casius Pealer, J.D.
Associate, Reno & Cavanaugh, PLLC
Co-founder, ARCHVoices

All architects must be able to communicate well in a variety of media. Other important skills include speaking, writing, critical thinking, and problem solving. Also, an understanding of business finance is important, as the measure of a successful project is more than aesthetics and function. My personal goal on every project is to learn at least one item that will enable me to increase my creativity or productivity.

Kathryn T. Prigmore, FAIA
Project Manager, HDR Architecture, Inc.

I believe the most useful skill or quality to ensure success is perseverance. Architects are

Rotunda — University of Virginia, Charlottesville. Architect: Thomas Jefferson. Photographer: R. Lindley Vann.

always trying to solve complex issues while balancing the demands of finance, site, owner, and self. They must be able to work through issues when the solution seems impossible. They must have faith in themselves and the peace within to press onward until the solution becomes evident. The design process is not linear but rather cyclical. Many times, architects find themselves back at the beginning and questioning whether they have moved forward in solving the problem. But good solutions do not come quickly. They need polish to make them shine.

Katherine S. Proctor, FCSI, CDT, AIA
Director of Facilities, Jewelry Television

Architects must have communication skills (both oral and written), flexibility, patience, the ability to work well under the stress of deadlines, the ability to work with many types of people, organization, a willingness to continue to learn, and a sense of humor.

Tamara Redburn, ASSOCIATE AIA
Intern Architect,
Fanning/Howey Associates, Inc.

Architects require collaboration, visionary ideas, persistence, optimism, and the scale of pragmatism and idealism, tipping more toward idealism.

Patricia Saldana Natke, AIA
Principal and President, Urban Works Ltd.

As cliché as it sounds, communication is the most important skill an architect uses. The language we use when we talk among ourselves is unintelligible to most clients. Even our visual expressions are often misinterpreted or misunderstood. The sophisticated computer programs we employ are no substitute for confident and articulate face-to-face communication.

W. Stephen Saunders, AIA
Principal, Eckenhoff Saunders Architects

The workplace and the field are multifaceted, far more so than most outsiders appreciate. With the diversity of needs and opportunities within the profession and allied areas of design and construction, one can become a successful architect in a variety of career paths. So it is difficult to identify specific, critical skills relevant throughout this breadth of alternatives. Of course, individuals have different perceptions of success in professional as well as personal life.

Most professional skills can be taught and developed, and no one can possibly possess them all. But it is difficult to make someone intelligent — and without that capability, and without passion, perseverance, good judgment, and high ethical standards, all of which are difficult to teach, success may be elusive.

Following graduation, if a person excels at even one thing and wishes to specialize, a lack of finely honed skills in other areas is probably not detrimental in becoming successful.

Roger Schluntz, FAIA
Dean, University of New Mexico

The future of architecture depends on the attainment of *all* architects, regardless of special expertise and focus in practice settings, of these knowledge areas and practice skills:

Knowledge Areas

- Design: aesthetics, synthesis, analysis, implementation planning, outcomes evaluations; holistic process, team-based methods
- Sustainability domains: materials, natural resources, human-invented systems
- Leadership: ideas, organizations, communities

Practice Skills

- Digital, electronic technologies: data, information, images
- Modeling and image making: virtual objects, spaces, and places
- Management systems/business practices
- Group dynamics and decision theories
- Effective communications
- Community visions facilitation
- Cultural reading and interpretation
- International development and economies
- Public regulations and governance
- Materials: content, manufacture and applications
- Continuous professional development

W. Cecil Steward, FAIA
Dean Emeritus, University of Nebraska — Lincoln

President/CEO, Joslyn Castle Institute for Sustainable Communities

Architects must be able to communicate visually and verbally; visualize three-dimensionally; distill a set of requirements to their essence; arrive at solutions that answer these requirements; and entertain many ways of looking at a problem/solution.

Eric Taylor, ASSOCIATE AIA
Photographer, Taylor Design & Photography, Inc.

Architects must have communication and team skills. While architecture school emphasizes drawing, model building, and other visual communication skill for presenting designs, in the real world I spend much more time interviewing my clients in order to understand their needs, goals, and objectives. I do spend time talking, but I spend much more listening. I also spend much more of my time writing than drawing or designing. Often that writing is to clients for proposals or project communications or internally to communicate with project teams I work with in our organization. These days, few architects work alone. Teamwork skills are critical to success. Architects must be able to work with not only other architects but also engineers, construction managers, owners' representatives, municipal officials, real estate professionals, and so on toward the successful completion of projects. Often they are called on to lead these teams as well.

Randall J. Tharp, RA
Senior Vice President, A. Epstein and Sons International, Inc.

Without any doubt, the discipline of architecture is becoming more and more complex. As Mark C. Taylor has commented, "We are living within a moment of unprecedented complexity, when things around us are changing faster than our ability to comprehend them." Architects today must develop a well-constructed mind and become fully conscious of themselves and their changing world. They must possess a high degree of intelligence, the mental flexibility and agility to tackle uncer-tainly, and must discover new ways to operate beyond a fixed system of values and conventions.

In addition, architects must embrace transdisciplinary collaboration and learn to collaborate effectively. They must develop the ability to plug into any project that presents itself and add value. This means not only possessing excellent communication and visualization skills but also possessing a fertility of ideas, a richness of imagination, and adaptive awareness. "Education is the ability to perceive the hidden connections between phenomena," as Vaclav Havel observed.

Max Underwood, AIA
Professor, Arizona State University
Architect and Principal, Underwood + Crisp

Being an architect takes an innate understanding of people and the way they use space. If you cannot understand people, then you cannot be an architect.

Lisa Van Veen, Associate AIA
Architectural Designer, Design Forward

Problem-solving skills are very important. You must teach yourself to see things in ways uncommon to most people. Dedication and eagerness to learn are also important traits. Seek out ways to learn and get the most out of school. Also, develop some interest or background in art, drawing, sculpture, and so on.

Brad Zuger
Student, University of Nebraska — Lincoln

From Verbal Concept to Fabrication

DOUG GAROFALO, FAIA

Professor, School of Architecture
University of Illinois at Chicago

President
Garofalo Architects, Inc.
Chicago

Why and how did you become an architect?
Initially, I wanted to become an architect because the field seemed to combine my interests in making, building, and the arts. I became an architect by attending a five-year bachelor of architecture degree program, working a few years in an office, studying for and passing the Architect Registration Exam (ARE), and then going to graduate school. I consider all four of these steps equally important.

Nothstine Residence, Green Bay, Wisconsin. Architect: Garofalo Architects.
Photographer: Garofalo Architects.

Why and how did you choose which school to attend for your architecture degree? What degree(s) do you possess?
I decided on Notre Dame for undergraduate school because it had one year entirely in Rome, Italy. I went to Yale for graduate school based on the strength of both the art and architecture schools.

What has been your greatest challenge as an architect?
Perhaps it is the necessity of protecting design concepts throughout the life of a project. That this integrity is maintained is not a given — quite the opposite, in many cases.

How do you balance the challenging demands of both an architectural practice and teaching in a program in architecture?
I would not refer to this situation as a balance but as a competition for time; it is something that continues to evolve as the work in the office changes.

You were involved with the award-winning Korean Presbyterian Church of New York, the first building truly conceived and executed with digital media. Please provide insight on the experience of designing by digital media.
We were able to exploit these relatively new digital tools, from email file transfer to complex manipulations of form and program over the Internet, to form a truly unique collaboration. Also, and perhaps more relevant to our current work, the use of multiple software programs (as opposed to one or two) enhances our interests in program over time, complex geometries, patterned space and surface, repetitive structure, and many other concepts. Increasingly, digital technology allows us to be more involved in fabrication and building.

What are your primary responsibilities and duties as an architect?
My office is run as a studio in the truest sense of the word, or at least my definition of it; everyone does everything insofar as possible, meaning everyone acts as a designer, and everyone runs projects. This makes me a sort of director, overseeing and collaborating.

What is the most satisfying part of your job?
It may sound simple, but the seemingly simple banter and exchanges in the office results in some very interesting concepts. We then develop these in a sophisticated way. The act of making, from verbal concept all the way through to fabrication, is most satisfying thing.

Hyde Park Art Center, Chicago. Architect: Garofalo Architects.

Spring Prairie Residence, Spring Prairie, Wisconsin. Architect: Garofalo Architects. Photographer: Nathan Kirkman.

What is the least satisfying part of your job?

The amount of so-called justification needed to complete a building is astounding; most of it is necessary and good, but some of it is absurd. A good example of this is how hard it is to obtain a building permit.

Another unique project during your career was the full-scale prototype newsstand at the Museum of Contemporary Art Chicago. Please describe this project.

The IN.FOrmant.system was a built response to a set of questions raised by the Museum of Contemporary Art Chicago for the exhibit "Material Evidence: Chicago Architecture @ 2000." We were asked to consider issues of materiality in relation to the program of a newsstand, which was constructed full-scale and installed at the museum. The IN.FOrmant.system refers to a future micro-urbanism of many structures in the city dispensing information in variable ways.

IN.FOrmant.system — Museum of Contemporary Art, Chicago. Architect: Garofalo Architects. Photographer: Garofalo Architects.

The prototype as constructed at the museum demonstrated three ideas relative to materiality: first, that the interaction of even a small palette of materials, both conventional and new, can be treated as a flow of matter; second, that this performance is conceived and constructed using parametric modeling techniques inherent to animation software; and, finally, that the material and spatial effects produced by these two ideas may collaborate with and expand the given program of a newsstand.

Who or what experience has been a major influence on your career?

I have had the benefit of many amazing teachers, so it is hard to single out even a few. Other influences include the opportunity to travel as a student in Italy and as an Skidmore, Owings & Merrill Traveling Fellowship recipient through India and Asia.

Teaches About People and Places

KATHRYN H. ANTHONY, PH.D.
Professor
School of Architecture
Department of Landscape Architecture
Gender and Women's Studies Program
University of Illinois at Urbana-Champaign
Champaign, Illinois

Why and how did you become an architecture professor?
I have had a lifelong fascination with architecture, especially the social and psychological relationships among people, places, and spaces. My father is a retired professor of city planning and also has a degree in architecture. I have early memories of visits to my father's office at Columbia University's Avery Hall, where I was intrigued by all the architectural drawings and models displayed throughout the corridors. I was also fortunate to travel with my family throughout Europe. Several visits were to contemporary urban design projects as well as new towns, topics of my father's university lectures.

Why and how did you choose which school to attend for your architecture degree? What degree(s) do you possess?
I was an undergraduate student in psychology at the University of California, Berkeley. During my final year, I discovered the new field of environmental psychology and enrolled in a course on this subject. After purchasing all three textbooks required for the course, I could not put them down. I read them all during the first week of the term. This had never happened before, and I realized I had found my niche. After I received my B.A. in psychology, I remained at Berkeley to complete my Ph.D. in architecture with a specialty in social and behavioral factors in design.

Why is the topic of diversity important for architects?
Diversity is one of the most important issues for today's architects. The built environment reflects our culture, and vice versa. If our buildings, spaces, and places continue to be designed by a relatively homogeneous group of people, what message does that send about our culture? The lack of diversity in the architectural profession impedes progress not only in that field but also in American society at large.

Discrimination in the architectural profession can lead to discrimination in how we all use the built environment, and it has done so for years. Architects must pay greater attention to the needs of women, persons of color, gays and lesbians, and persons with physical disabilities, all of whom — until recently — have been treated as second-class citizens in the built environment. So-called minorities have already become the majority in many American cities, and that trend will only increase.

You are a faculty member in architecture, landscape architecture, and gender and women's studies. Can you describe the differences among these three disciplines?

I enjoy having academic appointments in all three disciplines, although architecture is my primary affiliation. Architecture has traditionally been a male-oriented model of education; however, that is gradually changing as more women students and faculty enter the field. By comparison, landscape architecture has historically provided greater opportunities for women. Gender and women's studies, a much newer discipline, examines issues that the architecture profession until recently has ignored. Students in all three disciplines differ greatly. While design students excel visually and are attentive to their physical surroundings, gender and women's studies tend to be talented verbally and more widely read.

What do you like about research, teaching, and writing?

By far the most appealing aspect of research, teaching, and writing is creativity. Research and writing offer the opportunity to examine issues previously unexplored. One has a chance to carve out new ground, and this is exciting. For example, while *Design Juries on Trial* is by no means the final word on this topic, the fact that it is one of the first examples of empirical research on design juries is significant. This is also true for my second book, *Designing for Diversity,* one of the first books to address how women and persons of color fare in the architectural profession compared to their white male counterparts. It is also based on empirical research.

As a female scholar in architectural education, my writings have a special slant, and I believe I have made a mark in the field. My aim in both books has been to create a more humane environment in both architectural education and practice.

Teaching is another creative endeavor. One of my favorite aspects of teaching is seeing a student flourish outside the university. An idea that started as a casual discussion during office hours germinates into a significant body of work presented at a national venue. It is an amazing metamorphosis, and it is gratifying to watch students discuss their work with leading scholars from around the world. Similarly, I appreciate hearing from alumni long after they graduate and learning about their accomplishments, both professional and personal. It underscores how fortunate we are as educators to cross paths with these individuals in their formative years.

Architecture = Connectivity + Community

PATRICIA SALDANA NATKE, AIA

Principal and President
Urban Works Ltd.
Chicago

Why and how did you become an architect?
I grew up on the south side of Chicago, in an area called Back of the Yards — the famed stockyards of Chicago. I am a first-generation Mexican American; both of my parents are from Zacatecas, Mexico. One day, my parents needed to go to downtown Chicago to address passport issues. We took a long bus ride (or what appeared to be long for an eight-year-old). When we arrived in the center of the Chicago Loop area, I was mesmerized by the skyscrapers, the expanse of the green space in Grant Park, the reflectiveness of the windows and metal on the building skins. I recall being breathless as I entered the Federal Building (Mies) — the expanse of the lobby and the simplicity of the materials. I wanted to know why there were no majestic places and green spaces where I lived. I did not know what an architect did, but I knew I wanted to change my neighborhood for the better. Therefore, I became an architect at a very early age.

Why and how did you choose which school to attend for your architecture degree? What degree(s) do you possess?
I wanted to attend a school somewhat close to home. My choice was based on a limited knowledge of schools that had an architecture curriculum and a narrow view of the options available to me. Because I lived in Chicago, I applied to the Illinois Institute of Technology (IIT) and the University of Illinois at Urbana-Champaign (UIUC). I was accepted at both and chose UIUC after a visit to the campus and a minority recruitment event where my mother and I spent the weekend on the UIUC campus. I hold a bachelor of science in architectural studies.

Westhaven Development — Mixed Income Housing, Chicago. Architect: Urban Works Ltd. Photographer: Anthony May Photography.

What has been your greatest challenge as an architect/principal?
Time! I need time for design excellence, maintaining and running an office of ten, and searching for the next project. My greatest challenge right now is time management and prioritization. I own a firm while balancing a family and being mother to two young daughters.

My other great challenge is the education of clients. I find this one exhilarating. I enjoy inspiring clients to take risks, to think outside of the box, to visualize (although technology has finally made a leap), and to put full trust in us as designers.

How did you name your firm Urban Works Ltd.? Why *urban* and not *architecture*?
We work in the urban realm. By works, we mean all aspects of the city, although we focus heavily on architecture. We also do a lot of urban planning work, interiors, and assistance in grant applications and funding. The name Urban Works denotes our unique capacity to convey the shifting conditions of a modern urban city.

Why has the architectural profession been unable to attract more minorities, particularly Hispanics, to its ranks?
I believe the reason may be socioeconomic conditions as well as cultural issues. Few role models exist in schools, universities, and the workforce. I have always followed my career path with a mindset of overcoming all obstacles — and yes, the obstacles are greater and more regular than anticipated — but I never expected prescriptive solutions.

Benito Juarez High School Performing Art Center, Chicago. Architect: Urban Works Ltd.

You are a past National Diversity Chair of the American Institute of Architects (AIA), and your firm profile states "celebrate diversity." Why is diversity important in the architectural profession?
The profession has an obligation to the public, and the public is diverse. The AIA has finally implemented the funded 2020 Vision for Architecture, which is developing a cohesive system for collecting demographic data on the profession and a methodology for analyzing and publishing the information.

You have been involved with a number of community service projects, including professional associations, neighborhoods groups, and area schools. Why is it important for you to be involved with this community service?
Local communities are underrepresented in architecture; I merely want to assist in giving a voice to people who may not be able to express their opinion. In addition, diverse architects bring valuable perspective to the design and definition of livable communities. Build-

Benito Juarez High School Performing Art Center, Chicago. Architect: Urban Works Ltd.

ings become a part of history; they should reflect their time, place, and inhabitants. Currently, a large segment of society has little influence on becoming part of architectural history. It is a crisis!

What are your primary responsibilities and duties?

I am the principal in charge of design. I provide the design direction on key projects in the office. In addition, I handle the marketing and business development for my office.

What is the most/least satisfying part of your job?

Truly, the most satisfying moment is the completion of a space or building. I like to think back to its genesis and to the human thought and labor involved in making it into a physical object. The least satisfying part is negotiating contracts. Each time we must negotiate a contract fee, I am reminded that society views our work with a finite value.

Who or what experience has been a major influence on your career?

Quite a few inspirational architects/individuals have influenced my career. It is an honor to name them:

Carol Ross Barney, FAIA, Ross Barney + Jankowski, Inc. — I was employed at her firm in the 1990s. I am grateful for her vision and persistence.

Dan Wheeler, FAIA, Wheeler Kearns — I taught with him at the University of Illinois at Chicago (UIC) (2000–2001), and I value his brilliance and optimistic quest for excellence.

Rafael Hernandez — He was the executive director of the Hispanic American Construction Industry Association (and winner of the 2003 AIA Whitney Young Award). I appreciate his endless support and confidence in the potential success of my firm.

Stanley Tigerman and Eva Maddox, Archeworks (2002–present) — I taught with them at Archeworks, and I value their tireless commitment to socially responsible design.

Bradley Lynch, Brininstool + Lynch (2004–present) — I taught with him at Archeworks, where he taught me of the poetics of elegant minimalism.

Architect of Change

ROY ABERNATHY, AIA, IDSA, LEED AP
President
Jova/Daniels/Busby
Atlanta

Why and how did you become an architect?
To be honest, I tried medicine first. I come from a large family that was always involved in the community, and once I realized that a career in medicine involved listening to people complain about problems, I wanted a more creative career. Near the end of my first undergraduate degree, I went looking for a more creative way to work with people and use creativity to solve problems, and I found architecture. I began the traditional undergraduate degree in architecture the next semester.

Why and how did you choose which school to attend for your architecture degree? What degree(s) do you possess?
I entered the first year of an undergraduate program in architecture at North Carolina State University when I was a senior pursuing a bachelor of science degree in animal science. I chose the undergraduate and graduate program in architecture based on geography and the depth of the program. I have two bachelor degrees, one in environmental design and one in animal science. I also have a master of architecture, also from the same school. The combination seems odd, but today I am leading the team to design the new Randall B. Terry, Jr. Companion Animal Veterinary Medical Center at North Carolina State University, where I attended school, and have won awards for the design of spaces shared by animals and people.

What has been your greatest challenge as an architect?
The greatest challenge of my career thus far has been navigating the line between traditional practice and the fringes of design, creativity, and what those outside the profession expect from architects. I have found a position that allows me to work in the markets and with the people who see architecture as broader than the simple design and construction of buildings.

Randall B. Terry, Jr. Companion Animal Veterinary Medical Center, Raleigh, North Carolina. Architect: Jova/Daniels/Busby.

What exactly does a principal do on a day-to-day basis?

I act as the managing principal within the firm, handling the day-to-day management tasks like payroll, financial management, and staffing and human relations. I also lead projects, sell work, and lead our strategic and master planning practices.

What are your primary responsibilities and duties?

Management: I am responsible for the management leadership for the corporation. The controller, vice president of marketing, and directors of architecture, technology, and interiors all report directly to me.

Design: I am responsible for the design leadership of the firm, including marketing strategy, implementation, and staffing.

Strategic and Master Planning: I serve as the principal in charge of the planning group. Our focus is on pre-design and planning for projects, from macro regional to micro space initiatives. This group's goal is to advise the client whether or not an architecture project is on the horizon.

Research: I lead our research and development team. Over the past two years, since the group was created, we have worked on product development with a major furniture manufacturer and provided research support for the internal strategic and master planning studio.

What is the most satisfying part of your job?

The reason I love what I do is the chance to work with designers and clients who get it. By getting it I mean understanding that design and the products of design are tools, just like a hammer and nails. The way we use the tools takes design from just another project or space to a level of project collaboration that you cherish. Architecture is about people and how space supports who they are and what they do; when it's just about you, the designer, it's sculpture, and I don't want to do sculpture.

What is the least satisfying part of your job?

Working with people inserted into the process just to monitor it, not add to it. Because architects have traditionally not taken the responsibility, a wide range of other professions have developed to monitor the design and implementation process without adding any value to the process or the product. Architects should focus on managing the process, project, and expectations so the client has confidence in the delivery process.

Previously, you were the director of facilities and manager of geographic services at Accenture. How did your background as an architect prepare you for such a position?

Another amazing experience in my career, my time at Accenture showed me that my training as an architect was more marketable to clients than to other architects. At Accenture, my combined roles all related to the way Accenture used, built, and managed space internally and externally. At this point in my career I realized the strategic planning process was tailored to the skills inherent in archi-

Randall B. Terry, Jr. Companion Animal Veterinary Medical Center, Raleigh, North Carolina. Architect: Jova/Daniels/Busby.

tecture. The ability to work at the highest conceptual level and define a way to move from that concept to reality is the core of strategic planning. Our ability to communicate those macro concepts in a way that is both real and tangible makes us unique as a profession. Accenture understands that aspect of what architects can do and used it to expand from a consulting company to an international partnership that defines and creates its own markets.

In the past, you have been involved with various civic organizations. Why are you involved with these organizations, and how do you connect this involvement with your career?
I like to become involved and am always amazed at how much an active community can accomplish. I connect my involvement with my career through networking and social responsibility. Our firm allocates a portion of our fees and time to give back to the community and has as part of its mission doing architecture that improves the community.

On a recent project to renovate and add to the largest Jewish temple in Atlanta, the project scope displaced a number of community organizations, including a women/children's shelter and an organization that coordinates more than 25,000 volunteers annually. We helped both organizations relocate and donated a significant portion of our fees to help make it happen. I served on the capital campaign committee for Hands on Atlanta while leading the team to design their new space. They needed their space to be a tool to help them recruit, educate, and coordinate the volunteers, who are important to the local community, while giving them an identity in the city. The project and my experience with it have resulted in lifelong friendships and memories, all supporting a project that helps Hands on Atlanta do what they do better.

Who or what experience has been a major influence on your career?
The experience with the most persistent influence was the year I spent working for a combined architecture firm and sculpture studio, Clearscapes, which integrates real art into architecture. During that year, a large-scale project for a corporate headquarters included a number of artists who worked collaboratively on one large piece. As a production assistant, I had a chance to see more of what went into the collaborative and creative process than anyone else. The sculptor, Thomas Sayre, developed the concept, which centered on the history and future mission of the corporation, and he involved others in his vision, including other artists, the architecture team, the client, and those of us in the sculpture studio.

As a sculptor, Thomas described for me a connection between the senses and the brain that showed me how architecture, sculpture, space, and culture all influence perception. The experience helped me develop a perceptive nature whereby I look at things differently than many other people do.

Retail Design: Managing Change

CAROLYN G. JONES, AIA

Associate Principal
Callison Architecture, Inc.
Seattle

Why and how did you become an architect?

After I took a miniature Introduction of Architecture class at a summer camp program in junior high, architectural design became one of my favorite hobbies. I
spent summers at my table designing floor plans and building foam core models
of houses. Despite my interest in architecture, I never thought of it as a career I
wanted to pursue. I went to college as an international studies major without
giving architecture a thought. During the second semester of my freshman year, I
had one elective class open, and my mom talked me into taking Intro to Architecture. Three weeks later I was an architecture major.

**Why and how did you choose which school to attend for your architecture
degree? What degree(s) do you possess?**

Because I did not originally go to college to study architecture, it was pure luck
that I ended up at the only school I applied to that even had an architecture program. I chose the University of Notre Dame for its well-rounded liberal arts undergraduate program, its size, the campus atmosphere, and the student life it
provided. I was interested in schools that were a great overall fit for me personally, whether or not they had the best program in my field of study.

In the end, I believe the Notre Dame program provided me with a strong background and foundation for the study and practice of architecture. However, I truly
believe that the most important part of my education was based on my entire
Notre Dame experience.

What has been your greatest challenge as an architect?

My greatest challenge as an architect has been learning the skills necessary for
my job that were not taught in school, mainly management and leadership. One
of the main challenges has been learning to set individualism aside and make
teamwork a priority.

Right after leaving school, I had a tough time learning humility and recognizing how much I did not know. With ten years of experience, I now find it tough to have that earlier confidence in myself as I become more and more aware of what I do not know. I try to remember that experience has given me good judgment and decision-making capabilities and that these are the most valuable skills of all.

What is retail design, and how is it different from architecture design?

Retail design is focused on the interior architectural design as well as visual merchandising. The design of the entire environment, down to the smallest detail of a merchandise fixture, is part of what makes the space unique.

I have never felt that interiors and architecture are distinct fields, and in retail design, they are inseparable. Interior design *does* have an additional layer in the traditional sense of color and materials, which are also critical to retail design, but from the architectural standpoint, retail design must form a seamless connection between interior and exterior spaces and forms.

The key is remembering that in retail, the architecture serves as a backdrop for displaying the merchandise. You have to understand how product is displayed, how it best sells, how the customer interacts in or shops the space, the impact of lighting, and the importance of setting a certain atmosphere through a combination of built environment, furniture, fixtures, and finishes.

How have you been involved with the AIA at the local and national levels? Why are you involved with the AIA?

I began my involvement with the AIA as a way to network in my local architecture community. The AIA provided me with a way to meet other architects at all career levels and to find out about firms in town.

Although I initially got involved to give back to the profession, I stayed involved in an effort to help create the future of the profession, especially within the Institute. I also enjoyed the opportunity to meet and work with young professionals like myself and to develop a peer group to look to for support and guidance as I made my way into my career.

The AIA, and the Young Architects Forum (YAF) in particular, have given me a place to learn and grow with others, to see that I am not alone in my struggles, and to give support and a voice to young professionals. My involvement at the local and national levels has been my attempt to further that cause both for my generation and those to come.

Coldwater Creek International Plaza Retail Store, Tampa, Florida. Architect: Callison Architecture. Rendering: Brian Fisher, Presentation Arts.

Nordstrom, Canoga Park, California. Architect: Callison Architecture. Rendering: Amy DiMarco, AIA.

What are your primary responsibilities and duties?

As a project manager, my primary responsibilities are general oversight of the design and construction of a project from start to finish. I work with the client, my internal team, and the consultants to set the schedule for project documentation.

From there, we set the budget for the design and documentation services, which I monitor for the duration of the project, including working with our accounting department during the monthly invoice process. Internally, I work with my project team to keep to our schedule, help coordinate with our consultants, and review documents and design for quality assurance, coordination, and consistency.

I am primarily responsible for communication with the client's project manager, getting information we need to proceed, reviewing design decisions, and working through developer or landlord coordination issues.

What is the most/least satisfying part of your job?

The least satisfying part of my job is probably office politics. This has been an issue for me in five-person firms as well as 500-person firms.

The most satisfying part of my job is being in the field and solving problems with the client and contractors. I learn so much every day that I am on a job site, and being knowledgeable and creative in solving problems as they arise is very satisfying. It is a great feeling to be part of a team working together to make a project happen, and the reward is actually seeing something built and watching people use it.

A less measurable but still satisfying part of my job is being a role model for younger architects, especially women. I am honored to be one of the young leaders in my firm; it is important for the next generation to see that career growth and success are perhaps not as far off as they imagine.

Who or what experience has been a major influence on your career?

By far the greatest influences on my career are my two mentors. Both were extremely supportive of my career growth and champions for me within the firm. As a result, I have enjoyed rapid career development and a chance to expand my skill set and knowledge base. I am certain these would help fuel my success in other firms or with other project types.

One word of advice: Finding a great mentor is a two-way process. The more interest, initiative, drive, and enthusiasm you show in your career, the more likely you are to attract the attention of a mentor who can support you along the way.

Educator and Architect

ROGER SCHLUNTZ, FAIA

Dean and Professor
School of Architecture and Planning
University of New Mexico
Albuquerque

Why and how did you become an architect?
As a youth, I always enjoyed building things, both literally and in my imagination. In high school I showed a strong aptitude for math and science and a fairly accomplished skill in art. I had never met an architect before enrolling in the academic architecture program at college, so I knew very little of the reality of the profession or practice. My career choice was almost as much a process of elimination — that is, of what I knew did not interest me — as it was a declaration of what I wanted to be.

In the old days of the lockstep, five-year bachelor of architecture professional programs, once you embarked on that path it was difficult to turn and proceed in another academic direction. I was probably motivated as much by fear of failure as desire to succeed. Fortunately, and with a bit of luck, I think I chose wisely.

Why and how did you choose which school to attend for your architecture degree? What degree(s) do you possess?
I grew up on a farm in Nebraska, a son of Depression-era parents. Going to a college out of state was never a consideration, and I wanted to be at the University of Nebraska anyway. I expect I would have enrolled in engineering if Nebraska had not had an architecture program. I remember working construction one summer and observing the architect's visit to the building site. That's when I decided that, as much as I liked working with my hands, his position and situation was undoubtedly preferable.

I received the professional degree of bachelor of architecture at Nebraska in 1967 and completed the structural engineering specialization in the process. The only graduate program I applied to was the University of California, Berkeley, partly because of its fantastic reputation and partly because of its diverse and exceptional faculty. I visited the Berkeley campus and fell in love with San Francisco and the splendid geographic setting of the Bay Area on first sight.

I received my master of architecture degree from Berkeley in 1968, with an emphasis (if one might call it that) in urban design. I had the wonderful mentorship of the late Joseph Esherick, FAIA, while studying there, and the opportunity to work part-time in the Sausalito office of Sasaki Walker Associates. I was tempted to pursue a graduate degree in landscape architecture and might have chosen that career path were it not for the circumstances of the time. I have some regret, even today, that I did not pursue landscape architecture as a career. Perhaps it's not too late.

What has been your greatest challenge as an architect/faculty?
I have faced many challenges — that is, opportunities — and on any given day I would probably answer this question differently!

What is your primary responsibility as a dean? Why did you make this professional career choice?
Every day seems to bring a different primary responsibility. Being a dean is not unlike being an architect in that one is constantly required to seek the means and methods to optimize limited resources in managing and direction of professional design programs.

In most institutions, the dean is responsible for managing the programs and curriculum, overseeing almost every function within the college or school, and the school's budget. We are typically heavily engaged in outreach activities and fundraising. Collectively, the deans also play an important function as an advisory group to the provost or president of the university on broader institutional issues and directions.

Helping others (students, faculty, and staff) achieve their goals and objectives within the context, and certainly limitations, of the institutional setting is always challenging. But I find that being able to effect change and make good things happen is extremely rewarding.

I did not consciously choose academic administration as my professional career, but up to this point it seems to have turned out that way. Notwithstanding, I think most of us in higher education administration still consider ourselves, first and foremost, educators and architects. Although the hours are long and the problems and frustrations never cease, the job is certainly a challenge and, for the most part, intellectually stimulating. I might also note that the workday is seldom, if ever, boring.

You have served as director at Arizona State University and dean at both University of Miami and University of New Mexico. How has serving these three institutions shaped your professional career?

Prior to accepting the position with Arizona State University, I taught for a year at California Polytechnic at San Luis Obispo, then for eight years at the University of Nebraska, where I first received tenure. I have always enjoyed teaching and expect to return to the academic faculty on a full- or part-time basis after I stop being a dean.

I left the University of Nebraska faculty to become the executive director of the Association of Collegiate Schools of Architecture (ACSA) in Washington, D.C. This three-year assignment probably focused my interest in program administration and leadership, and the position offered at Arizona State University seemed a logical progression in my academic career.

The university setting provides considerable opportunity for creative work and sponsored research activities. For example, a colleague and I received an Honor Award in Urban Design from *Progressive Architecture* magazine for our efforts in developing the Nebraska State Capitol and Environs Plan. At Arizona State University, I was able to institute the Joint ASU/City of Phoenix Urban Design Program, and a similar initiative at the University of Miami resulted in the school's Center for Urban and Community Design.

Having the opportunity to live in many parts of the country (as well as overseas, briefly) most certainly broadened my experiences and perceptions of society as well as my understanding of the architecture profession. Throughout my career(s), I have learned from my students and have had the good fortune of meeting and often working with incredibly interesting and talented individuals in architecture, related fields, and other disciplines. All of this has provided me a wonderful feast, and each experience has uniquely contributed to my career and development.

One part of your professional career was serving as the professional adviser for number of major design competitions. What does that entail? What do design competitions bring to a project?

I found it extremely difficult to balance the demanding and sometimes competing needs and expectations of academia and a private practice. So I could focus on my university assignments, I decided some time ago to engage in limited consulting and forgo the attempt to develop and run a small firm. In working with public agencies in developing design review procedures, urban design guidelines, and procurement processes for professional design services, almost inadvertently I became involved in serving as the professional adviser to what has now become a fairly extensive list of major design competitions throughout the United States.

The primary purpose of a professional design competition is to increase the probability of the completed project achieving design excellence. With that in mind, and acting as the agent for the competition sponsor (client), the professional adviser must ensure the fairness of the process and safeguard the interests of the competing architects and the profession. Being able to organize, direct, and observe the competition process as well as the work of inspired architects engaged in the competition is a marvelous experience. And it is really great to be paid to do something I would probably be willing to do for nothing.

As a professional adviser for a design competition, my specific role might include some of the standard preliminary design services that are part of any architectural project — for example, programming, site selection, scheduling, and review of owner-architect contract forms. In organizing a design competition, a major and critical task is the development of the competition rules — essentially the contract between the sponsor and the participants that details the process, schedule, submission requirements, and evaluation criteria. I am usually very much involved in the selection of jurors and other advisers. I often assist with post-competition publicity, exhibitions, and publication of the submitted entries.

Who or what experience has been a major influence on your career?
An astonishing number of individuals and experiences have directly impacted my career as well as how I view the world and the profession. If I had to select the one person who has had the most lasting impression and impact, I would probably choose Joseph Esherick, FAIA. He was an exceptional architect, extremely thoughtful, and very patient. He was probably not the most gifted teacher in the traditional sense, but knowing him and seeing how he thought, worked, and lived his life was extremely enlightening for me.

Teaching Architect

MAX UNDERWOOD, AIA

Professor of Architecture
School of Architecture and Landscape Architecture
College of Architecture and Environmental Design
Arizona State University
Tempe, Arizona

Architect and Principal
Underwood + Crisp
Tempe, Arizona

Why and how did you become an architect?
Because my father was involved in construction as a high-voltage electrician, I grew up within the building industry and became an architect primarily by osmosis. Some of my fondest childhood memories are of accompanying my father to his construction sites at Disneyland, Kaiser Steel, MGM studios, and the Huntington Library Gardens.

In addition, I spent many hours of my youth working with my hands, building custom furniture and rebuilding my 1955 Oldsmobile, in our well-equipped shop in the family garage. In high school, I excelled in chemistry and physics. Because I love conceptual thinking, open-ended discovery, plus art and drafting, I worked summers for several local architects and contractors.

Why and how did you choose which school to attend for your architecture degree? What degree(s) do you possess?
During my senior year of high school, I was recruited in physics by Caltech and the University of Southern California (USC). After attending their respective open houses, I decided to enroll in a dual physics and architecture major at USC.

In the mid-1970s, the architecture program at USC had a wonderful mix of European and Southern California professionals who had commissions throughout Los Angeles. In addition, the larger university offered exciting classes in film, urban geography, computer science, and, of course, physics, taught by leading physicists of the NASA Jet Propulsion Lab in Pasadena.

Spaces of Silence, Kyoto,
Japan. Architect: Soami.
Photographer: Marc Monty.

The larger architectural and physics cultures of Los Angeles were exhilarating at
the time, with Aldo Rossi visiting at the University of California at Los Angeles
(UCLA), the newly formed energy of Southern California Institute of Architecture
(SCI-ARC), and Richard Feynman lecturing at Caltech. During my junior year of
the bachelor of science in architecture program, I worked in the office of Charles
and Ray Eames. This was a life-altering and formative experience that affected
my subsequent career as both an architect and an educator.

I attended Princeton University and received my master of architecture degree
within its small, intimate program. Princeton is close enough to New York City so
I could be part of its vital energy and still get my work done.

**What are your primary responsibilities and duties as a teaching architect, an
architect, and a faculty member?**
True education is not only imparting a body of professional knowledge but also
questioning and advancing it through a collaborative investigation of the discipline by both student and teacher, whether in school or in a professional office.

Education is a forum where the distinctions between teacher and student are
replaced with the notion of collective inquiry and discourse. The condition is not
one of students in competition with one another but rather one where everyone
is discovering something that was unfamiliar a moment before and where everyone is willing to help one other clarify ideas, methods, and work.

Education begins with a response to each student's individuality and talent. The student and teacher must first jointly find out where the student is relative to his personal growth and then establish how to develop his self-discipline, motivation, expertise, and individuality. Education, like design, is an act of faith and discipline where the limits are not clearly defined and the student must discover, define, and act on them. Outstanding students constantly reach beyond themselves to develop new ideas, cherishing the difficulties of work that asks hard questions and forces them to experience the world differently and to change. The pleasure of teaching comes from firsthand participation in a student's discovery of the previously unrealized power of his innate ability to form his own ideas, investigations, and self-criticism.

Next, education should focus on the development of each individual's processes of inquiry, invention, and making, grounded by an emphasis on making connections between cross-cultural references, other disciplines, and architecture. Therein lies a concern with integrating interdisciplinary knowledge and critical inquiry from the arts, humanities, and sciences alike, but in ways that suit the problems and purposes of the present.

Students should develop a personal attitude and vision in their inquiry of architecture, test it, and realize it through their critically made work. They must be encouraged to doubt, question givens, and generate acute alternatives to what architecture is today. Familiarity with that evolving body of knowledge we call *tradition* and its progression of ideas helps students obtain a critical breadth of personal vision and understand why certain questions being explored by other disciplines are essential to their evolving body of work. Students must develop representational media and notational devices that capture the spirit of their design inquiry and allow them to visualize, refine, and communicate its qualities to other people. They must remember that the most challenging professional and intellectual problems of contemporary architecture require the integration of several disciplines into broader understanding, insight, and action.

Who or what experiences have been major influences on your career?
Working for Charles and Ray Eames in the mid-1970s was one of the most profound and life-altering experiences of my career. Their office allowed me to experience firsthand exemplary professional practice and what happens if you "make design your life, and life your design." It was a rich and provocative environment for celebrating the inquiry into the unknown. Everyone in the office was personally engaged in thinking deeply and differently, going beyond the point where others had stopped, satisfied. I saw endless speculation, prototyping, and, when a promising revelation was arrived at, the celebration of its beauty through film so anyone, even a child, could share in the enjoyment of the discovery. Charles always asked one question at a desk critique: "What is interesting?"

A Privilege and Blessing

JACK A. KREMERS, AIA

Professor of Architecture
Judson College
Elgin, Illinois

Why and how did you become an architect?

My father was small homebuilder. I never thought in terms of becoming an architect but was aware at a very early age of the processes and technologies of wood frame construction. My father gave the designers sketches that he envisioned and asked them to provide a buildable design. The transition from Dad's sketches to the final drawings made me aware that with experience, education, and skill, one could greatly impact the creation of building forms and physical environments.

I was the first in my family to go to college. I decided I enjoyed math and did not want to take any foreign language courses. The engineering program was the only one that focused on math *and* did not require foreign language courses. Thus began my college career.

However, I soon realized that something was missing. Engineering did not address all of my interests and how I hoped to spend my career in a productive and fulfilling way. A student in the architecture program at the University of Michigan explained how architecture integrated engineering ideas with the fulfillment of real human needs and expressions. The idea excited me immediately, and I began to explore my chances of entering the University of Michigan architecture program. I was accepted.

Although I found the architecture program tough, I discovered that I thoroughly enjoyed bringing together technology, function, and aesthetics. As I progressed in the curriculum, I found my strengths in the technology areas and the then emerging subdisciplines of lighting design and acoustics. I also enjoyed presenting my ideas. Organizing the ideas and then formally presenting a project for review was exciting and motivating.

Why and how did you choose which school to attend for your architecture degree? What degree(s) do you possess?

I attended the University of Michigan because it was the best architecture program near my home in Grand Rapids. I considered Michigan the ideal; they were the Wolverines. I grew up listening to their football games on the radio, and that excited me. The color and pageantry of the whole university probably played a bigger role in my choice of school than the content of the curriculum or program.

In 1974 I received the bachelor of architecture degree, the accredited degree at that time. Upon graduation, I began working at an office in Ann Arbor, but I found the office experience boring after the academic environment. After a year, I returned for the master of architecture at Michigan. My interest was in exploring architectural technology. While in graduate school, I had the opportunity to teach as a teaching assistant. At the time, teaching was only a way to help pay the bills, but I found I enjoyed the classroom. I always enjoyed academic life, and teaching provided a splendid opportunity to combine my interests in architectural technology, the academy, and the practice of architecture. I determined that I would at some point seek an academic position.

What has been your greatest challenge as an architect?
The biggest challenge I have faced was the opportunity to create an accredited program in architecture at Judson College, a small evangelical Christian college in Elgin, Illinois. The forty-year-old college was built as a liberal arts college. In 1997, the college determined to create a program in architecture. Judson was a most unlikely place to establish a new architecture program, and even its biggest supporters were not convinced it could be done.

I arrived at Judson in the fall of 1998, when the program was in its second year. Shortly thereafter, I was asked to chair the new program.

The college made its commitment clear through the provision of adequate resources and the encouragement and support of upper administration, but it was difficult to satisfy the Judson academic community. An architecture program is unique in that the National Architectural Accrediting Board (NAAB) establishes the content and standards. One of the issues was that this new accredited degree would have to be a master's degree. Judson College had no previous graduate programs.

The difficult steps in the accreditation process were convincing the academic community, steeped in the tradition of a liberal arts environment and the Judson College image of what an academic environment and standards should be, to support and approve the content of the program. It was also a challenge to bring together a diverse new architecture faculty with great skills and credentials but little teaching experience in higher education.

The goal was achieved in summer 2004, when NAAB awarded the program full accreditation at the first opportunity. I am proud that the program is not only accredited but also a superior program, as demonstrated by our first graduates working and fulfilling their dreams and the dreams of all the people at Judson College.

My first year teaching (1969–1970) at Kent State University was also a large challenge. The infamous shootings by the National Guard occurred on May 4, 1970, immediately outside of the architecture building. Somehow we survived it, but the challenge included completing classes for the second half of the spring quarter when the campus was locked to all and returning to classes for the next several years in an environment that had lost confidence in its purpose, let alone the achievement of excellence. That experience pretty well prepared me for the next thirty years of teaching in higher education. I learned to not give up but to remain faithful to the challenges that always develop.

What are your primary responsibilities and duties as an architect and a faculty member?
My primary responsibility as a combined architect and faculty member is to understand and know the material I teach as well as I possibly can and then to make it understandable and appealing to the beginning architect in a way that fits in the context of the total discipline. I need to truly know, and I need to be able to communicate effectively. John Flynn, my mentor when I began to teach at Kent State, told me that a teacher could never make an idea or concept too simple. That has stuck with me over the past thirty-five years.

The details and conventions of the building industry can be confusing to someone new to the field. The theory or basis behind many applications can be lost or undecipherable. A good architecture teacher makes the theory understandable and connects it to the culture of the built environment and culture as a whole.

How does teaching architecture differ than practicing architecture?
Teaching requires patience. Ideas that seem obvious to me are not always obvious to students. In architectural practice, one grows and becomes the leader, and others follow because of one's experience. In teaching, the student body is new each year. Each class has different experiences and background. The culture changes rapidly. A teacher must first understand where the students are at and then provide the leadership in their education. The students are refreshing and raise questions and issues that people of my age and background do not consider.

Teaching is concerned with theory and ideas. Practice is concerned with application and client needs. Both roles contain all aspects, but to differing degrees.

After a substantial teaching career at Kent State, you chose to change to Judson College, a new program. Why did you make that change?
After initially considering me for the Advisory Council, Judson College invited me to become a faculty member. I was completing my thirtieth year of teaching at Kent State.

Judson is an evangelical Christian college and probably the only other program I would have considered teaching in. I am an evangelical Christian. It had become increasingly clear to me over the thirty years at Kent State that political correctness was less and less tolerant of a commitment to Christian faith in the secular classroom.

Who or what experience has been a major influence on your career?
Faculty members who have influenced me are John Flynn, Willard Oberdick, Peters Oppermann, Robert Darvas, and Gunnar Birkerts, FAIA. Jerry Cain, the president of Judson College, has been a great encouragement and leader in bringing the Judson Architecture Program to accreditation.

The opportunity to teach environmental technology at Kent State, in courses created by John Flynn, allowed me to research lighting, acoustics, alterative energy sources, and resource conservation.

Notes

1. Rand, Ayn. (1943). *The fountainhead.* New York: Penguin (p. 16).
2. *The American Heritage dictionary.* (2000). Boston, MA: Houghton Mifflin.
3. Kostof, Spiro. (1986). *The architect: Chapters in the history of the profession.* New York: Oxford University Press (p. v).
4. Cuff, Dana. (1991). *Architecture: The story of practice.* Cambridge, MA: MIT Press (p. 153).
5. Raskin, Eugene. (1974). *Architecture and people.* Englewood Cliffs, NJ: Prentice-Hall (p. 101).
6. U.S. Department of Labor. Bureau of Labor Statistics Occupation Report. (2002). Retrieved February 20, 2005, from http://www.bls.gov
7. NAAB statistics report. (2004). Retrieved June 28, 2005, from http://www.naab.org
8. National Council of Architectural Registration Boards. 2004 Survey of registered architects. (2004). Retrieved June 12, 2005 from http://www.ncarb.org
9. U.S. Department of Labor. Bureau of Labor Statistics. Occupational outlook handbook. (2004–2005). Architects, Except Landscape and Naval. Retrieved June 29, 2005, from http://www.bls.gov/oco/ocos038.htm
10. American Institute of Architects. (2003). *The business of architecture: The 2003 AIA firm Survey.* Retrieved June 28, 2005, from http://www.aia.org
11. Anthony, Kathryn. (2001). *Designing for diversity.* Urbana: University of Illinois Press (p. 22).

Alexandria Central Library, Alexandria, Virginia. Architect: Michael Graves + Associates/PGAL. Photographer: Eric Taylor, ASSOCIATE AIA. Photo© EricTaylorPhoto.com.

Chapter Two

The Education of an Architect

From a legal standpoint, there are three major steps to becoming an architect: education, experience, and exam. The most critical may be education. While completing your formal education (obtaining a degree) may last five to seven years in college, your architectural education will continue throughout your lifetime. This chapter will help you learn how to prepare for education, discuss the different degree paths, outline the selection process, and describe the experience of an architecture student.

But first, how can you prepare for a career in architecture if you are younger than high school age? As you may already know, a number of toys, books, activities, and resources can introduce you to architecture.

Preparation: Pre-High School

TOYS

Over the past century, numerous toys with an architectural theme have been developed. Many are variations of blocks; all provide children a sense of design, discovery, and creation. For example, Legos® are one of the more popular children's toys that architecture students say helped them become interested in the field. John Lloyd Wright, the son of the famous architect Frank Lloyd Wright, invented Lincoln Logs in 1916. Introduced just prior in 1914, Tinkertoys® and Erector Sets allow children to construct and build their ideas. A more basic toy that almost all children play with is blocks. Sets of purchased wooden blocks can be used to build everything from patterns to elaborate structures, houses, and skyscrapers.

A less well-known toy, used by Frank Lloyd Wright as a child, is Froebel Blocks, a series of wooden stacking blocks developed in the 1830s by Friedrich Froebel, a German educator and the originator of the kindergarten, for children to learn the elements of geometric form, mathematics, and creative design. Wright described their influence on his work: "The smooth shapely maple blocks with which to build, the sense of which never afterwards leaves the fingers: so form became feeling," and "A significant idea behind the blocks is the importance for developing minds of examining things around them in a freely structured manner."

BOOKS

Many books tell stories featuring architecture or buildings. Some targeted at younger children have good illustrations of architecture, while others have plots that engage the reader with houses, castles, trees, and imaginative environments.

ACTIVITIES

Cultural institutions in some areas sponsor events or activities meant to expose children to the world of architecture. For example, the National Building Museum in Washington, D.C., holds a Festival of the Building Arts each fall. During the festival, visitors of all ages can build a brick wall, participate in a nail-driving contest, try stone carving and woodworking, learn the techniques involved in surveying, build a city out of boxes, or create a sculpture out of nuts and bolts. The Frank Lloyd Wright Home and Studio near Chicago offers an opportunity for young teens to serve as tour guides. Contact local museums or other organizations in your area for exhibits, lectures, or classes related to architecture and the built environment.

Selected Books on Architecture for Children

Architects Make Zigzags: Looking at Architecture A to Z by Diane Maddox (ISBN: 047114357X)

Draw 50 Buildings and Other Structures by Lee J. Ames (ISBN: 0385417772)

Frank Lloyd Wright for Kids: His Life and Ideas by Kathleen Thorne-Thomsen (ISBN: 155652207X)

Houses and Homes by Ann Morris (ISBN: 0688135781)

Housebuilding for Children by Les Walker (ISBN: 0879513322)

How a House Is Built by Gail Gibbons (ISBN: 0823412326)

Math in the Real World of Architecture by Shirley Cook (ISBN: 0865303428)

Round Buildings, Square Buildings, and Buildings That Wiggle. by Phillip M. Isaacson (ISBN: 0394893824)

The Architecture Pack by Ron Van Der Meer (ISBN: 0679431004)

Under Every Roof by Patricia Brown Glenn (ISBN: 0471144282)

RESOURCES

Organizations such as Center for the Understanding of the Built Environment (CUBE), Built Environment Education Program (BEEP), Chicago Architecture Foundation, Learning by Design in Massachusetts, and Architecture in Education serve as resources for both individuals and teachers who desire to help younger children learn about architecture. CUBE brings together educators with community partners to effect change that will lead to a quality built and natural environment. A program of the AIA Philadelphia, Architecture in Education brings architects, landscape architects, and other design professionals into classrooms to help young people understand what it takes to make buildings and communities work for the people who live in them. BEEP, a program for young students sponsored by the AIA California Council,

Willits House, Highland Park, Illinois. Architect: Frank Lloyd Wright. Photographer: R. Lindley Vann.

encourages in elementary students an awareness of the built and natural environments, architecture, urban planning, seismic safety, and how citizens can influence growth and planning in California.

An element of the Boston Society of Architects, Learning by Design gives young people the opportunity and the skills they need to communicate their ideas about the built and natural environments, about community, and about themselves. This organization has developed children's design workshops with themes including designing dream houses; designing the community; neighborhood walking tours; places to learn; history through structures; block play; and block design.

Preparation: High School

The process of becoming an architect can take ten to fifteen years from entering an architecture program to passing the Architect Registration Examination (ARE).

Where does this process begin? Based on interactions with students wishing to become architects, it starts very early. Some students say their interest in becoming an architect began in elementary school or even earlier. For others, it was later — after college or later in life.

Where does their desire to become architects come from? Students say they enjoyed drawing; they enjoyed constructing or building with blocks, Legos, Erector sets, and similar toys. In addition, a drafting course may have piqued an interest in architecture.

What should you do if your desire to become an architect emerges in high school? From the academic coursework you choose to a part-time position in an architectural firm, you can pursue many activities to further your interest in architecture and begin the process of becoming an architect. If you completed college, many of these same activities can be helpful.

ACADEMIC COURSEWORK

Because becoming an architect requires a college education (in most states), your high school academic curriculum should focus on college preparatory courses, including four years of English and mathematics. Pursue as many honors and advanced placement (AP) courses as possible; by taking and passing advanced placement exams, you receive college credit and bypass required entry-level courses. (*Note:* The number of credit hours you can receive varies by college.) As well, AP credit allows you to carry a lighter academic load or pursue additional coursework such as electives or minors.

While the mathematics requirement varies among architecture programs, most either require or encourage you to take calculus. You should pursue or take the highest-level math course your high school offers.

Although some high schools do not require or offer physics, you should take an entire year of high school physics rather than biology or chemistry if you can possibly arrange it. A good year-long physics course is excellent preparation for college physics and structures courses.

In addition, take art, drawing, and design classes rather than architectural drafting or CAD. Your interest in architecture may surface due to a drafting course, but drafting is not as helpful in your skill development as art classes. Art, drawing, and design courses develop visual aptitude and literacy while expanding your ability to communicate graphically. Take a freehand drawing course or a three-dimensional course such as sculpture or woodworking. In addition, art courses provide you with materials for your portfolio, a requirement for some architecture programs.

Do your best with every academic course you take! While grades are not the only criterion by which college admissions offices judge applications, it certainly is one of the more important ones.

Beside academics, what can you do to begin your preparation for a career in architecture? Consider the following: (a) exploration of the built environment; (b) visits to architecture firms and schools; (c) participating in a summer program sponsored by an architecture program; and (d) participating in an after-school program. All these provide you a head start on the path to becoming an architect.

EXPLORATION

An important skill to acquire in becoming an architect is the ability to see. By learning to observe buildings, spaces, and their relationships, you become sensitive to issues that concern architects. Explore your surroundings by looking closely at the built environment every day.

Piazza d'Italia, New Orleans, Louisiana. Architect: Charles Moore. Photographer: Isabelle Gournay.

What detail can you describe from memory about a building you know well — a school or nearby store, for example? Now, visit the building and note all the details you did not remember or notice before. Draw sketches of the overall building or details.

MARGARET DeLEEUW, UNIVERSITY OF MARYLAND

Tour and observe your neighborhood or city and take visual notes about the architecture you encounter. Seek out guided tours of significant buildings in your city and learn about their architectural features.

Purchase a sketchbook and begin to teach yourself to draw. Sketch from real life to develop your drawing skills and sharpen your awareness of the existing environment. Sketching from life trains you to observe, analyze, and evaluate while recording your surroundings. Do not worry about the quality of the sketches; focus instead on developing your skill of seeing.

When I was a summer intern, I sat outside and sketched during my lunch break. One day I sketched a landscape, as the office overlooked a waterfall. Another day I drew my shoe or my handbag. Yet another day I found some object in the office to draw, like a lamp. Some days I sketched my hand or my foot. This simple exercise was greatly beneficial, as it taught me that the key to producing an excellent drawing is to train your eyes to see.

MARGARET DeLEEUW, UNIVERSITY OF MARYLAND

One way to develop your drawing skills is to dedicate a specific amount of time — one or two hours — per day to sketching. Be committed to drawing each day. Practice, practice, and practice!

Begin reading books, magazines, and newspapers articles on architecture and the profession of architecture. Check your local public library for ideas.

VISITS

Tour the design studios of a nearby school of architecture to become acquainted with the experiences of an architecture student. Speak with students about what they do. If possible, attend a few classes to learn about the courses you may take. Additionally, consider attending a lecture sponsored by the school. Most schools sponsor evening lectures highlighting architects and their work.

Typically, these are free and open to the public.

Visit with local architects to gain a broader understanding of the nature of an architect's work and the value of the profession. To locate an architect, contact the local chapter of The American Institute of Architects (AIA), listed in the phone book, or use the yellow pages. Ask your parents, teachers, or friends of your family if they know any practicing architects. Try not to be intimidated as you call to meet with an architect. Remember, these connections may be valuable when you apply to architecture programs or for possible summer employment opportunities.

Visit construction sites to learn how buildings are constructed. Talk with carpenters, builders, and others in the building industry to learn their perspectives on architecture. In addition, travel throughout your community, your region of the country, or to other countries to experience architecture from various perspectives. As you visit, sketch!

SUMMERS

Many colleges and universities offer summer programs designed for high school students who desire to learn about the field of architecture. Lasting from one to several weeks, these programs are an excellent opportunity to determine if architecture is the right career choice. Most include design, drawing, and model-building assignments, field trips to firms or nearby buildings, and other activities. These can all assist you in determining if architecture is for you. Summer programs are also a good way to learn about the regular architecture program of that particular school.

Each summer, the Graduate School of Design at Harvard University offers Career Discovery, a six-week program during which students are introduced to design through a core program of morning lectures, panel discussions, and field trips. Over forty schools nationwide offer such summer programs. Entities such as museums and community park districts may also offer such programs.

While growing up, I wanted to be an architect, but I really did not know much about the profession or architecture school. To learn more, I attended the Discovering Architecture Program at the University of Maryland the summer before my senior year of high school. Completing the program solidified my interest in architecture. During the three-week program we took field trips to Baltimore and Washington, D.C., listened to lectures about the basics of architecture, and designed and modeled our own memorial. I loved how the program was hands-on and encouraged interaction with faculty and graduate students. Most important, it was located in the architecture building on campus so I could experience architecture school and college life.

DANA PERZYNSKI, UNIVERSITY OF MARYLAND

If you take a summer internship with a construction company or architectural firm, you may be limited in the tasks you do, but the experience will be far more rewarding than typical summer positions. If you are unable to secure a summer internship, find an architect to shadow for a day or a week. Many high schools offer programs designed to connect students with career professionals.

Seaside, Florida. Photographer: Isabelle Gournay.

AFTER-SCHOOL PROGRAMS

Another program that exposes you to the profession is the ACE (Architecture, Construction, and Engineering) Mentor Program of America. ACE is an after-school program for high school students interested in learning about career opportunities in architecture, engineering, and construction management. Throughout the school year, students are matched with professionals on a project that suits their interests. Other extracurricular programs include the Boy Scouts of America Explorer Post, Odyssey of the Mind, and others. Additionally, the Newhouse Program and Architecture Competition, sponsored by the Chicago Architecture Foundation and the Chicago Public Schools, offers opportunities year-round for students interested in architecture and design.

What Advice Would You Provide to Someone Who Wants to Be an Architect?

Have passion and patience. Is that enough advice?

> **Robert M. Beckley,** FAIA
> **Professor and Dean Emeritus, University of Michigan**

Architecture is a vocation as well as a profession. It cannot be done casually. You must have a passion for it.

> **Carol Ross Barney,** FAIA
> **Principal, Ross Barney + Jankowski, Inc.**

Draw, read, or write about architecture every day. Create! Take all the art, math, and science classes you can. Don't waste a moment!

> **Dianne Blair Black,** AIA
> **Vice President, RTKL Associates, Inc.**

Pursue a basic college preparatory curriculum, including math and the sciences, and engage in freehand drawing. Travel to develop a good sense of inquisitiveness about what you see. Ask why the cities, neighborhoods, buildings, and landscapes you visit resulted in their present condition and form. Develop a broad interest in the humanities; learn to write and speak. Read, read, and read!

Undertake summer employment in a firm before graduation. Each summer experience even tangentially related to the profession enables you to access increasingly directed work. By the time you graduate, you will have a competitive advantage with potential employers and access to the best architectural firms.

> **Roger Schluntz,** FAIA
> **Dean, University of New Mexico**

Keep your eyes open and look at the full spectrum in which architects operate. Seek where you can best use your unique education and individual talents and grow.

> **Randall J. Tharp,** RA
> **Senior Vice President, A. Epstein and Sons International, Inc.**

Take a design course, intern with a firm, read architectural magazines, visit buildings, and, once you are confident with your decision to pursue architecture, identify schools that provide what you want from your education. Choose a school with a curriculum that is strong in your interests — design, sus-

tainability, theory, technology, urban planning, historic preservation, etc.

> **Margaret DeLeeuw**
> **Graduate, University of Maryland**

Have a passion for observing the environment around you. Learn to translate what you see into lines on paper.

> **H. Alan Brangman,** AIA
> **University Architect, Georgetown University**

I would stress the importance of two points: that architecture is very much an intellectual pursuit, and that architects must be interested in craft, making, etc.

> **Doug Garofalo,** FAIA
> **Professor, University of Illinois at Chicago**
> **President, Garofalo Architects, Inc.**

I recommend that everyone, no matter what his or her aspirations, seek one or more individuals for help with career development. I have had two primary mentors — one for nearly thirty years and one for almost twenty-five years — and many friends and associates along the way who contributed to my success. I would not have achieved as much as I have without their support. I also developed a twenty-five-year plan early in my career. This too has been invaluable.

Kathryn T. Prigmore, FAIA
Project Manager, HDR
Architecture, Inc.

Shadow an architect before deciding to attend an architecture school; several shadowing experiences is ideal. Take all classes available in freehand drawing, painting, photography, sculpture, furniture making, and related arts and crafts. Invest in a sketchbook. Explore a new part of your city, or take a trip to a different city. Participate in the summer high school programs offered by many architecture programs.

Elizabeth Kalin
Architectural Intern, Studio
Gang Architecture

Talk to individuals in the profession, both those pursing a traditional career in a design firm and those following an alternative career path. Realize that architecture can take you on paths as varied as publishing, graphic design, and documenting historical buildings. The problem-solving skills inherent in an architecture degree are valuable in many occupations that have nothing or little to do with architecture.

Tamara Redburn, ASSOCIATE AIA
Intern Architect,
Fanning/Howey Associates, Inc.

Develop a passion for architecture and design in order to truly enjoy the field. As you will invest much time in becoming an architect, you must enjoy and learn from this time-consuming, dedicated work. Although becoming an architect is not easy, you will learn from the process.

Brad Zuger
Student, University of
Nebraska — Lincoln

Try architecture, but do not rule out other careers without adequately exploring them. Keep an open mind about your future — but once you have decided on this field, do not let anything stop you.

David Groff
Intern Architect, Dalgliesh,
Gilpin, and Paxton Architects

Fishing Boats, Styrso, Sweden.
Photographer: Michael R.
Mariano, AIA.

First, you must always remember that there is more to life than a career. The education of an architect must begin with a framework for developing personal consciousness — that is, an avenue for instilling the value and manifestation of being fully awake and aware as a thinking, feeling, and contributing member of our evolving world.

Be encouraged to doubt, question givens, and generate keen alternatives to what architecture is today. In the real world, enlightened clients seek the conscious architect, rather than the trained architect, to identify and propose solutions to the unprecedented conditions of our rapidly changing world.

Second, immerse yourself in the emerging conditions of the world around you. Ask yourself what is changing, and why. What forces and conditions are causing these changes? The broader your understanding of the human experience, the better design you will produce.

Max Underwood, AIA
Professor, Arizona State University
Architect and Principal, Underwood + Crisp

Motivation is paramount. Studying and practicing architecture takes an enormous amount of time and energy. The academic studio environment is a microcosm of the profession. Not all students instantly take to the studio setting, but when used creatively, it has a great deal to offer.

Kathryn Anthony, Ph.D.
Professor, University of Illinois at Urbana-Champaign

Be open; do not limit yourself to the traditional definitions and boundaries of the practice of architecture. Learn to observe and to be a good listener. Understand the design process and become a master of your own process. An architecture degree is rich and diverse training for many design-related careers. The process of solving problems creatively translates broadly and does not limit your career possibilities. Because opportunities present themselves unexpectedly and often, be open to them. Know and believe in your unique talents and how these opportunities can be best used.

Barbara Crisp
Principal, Underwood + Crisp

Be confident in yourself and your ideas; filter through your ideas to identify those most pertinent to your objective; recognize that your architecture, in most instances, is serving others. Most of all, have fun with it!

Monica Pascatore, LEED
Freelance Designer, P Inc.

Do not look at buildings; instead, look at the way people react to them and move through them.

Trinity Simons, ASSOCIATE AIA
Vice President (2004–2005), American Institute of Architecture Students

Intern, intern, intern. Do whatever it takes to gain a summer position in an architecture firm and discover what professional practice is really like. Find out as much as you can about the profession and the career paths you can pursue, but be open to all sorts of experiences. Stay flexible and open to new challenges. Realize that, even after college, your education in architecture has hardly begun; your career path can be a rewarding adventure.

Carolyn Jones, AIA
Associate Principal, Callison Architecture, Inc.

To become an architect and function as an architect, you must be prepared to accomplish the most difficult thing you have ever done. Architecture does not get easier when you graduate, but it does get more interesting.

To study architecture is a great general education. It is a rigorous foundation from which to pursue many fields as your interests develop over the years.

**Richard A. Eribes, Ph.D., AIA
Professor and Dean Emeritus,
University of Arizona**

While in school, partner your undergraduate architecture degree with another degree. Many architecture students spend too much time with architecture students only; diversify your contacts and general education. Question design, authority, and the boundaries created by your education and this profession. Architecture is a lifelong discovery of how creativity can change the world.

Do not forget to keep your eyes open.

**Roy Abernathy, AIA
President, Jova/Daniels/Busby**

Set your sights high! Go find amazing architects and work with them. Go knock on Alvaro Siza's door or travel to London and work for Hadid.

**William Carpenter, Ph.D., FAIA
Associate Professor, Southern
Polytechnic State University
President, Lightroom**

Architecture is a fabulous profession with social relevance. The field is so multifaceted that anyone with an inner drive for building in the physical environment will succeed.

**Patricia Saldana Natke, AIA
Principal and President, Urban
Works Ltd.**

Architecture is passionate. Being an architect is not just a career decision — it is a lifestyle. Architecture can be rewarding if you have realistic expectations about what to expect from it. Truly understand what an architect does, and commit your life to that.

Know why you want to be an architect — to end homelessness, to become rich and famous, to serve others, to get published. This goes back to the passion. Talk to practicing architects to see if the profession can really meet your career objectives.

**Grace H. Kim, AIA
Principal, Schemata Workshop,
Inc.**

Celebration, Florida. Architects: Cooper, Robertson with Robert A.M. Stern Architects. Photographer: Guido Francescato.

Gain a liberal arts training; do not focus exclusively on skills that apparently are required to be an architect (e.g., drafting). Written communication is a large part of being an architect and should not be overshadowed by drawing or computer skills.

> **Lynsey Gemmell**
> **Architect II, Holabird & Root**

Discover more about what architects do beyond the naïve things you hear. Take as many drawing, painting, and sculpture courses as you can. Learn software applications that expand your ability to tell a compelling story about what you are trying to do. Even though the ability to write well is not usually emphasized, it, along with the ability to speak well, is of great importance. A clear narrative, whether written or oral, has the most impact.

> **Thomas Fowler IV**
> **Associate Professor and Associate Head California Polytechnic State University — San Luis Obispo**

You must love buildings. You need many skills to become an architect, including drawing, math, and other creative problem-solving capabilities. However, a passion for the art of building is essential to being an architect.

> **Edward Shannon, AIA**
> **Assistant Professor, Judson College**

First, develop a facility for visualizing nonexistent (abstract) three-dimensional objects in space and the ability to visually represent (communicate) that object and space to another person.

Second, through both personal and intellectual experience, familiarize yourself with the conditions and histories of world cultures foreign to your own. The ability to read and interpret diverse and disparate cultures is becoming ever more essential to peace and prosperity in a sustainable world.

Third, develop an analytical and intellectual capacity for making order out of chaos and ambiguity — order and logic in analysis, order and logic in work process, and order and logic in communications.

Fourth, cultivate a strong personal goal of service to the public good, a healthy attitude of self-confidence, a commitment to team engagement, and a willingness to lead when the conditions call for leadership.

> **W. Cecil Steward, FAIA**
> **Dean Emeritus, University of Nebraska — Lincoln President/CEO, Joslyn Castle Institute for Sustainable Communities**

Identify why you want to be an architect. What interests you? What inspires you? Research the requirements for becoming an architect and which direction best supports your goals. The rewards far outweigh the challenges.

> **Joseph Nickol**
> **Graduate, University of Notre Dame**

Keep in mind that the architecture profession encompasses many careers and many firms, each with its own distinctions.

> **Eric Taylor, ASSOCIATE AIA**
> **Photographer, Taylor Design & Photography, Inc.**

Try it. The reality is different from the popular idea of the profession. Architecture is a diverse discipline with a wide range of opportunities for specialization.

> **Lois Thibault, RA**
> **Coordinator of Research, U.S. Architectural and Transportation Barriers Compliance Board (Access Board)**

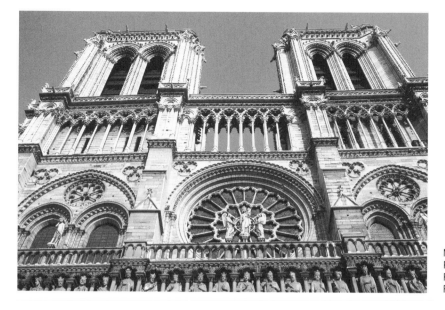

Notre Dame de Paris, Paris, France. Photographer: R. Lindley Vann.

Be passionate! You must feel in your heart that you want architecture to be a part of your life. Learn to be creative and to challenge linear thinking. Expand your world through travel, reading, drawing, conversation, music, and every other way possible. Learn to enjoy and be rewarded by the challenges of discovery and risk.

> **Clark Llewellyn, AIA**
> **Director, Montana State**
> **University**

As the profession of architecture is vast, do not be afraid to take an unusual path. Often we are taught we have just a single path to take in order to be a successful architect, but this is not so. Succeeding at architecture requires you to make your own path. Individuality is rewarded in this profession.

> **Lisa Van Veen, ASSOCIATE AIA**
> **Architectural Designer, Design**
> **Forward**

To be an architect, you need desire. You must be willing to work hard, as architecture is not easy. Establish a good academic record and study habits. Although desire is important, it cannot ensure your entry into an architecture program. Gain a broad academic experience that includes the traditional liberal arts but also fine and applied arts such as woodworking, photography, sculpture, sketching, and drawing.

Finally, explore and apply to more than one architecture program. Accredited programs are similar in curriculum and course content, but they vary considerably in philosophy, worldview, campus environment, and scale. Find the program that best fits you.

> **Jack Kremers, AIA**
> **Professor, Judson College**

Take time. Take a great deal of time to understand what undergraduate education and institution is the best fit for you. Select an education that gives you a broad understanding of the world so your work in architecture can engage as much context as possible.

Admit no money barrier. Go to both the best-fit and finest school you can possibly attend without regard for the expense—you can pay it back.

Seek out faculty. Get to know your teachers well and try to have work experiences that confirm the nature of practice. Verify what works and what does not with respect to your developmental needs; if you discover you really like to be in the woods, or in nature, another profession may be a better fit for you.

Travel. Observing and talking to people may be the greatest teacher.

It is okay to fail. Follow the maxim of IBM's Thomas Watson Jr.: "Want to succeed faster? Accelerate your rate of failure!"

**Joseph Bilello, Ph.D., AIA
Dean, Ball State University**

Earn a professional degree if you want, but don't let anyone tell you what to do with it or how to use it. Get out in the real world—by which I do not mean corporate practice. The real world requires you to get your hands dirty. The real world expects you to take initiative in doing mundane jobs. And the real world exists within, but also beyond, the borders of the United States and other Western nations. The corporate world will still be here and will value the real-world experiences you bring back.

**Casius Pealer, J.D.
Associate, Reno & Cavanaugh, PLLC
Co-founder, ARCHVoices**

Obtain a liberal arts education. Become intimate with a dozen fields of study. Maintain hobbies and friendships outside of architecture. Take an engineering course, a landscape architecture studio, English classes, botany classes, and Asian-American literature courses. Get involved with student government, student organizations, fraternities, sororities, choir. Spend time learning about people and thinking about how to design for them and serve them. Learn and appreciate the intricacies of the world around you.

**Jacob Day
President (2004–2005),
American Institute of
Architecture Students**

First, choose the right school for you. Speak to architects about what they do, visit their offices, and ask where they went to school and why. Most important, explore the physical world around you. Do you want to change it? Then, think about what part of architecture interests you—design, planning, engineering, business, development, preservation, residential, commercial, or something else. You need not choose right away but, with direction, the course of your training and work experience can be adjusted periodically to be sure you stay on track.

**Christopher J. Gribbs,
ASSOCIATE AIA
Senior Director, The American
Institute of Architects**

Studying architecture and practicing architecture are different. When you study architecture, you focus solely on the expression of your vision. As a professional, however, you cannot escape service and the imperative to accommodate other people's visions. If you wish to become an architect, be tolerant and flexible. Seek people who are doing what they want to do and spend time with them.

**W. Stephen Saunders, AIA
Principal, Eckenhoff Saunders
Architects**

Become a student of life and be familiar with the realms of design, communication, marketing, philosophy, history, computers, psychology, and engineering, to name a few. You should be knowledgeable not just about the design and construction industry but about nearly everything you experience with your senses.

Finally, you do not have to become an architect if you do not want to. If you are in the process of becoming an architect and want to take another path, *do it!* Use the diversity of your architectural education to your advantage and find a career path that really fits.

F. Michael Ayles, AIA
Director of Operations,
Antinozzi Associates

Talk first to several successful practicing architects and listen carefully to what they have to say. Architects have many opportunities to contribute in a meaningful way to the creation of good architecture. Whether or not you have splendid design ability, however, you cannot sell yourself to clients who want good architecture without an exceptional capacity to communicate.

Gaines Hall, FAIA
Vice President, Kirkegaard &
Associates

Architects come in many forms. Some are public architects working for communities and city governments; others design skyscrapers, schools, hospitals, churches, houses, and everything in between. Reach out to architects and ask questions. Develop a feel for the challenging and rewarding world that lies before you.

As you follow your dreams, reach out to an architect in your community. Even if you do not know one, pick up the phone book and look some up, give them a call, and simply ask to tour the office. Ask lots of questions — what they like and dislike, what school they went to, what type of projects they work on. Stay in touch with them as you go through your education.

Last, be a heads-up professional. While the profession emphasizes mentorship, know that you must be responsible for your own development by being aware of what you are working on and how it fits in with the overall process, and by asking questions. When you seek increased responsibilities in the office and exercise your judgment when needed, you will find your opportunities to grow are limitless.

Shannon Kraus, AIA
Associate Architect, HKS

Seizing a Leadership Role

TRINITY SIMONS, ASSOCIATE AIA
Vice President, 2004–2005
American Institute of Architecture Students
Washington, D.C.

Why and how did you become an architect?
I studied architecture so I could have a better idea of influences on space.

Why did you choose the school you did — University of Arkansas?
Growing up in Arkansas, I never thought I would go to school there. A series of events during my senior year of high school led me to Fayetteville with a full scholarship. In the beginning, I was planning to major in biochemical engineering and go on to medical school and do medical research in a lab setting (lofty goal for an eighteen-year-old?), but along the way I witnessed the architecture studio and could not think of doing anything else. Funny, I thought about architecture studio before I thought about being an architect.

What was your greatest challenge as an architecture student?
The greatest challenge was designing under the pretense that I could never know all of the answers.

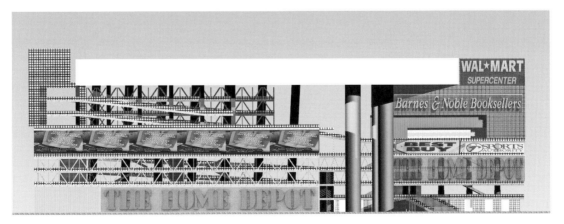

Vertical Power Center Studio Project, by Trinity Simons at University of Arkansas.

Why did you choose to pursue the five-year pre-professional bachelor of architecture degree?

Like most eighteen-year-olds, I was unaware of the many available degree paths in architecture. Looking back, I might have pursued an undergraduate degree in another discipline and then obtained my master of architecture.

What have been your priorities as American Institute of Architecture Students (AIAS) vice president?

Internship and architecture education.

Vertical Power Center Studio Project, by Trinity Simons at University of Arkansas.

During summers in school, you did academic research and taught rather than undertake the traditional internship. What exactly did you do, and why did you choose these experiences rather than work in a firm?

My summer experiences varied, but two stand out. The first was a summer workshop I did in Clarendon, Arkansas, with the Delta Regional Design Center and the University of Arkansas Community Design Center. We lived and worked in Clarendon and provided revitalization strategies that centered on ecotourism development. The second was researching and identifying readings for a class on Venice and the culture of consumerism.

What has been the most/least satisfying part of your education?

I feel strongly that architecture school provided me with the stamina, critical thinking skills, and intellect to attempt an array of other careers (maybe this is why many architecture graduates pursue other fields — our education is stellar). Our methodologies can be applied to a multitude of educational tracks, and other fields benefit. The studio environment is dynamic, collaborative, invigorating. I could go on and on. I crave it.

What do you hope to be doing five to ten years after graduation with regard to your career?

(1) Be licensed. (2) Return to school to obtain my master of architecture (post-professional), a master in urban design, or perhaps a master in theory and criticism. I would be happy to be a lifelong student. (3) Teach.

After your tenure with AIAS, you stated that you want to research ecologically sensitive methods of rural and urban development. Can you elaborate?

I am primarily interested in recombinant design methodologies as applied to anonymous architecture. The Dutch do this quite well. I think it is important that architects take a stand on anonymous architecture—big box, massive infrastructure, suburbia, etc. In our late capitalistic society, it is not reasonable for architects to simply shun them and hope they go away. That will never happen.

Architects must take the lead in creating these spaces, and they must do so in a way that acknowledges context is rarely unique or vernacular any longer (at least not in a meaningful way). My desire is to research recombinant models that give the consumer and client choice and opportunities for collaboration.

Good Shepherd Ecumenical Housing, by Trinity Simons at University of Arkansas with Community Design Center.

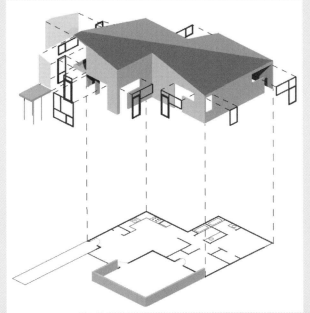

Good Shepherd Ecumenical Housing, by Trinity Simons at University of Arkansas with Community Design Center.

Explorations: A Student Perspective

CHRIS GLAPINSKI

Student, University of Miami
Oconomowoc, Wisconsin

Why and how did you become an architect?
During high school, I began to think architecture might be interesting to pursue.
I read more about it, and the more I read about it, the more I liked it. In addition, I gained an interest in art. I was always interested in math and science, so
drawing classes were refreshing.

Hometown Map — The Lakes
of Oconomowoc, Wisconsin,
by Chris Glapinski at University of Miami.

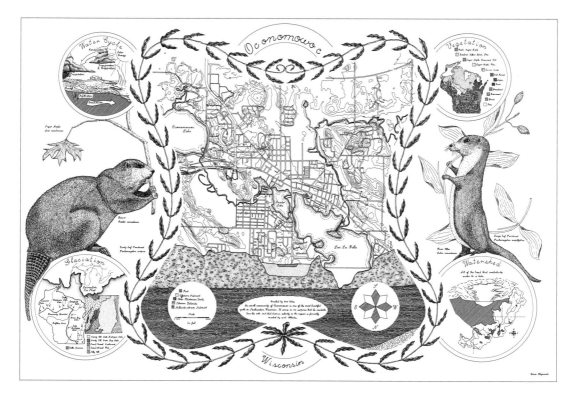

During the summer before my senior year, I took an architecture course called Explorations at the University of Miami. It was an intense, three-week experience of college and architecture. Afterward, I seriously considered majoring in architecture in college. I grew confident with my choice because I fell in love with architecture. For me, it has always been a constant discovery.

What has been your greatest challenge as an architecture student?

My greatest challenge as an architecture student is managing my time. Each design project involves so many things to think about and do, not to mention juggling other activities. It's a mental game to choose what work I want to do, and at what level. I try different strategies each semester. I have found a decent balance this semester, but I still work on it.

Why did you choose the school you did — University of Miami?

During my last two years of high school, I researched colleges on the Internet. I had only two criteria: that the school not be in Wisconsin — I was eager to leave and experience something new — and that it have an architecture program.

I considered schools with both types of degree programs, the five-year bachelor of architecture and the four-plus-two master of architecture, including Arizona State University, Ball State University (BSU), Illinois Institute of Technology, University of North Carolina — Charlotte (UNCC), University of Notre Dame, Washington University in St. Louis, and University of Miami. I tried to imagine myself at each of these schools, and I thought about each school's size, the student activities offered, the diversity of the student body, and cost. I honestly did not decide where I would go until a few weeks before the deadline. In the end, I narrowed my choice to three schools: UNCC, BSU, and Miami. These schools offered me scholarships, and I liked their campuses and students.

I debated and debated and compared the schools hundreds of times. Finally I just went with my gut feeling. I felt the best about Miami.

Why did you choose to pursue the five-year professional bachelor of architecture degree?

I did not necessarily *choose* the five-year B.Arch. degree; rather, I chose the University of Miami School of Architecture, which offers the five-year B.Arch. program. I see merit in both degree types, but I think the five-year program is good because it involves only one application to get an accredited degree. The worry with the four-plus-two is possible failure of admission to a graduate program after attaining a four-year degree.

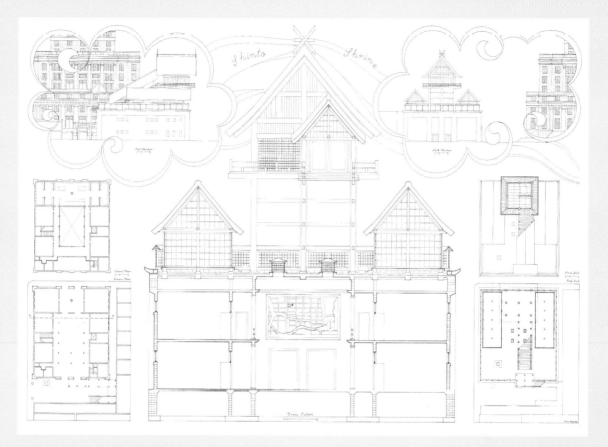

Shinto Shrine, by Chris Glapinski at University of Miami.

How was the summer course, Explorations, helpful in your pursuing architecture in college?

Explorations was an invaluable experience. It was a three-week preview of college in general and the School of Architecture in particular. During the week, we had classes in graphics, history, and design. On weekends, we took field trips to architecturally significant sites around Miami and Key West. From Explorations, I learned about architecture, about college in general, and about what direction in life I wanted to take. Explorations taught me what architecture is — before, I literally knew nothing.

What has been the most/least satisfying part of your education?

The most satisfying part of my education is the design studio. It can be agony at times, but after only two years of school, I already notice a great improvement in my work quality. I have been trying to put together a portfolio recently in hopes of getting a summer job, and looking back through my past projects has been interesting.

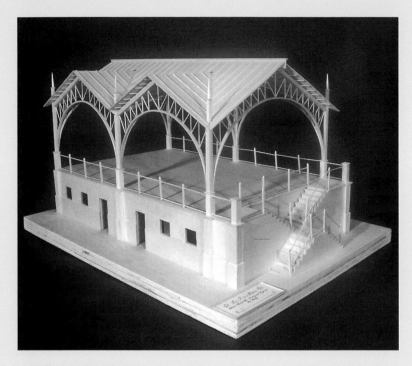

Le Pavillon, by Chris Glapinski, Margaret Wyman, Lee Graf at University of Miami.

I feel least satisfied with my choice of major when I think about what I may be missing. I have many other interests besides architecture for which I do not have time. I do not often have the opportunity to take other classes just for fun.

I also feel sometimes that I am missing out on life by putting so much work into architecture — even when I'm not working and I hang out with friends, they all study architecture as well.

What do you hope to be doing five to ten years after graduation with regard to your career?
After graduation, I may choose to attend graduate school because I am thinking about becoming a professor of architecture. I would like to pass the ARE and become licensed as well. I hope to have a family in ten years, too. I am not sure yet, however. This is just one possibility.

Who or what experience has been a major influence on your education/career?
Thus far, faculty and traveling have been the major influences. I admire my faculty's dedication to the profession, and their enthusiasm for architecture is contagious. They are great role models.

My trip to Bangkok, Thailand, last summer was one of the most profound influences on my education. Learning up close about another culture and building tradition has been the highlight of my education thus far, and I am just as excited for Japan next summer!

Exploring, Learning, Making an Impact

BRAD ZUGER

Student, University of Nebraska — Lincoln
Springfield, Nebraska

Why and how did you become an architect?

I was always interested in architecture and engineering. I first developed an interest in the design of buildings and homes in middle school, when we did small-scale architectural projects. I love architecture and design because it is an expression of form and composition, yet it requires attention to function and design issues. Also, I wanted a profession that would impact the community and allow me to work with others.

Why and how did you choose which school to attend for your architecture degree? What degree(s) do you possess?

I decided on the University of Nebraska for three main reasons: location, price, and people. I was impressed with the faculty, which is extremely dedicated to the students as well as inviting. It seemed as though the faculty was interested in the students and excited about teaching them. Currently I am seeking a bachelor of science degree and will continue with the master of architecture.

Chair with Jacket — Charcoal Drawing, by Brad Zuger at University of Nebraska.

What has been your greatest challenge as an architecture student?

Being an architecture student continues to challenge me, which I truly enjoy. My greatest challenge is the long nights at architecture hall, common to most students. Each project presents a new challenge, and solving all of the issues involved in a design project takes much time.

Why did you choose to pursue the four-plus-two master of architecture degree?

My decision did not depend on whether the school was a five-year or six-year program because I figured that both were professional degrees. However, I did think I would get more out of a program with a masters degree because I would be spending more time on my education.

As an architecture student, what are your primary tasks?

I must take a studio class every semester. These classes are set in a sequence, so they must be taken one after the other. In the pre-professional program (years one and two), the studio class is design-oriented and focused on composition, analysis, drawing, drafting, and simple design projects.

The University of Nebraska has a unique program for first-year students called visual literacy; it is an interdisciplinary design studio with students from art, graphic design, journalism, and interior design in the same studio. In the professional program (years three and four), a studio class involves usually one or two design projects per semester, and each studio focuses on a topic such as structure, programming, site, or systems. Other required classes include, in this order, physics, calculus, statistics, strength of materials, and systems. We are required to take five semesters of architectural history and, in the professional program, an adjunct to our studio. First-year students also take a computer class focusing on AutoCAD and 3-D Viz.

The two-year masters program includes a studio option or thesis option for the final year. Most students choose the thesis option, which gives them more freedom with their project.

Domino Frame — Sketches, by Brad Zuger
at University of Nebraska.

What has been the most/least satisfying part of your education?
The most satisfying part is the people I have met and interacted with. The professors have had the greatest impact on me and have really exposed me to the field of architecture.

Although my education is satisfying, it can be strenuous and time-consuming. Architectural education is demanding, with studio projects and course projects going on at the same time.

What do you hope to be doing five to ten years after graduation with regard to your career?
I want to be involved with my community, the university, and the AIA. Also, I want to gain a wide variety of experience with different firms in different areas with different specialties. Eventually, I want to work in my own design firm.

Who or what experience has been a major influence on your education/career?
As a first-year student, I had a professor who had a large impact on my education. She inspired me to be a passionate and hard-working student and really helped me see the design field in new and exciting ways. As a professor, she shows much interest in and dedication to her students and continues to advise and take interest in the students she has taught. She is an architect from South America with whom I work as a research assistant. Inside and outside of the classroom, she has taught me more than any other teacher, and I continue to look to her for guidance and advice. I think she has had the most impact on my excitement about architecture.

Fallingwater—Frank Lloyd Wright—Compositional Analysis, by Brad Zuger at University of Nebraska.

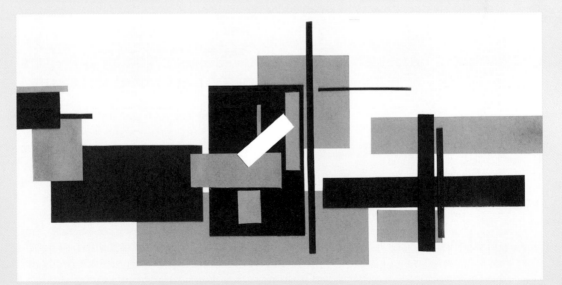

Routes to an Accredited Degree

Before selecting an architecture program, you must understand the different routes to obtaining an accredited degree. Because there is more than one route, this can be confusing. Each route is designed to offer a particular level of expertise and enable you to make a variety of career and educational choices. If your intent is to become an architect, your educational goal will be to obtain a professional degree accredited by the National Architectural Accredited Board (NAAB).

There are three routes to obtaining an accredited professional degree: the five-year bachelor of architecture (B.Arch.); the four-year pre-professional undergraduate degree followed by the two-year master of architecture (M.Arch.); and the four-year undergraduate degree in a field other than architecture followed by the three- or four-year master of architecture (M.Arch.). Another degree, recently accredited, is the doctor of architecture (D.Arch.), available only at the University of Hawaii at this time.

BACHELOR OF ARCHITECTURE (B.ARCH.)

The bachelor of architecture is an undergraduate five-year degree selected by students coming directly from high school. It is the oldest professional degree offered at the university level in the United States. Some schools, including Drexel University, the University of Detroit, and the Boston Architectural Center (BAC), offer the B.Arch., but completing the degree takes more than five years because of work programs required by these schools.

At most schools, enrolled students begin intensive architectural studies in the first semester and continue for the duration of the program. If you are highly confident in your choice of architecture as your academic major, pursuing a B.Arch. may be the ideal choice. If, however, you think you may not ultimately choose architecture, the five-year program is not forgiving, meaning that changing majors is difficult. Of the institutions offering an accredited degree in architecture, approximately sixty-five offer the B.Arch.

Recently, a handful of institutions began offering a five-year master of architecture. How are these degrees different than the traditional bachelor of architecture? Contact each institution and ask.

PRE-PROFESSIONAL BACHELOR OF SCIENCE (B.S.) AND MASTER OF ARCHITECTURE (M.ARCH.)

Sometimes known as a four-plus-two, this route to the accredited degree involves first obtaining a pre-professional architecture bachelor of science (B.S.) degree followed by the professional master of architecture (M.Arch.). Pre-professional degrees are four-year degrees that prepare candidates for pursuing a professional degree. These degrees may have different actual titles — bachelor of science (B.S.) in architecture, bachelor of science in architectural studies (B.S.A.S.), bachelor of arts (B.A.) in architecture, bachelor of environmental design (B.E.D.), or bachelor of architectural studies (B.A.S.). The amount of architectural work in the program varies from school to school and determines the length of time required to complete further professional architectural studies, typically the M.Arch. Some pre-professional degrees are within universities that also offer the professional M.Arch. degree; however, others are within four-year liberal arts institutions.

Another viable option for this particular route is to begin your studies at a community college. Often, the first two years of a B.S. degree are predominately general education courses that can be taken at a community college. It is important, however, to be in touch with the institution at which you plan to continue studies about what courses to take and when to apply. Depending on the institution, it may be worth transferring early rather than receiving an associate's degree from the community college.

Note that if you graduate with the pre-professional degree, you may not be eligible to become licensed in most states. Therefore, if you desire to be a licensed architect, you should continue your studies in the professional M.Arch. degree program. There are a few states in which you can pursue licensure with a pre-professional undergraduate degree, but you would not be able to obtain the NCARB Certificate necessary for reciprocal licensure.

The professional M.Arch. is a graduate-level degree that typically lasts two years and offers a comprehensive professional education. This combination of the B.S. degree with the M.Arch. offers flexibility, as you can choose to take any number of years off to gain experience between the two degrees. Plus, you may choose to attend a different institution for your graduate studies.

A handful of schools offer a master of architecture lasting less than two years that follows a pre-professional undergraduate degree. However, these degree programs may be limited to candidates from the same institution. For example, The Catholic University of America (CUA) offers a master of architecture with advanced standing (1.5 years) for individuals who graduate with the B.S. in architecture from CUA, but those with a B.S. in architecture from other institutions must take two years to complete the master of architecture.

UNDERGRADUATE DEGREES (B.A./B.S.) IN FIELDS OTHER THAN ARCHITECTURE AND MASTER OF ARCHITECTURE (M.ARCH.)

A master of architecture program is available for candidates with an undergraduate degree in a field other than architecture. It offers a comprehensive professional education. Depending on the institution, this accredited M.Arch. will take between three and four years of study to complete. Some institutions require that calculus, physics, and freehand drawing be taken before admission. Depending on your particular educational background, you may need to fulfill these prerequisites. Of the institutions offering degree programs in architecture, approximately sixty offer this M.Arch.

Some of these programs have the student begin work in the summer before the first semester, while others require full-time study during a later summer semester. Be sure to explore the differences among the programs you are considering.

DOCTOR OF ARCHITECTURE (D.ARCH.)

The doctor of architecture (D.Arch.), as a professional degree, is currently available only at the University of Hawaii. The program is seven years in length and is unique in that it allows the graduate to fulfill the education requirement for taking the licensing exam, whereas the post-professional doctoral degrees do not. As the D.Arch. is an accredited degree, you are encouraged to contact the University of Hawaii if you are interested in this route.

POST-PROFESSIONAL DEGREES

Besides offering professional degree programs, many institutions offer post-professional degree programs intended for study as an advanced degree after the professional degree. Although these degrees go by different names, they all allow candidates to focus on a particular field of study — for example, urban design, architectural theory, computer-aided design, housing, sustainability, or tall buildings. The typical candidate pursues this degree after work-ing within the profession for a few years. In addition, a handful of institutions offer a doctor of philosophy (Ph.D.) for those with the master of architecture.

Decision-making Process

Regardless of the degree you pursue, how do you select an architecture program? After learning about the many degree programs, choosing among them may seem a daunting task; over 100 institutions in the United States and Canada offer professional architecture degree programs. However, if you analyze the criteria that are most important, you can quickly narrow your search and manage this process.

Consider that your education in architecture is only one-third of the path to architectural licensure. There are three *E*s to complete before becoming an architect: (1) education — a NAAB-accredited degree (Canadian Architectural Certification Board [CACB] in Canada); (2) experience — fulfilling the requirements of the Intern Development Program (IDP); and (3) exam — satisfactorily passing the Architect Registration Examination (ARE). All told, it may take eight to twelve years to complete the three *E*s.

When choosing the institution where you will pursue your architecture degree, strongly consider the following:

Ensure that the degree program is accredited. Degree programs are accredited by the NAAB (or CACB in Canada), not the institution itself. (For a current list of institutions offering accredited programs, see Appendix B).

Be sure to understand the possible routes to obtaining your professional degree: (1) bachelor of architecture; (2) master of architecture following a pre-professional architecture degree; and (3) master of architecture following a degree from another discipline. Each route has advantages and limitations. Consider which is best suited for you, which will help narrow your choices.

Identify the typical coursework offered in most, if not all, architecture programs: design studio, structures, systems, graphics/drawing, architectural history, general education, computer, site, professional practice, programming, and architecture electives.

You know the degree programs, the list of architectural programs, and the typical courses offered, but what is most important to you? Think about the criteria listed below in the following categories: You, Institution, and Architecture Program. Take time to think about answers to the questions posed and write them down.

By going through this process, you will be better matched with your eventual college choice and more confident in your decision. As you develop criteria on which to base your decision, certain degree programs and universities will surface as logical choices.

National Museum of Canada, Ottawa, Canada. Architect: Moshe Safdie. Photographer: Ralph Bennett.

You

Consider the following attributes prior to selecting a school:

Level of confidence: How confident are you in your choice to become an architect? Do you want options as you progress through college, or do you want to dive right into architecture?

For example, if you are not completely confident in becoming an architect, you may consider a program that offers the pre-professional four-year bachelor of science; this way you can begin to explore architectural studies, but not full force, as in a professional B.Arch. program.

Personality type: What type of person are you? Will you feel more comfortable at a large school or a small school? This is a difficult criterion to nail down, but also a critical one. Ask yourself, "Will I be comfortable here?"

Closeness to home: How close do you wish to be to home with respect to miles or time? Proximity to home is typically a top reason for selecting a school by many students. If it is important to you, draw a circle on a map around your hometown indicating your desired distance from home.

What schools are inside the circle you have drawn? However, challenge that notion and select the school that is best for you regardless of its location. You should consider each of the over 100 accredited architecture programs. Narrow the choices later based on other criteria.

Budget: Do you and your parents have a specific budget for college? Obviously, with college costs increasing at a rate greater than inflation, cost is an important criterion. Recognize that your college education is an investment in your future and not something that disappears, like a pizza. Remember, once you have your education, no one can take it away.

Institution

Attributes to consider when selecting an institution include:

Type of school: While most individuals refer to all post–high school institutions as *colleges,* there are different types from which to choose. Most probably consider the university, typically a cluster of colleges under a single administration. However, just as possible is a four-year college, which is usually smaller and places less emphasis on research. Other choices include an institute of technology or polytechnic institute; these focus primarily on engineering and the sciences. Another choice is a two-year college or community college — a viable option, but one that will require transferring to a four-year program to complete your undergraduate degree.

Locale: Where is the institution located? Is it in an urban or a rural setting, or somewhere in between? To what extent is a program's location important to you? Programs located in cities such as New York, Chicago, or Philadelphia consider this urban location an asset, as it gives proximity to architecture to be studied and to architects and other professionals.

Institution size: How many students attend the institution? What is the faculty-to-student ratio for courses, both in the major and in other fields? How much do class and institution size matter to you? For example, a small number of architecture students may be an advantage of a small school, but a larger institution may have more robust resources to offer.

Public vs. private: Is the school private or public? Public institutions tend to be less expensive than private institutions because of the support they receive from the state, but they also typically have higher student enrollments. For international and other out-of-state students, tuition differences between public and private schools may be insignificant.

Cost: What is the overall cost of tuition, room and board, and other expenses? Be careful of using cost as the primary criterion for your initial selection (see Financial Aid, below). Cost is and will always be an important consideration, but do not eliminate an institution because of the advertised tuition rate alone. Be sure to gain complete cost information that includes tuition, room and board, books and supplies, travel, and personal expenses.

Financial aid: What amount of financial aid will you receive in the form of grants, scholarships, and loans? Financial aid should be an important consideration, especially at the beginning of the search process. Realize that at a given institution, a large percentage of students receive financial aid. Many schools have full-tuition scholarships that save you as much as $100,000. You will never be eligible for such scholarships if you do not apply or consider these schools. Also, do not only consider financial aid upon entry to the program; ask what financial aid is available for upper-class students. Many programs award scholarships on a merit basis.

Architecture Program

Because you will spend the largest portion of your college career within the architecture program, consider the following factors:

Degree: What types of the professional degree programs are offered? Does the school have joint degrees with other disciplines? The type of degree program varies from institution to institution. Many academic units have joint degrees with engineering, business, urban planning, and so on. These opportunities may be attractive to you but not available at all schools.

Academic structure: Where is the architecture degree program housed within the institution? Is it within its own college, school, or department? Is it with other departments in a school of engineering, art, design, or other discipline? The location of the architecture program can impact its culture.

During my graduate studies at Arizona State University, the School of Architecture was housed in the College of Environmental Design. Beside architecture, the college offered degree programs in interior design, industrial design, and landscape architecture. We had the chance to study in close proximity to students who would eventually be our professional peers in the workforce. In addition, courses in these other programs were easily available to us as electives.

LEE W. WALDREP, PH.D.

Philosophy/approach: What is the philosophy of the academic unit and of particular faculty? Some schools are technically oriented, while others are design oriented. Does the school lean in one direction more than the other? What is the mission statement of the architecture program? The approach of the programs you consider should be in concert with your own ideas of architecture. Learn about these differences in approach and decide which fits you.

Reputation/tradition: How long has the school been in existence? What is the reputation of the school among architecture professionals? Reputation is difficult to measure. Decide how important reputation is to you. Ask architects in the profession if they have heard of the school. If possible, contact alumni or current students to obtain their perspective.

Enrollment: How many students are in the architecture program or in each academic class? Just as institution size can affect your decision, so can the enrollment of the program itself. Consider the overall enrollment of the program and the number of students in each graduating class as well as the student-faculty ratio for architecture courses, especially the studio courses. The number of students in a program could be a reason to strongly consider or not consider a particular school.

Academic resources: What kind of studio space is available to students? What other spaces or resources exist for students — resource center (library), shop, computer labs? What is campus housing like? What about recreational facilities and other campus buildings? Because you will be provided a personal workspace in a studio, the quality of the facilities must be considered carefully — more so than for many other majors. The environment of the studio space and access to it can directly affect your choice. What are the hours of the studio? Other facilities such as the shop, architecture library, and computer labs are also worth investigating.

Special programs: What opportunities beyond the classroom does the school offer its students? Lecture series? Study-abroad programs? Dual-degree programs? Minors? Individually designed programs? Experienced-based programs (co-ops, internships, preceptorships)? What special enrichment programs appeal to you? The notion of enrichment programs is a catch-all category. Do you wish to study abroad during college? If so, attending a program with a required study abroad program might be essential. How about a lecture series? Although not a formal part of the academic coursework, an engaging lecture series can be a plus.

Faculty: Who are the faculty? How many are pure academicians versus practicing architects? Are they young or old? What is the diversity of the faculty? Faculty bring academic courses to life. Read the faculty biographies in the catalog or online and ask to attend a class or meet a faculty member when you visit the school. Do the faculty seem like they would inspire you, motivate you, help you learn? Pay attention to how many faculty members are practitioners first and edu-

Duomo, Florence, Italy. Photographer: R. Lindley Vann.

cators second. What difference does that make in the quality of teaching?

Student body: Who are the students? Where are they from? What are the demographics of the student body (gender, age, ethnicity, etc.)? For graduate studies, consider the educational backgrounds of your fellow classmates. What proportion are international students, and from what countries do they come? Attending a program with international students can enhance your architectural education. You will spend a great deal of time with your fellow students, and you should be comfortable with them. Consider that many institutions have more than one architecture degree program, which means you may interact with students in degree programs other than your own.

Career programs: What programs are in place to assist you in gaining direct

experience in the field? Cooperative education? Internships? Exposure to practicing architects? What programs are in place to assist you in gaining direct experience in the field during summers or after graduation? Some schools, including the University of Cincinnati, Drexel University, University of Detroit — Mercy, and Boston Architectural Center, have cooperative education programs that require students to work in the profession while in school. For more details on these school/work programs, refer to the next chapter.

Postgraduate plans: What happens to the school's graduates? Where are they employed? How long did it take them to find a job? Ask the career center for the annual report on graduates, or obtain the names of recent alumni from the alumni office and contact them.

Resources

The following are resources to assist you in your decision-making process:

PROMOTIONAL MATERIALS, VIDEOS, CATALOGS, AND WEBSITES

The first resource you are likely to receive from any school is the promotional materials that accompany the application for admission. Be sure to contact the architecture program as well as the central university admissions office. In some cases, the program provides additional information or materials. All of these materials are helpful in learning more about the university or its architecture program; however, recognize that they are designed to persuade you to select the institution. Review the materials alongside materials not produced by the program, or visit the campus to see for yourself.

GUIDE TO ARCHITECTURE SCHOOLS

Compiled approximately every five years by the Association of Collegiate Schools of Architecture (ACSA), the *Guide to Architecture Schools* ([6th ed.]. Washington, D.C.: Association of Collegiate Schools of Architecture [$24.95; 298 pages]) is a valuable resource. Its primary content is a compilation of two-page descriptions of the over 100 universities offering professional degree programs in architecture.

NEW ENGLAND CAREER DAY IN ARCHITECTURE

Typically held each October, the New England Career Day in Architecture is a great opportunity to learn more about a career in architecture by interacting with professionals; attending workshops on selecting a school, career options, and financing your education; and meeting with admissions representatives from over thirty-five programs.

For more information, contact the Boston Society of Architects (BSA), www.architects.org.

CAMPUS VISITS

One of the most helpful resources is the campus visit. Campus visits are an absolute must, especially for your top choices. When arranging one, consider spending the night with a current student to get an inside feeling about the institution. If possible, request that your stay be with an architecture student. In addition, visit with a faculty member or administrator within the academic unit; ask for a tour of the program facilities; and monitor a class.

In the fall, most schools host open houses as an opportunity for prospective students to meet with faculty and students and to learn more about curricular opportunities. While these are excellent opportunities, recognize that they present the campus at its best. In addition to these planned events, visit unannounced, including the design studios, to see the campus in its normal setting.

ADMISSIONS COUNSELOR/ ADMINISTRATOR

As you narrow your choices, one of the best resources is an admissions counselor or an administrator (director, advisor, faculty member) from the architecture program. Remember, the task of these people is to assist you in learning more about their university and the architecture program. Develop a personal relationship with them to obtain the information you need to make an informed decision. Do not hesitate to keep in touch with them throughout the admissions process.

STUDENTS, FACULTY, ALUMNI, AND ARCHITECTS

Often neglected, an important resource is conversations with individuals associated with the architecture program — students, faculty, alumni. During campus visits, ask for an opportunity to speak with students and faculty. Request the names of a few alumni in your area, both recent and older graduates, to ask their impressions. Finally, seek out architects and ask them their opinion about the schools you are considering for admission.

NAAB ARCHITECTURE PROGRAM REPORT (APR)/VISITING TEAM REPORT (VTR)

As part of the accreditation process, a reviewing team visits each program in architecture approximately every five years. Each institution under review prepares a related document called the Architecture Program Report (APR). The APR is an excellent resource as you make your decision. It provides details of the program and describes its institutional context and resources; it is public information and available from the academic unit on request. It is too long for the institution to send it to you, but it may be available in the institution's library or online.

Another document, the NAAB Visiting Team Report (VTR), also should be available to you on request. The VTR conveys the visiting team's assessment of the program's educational quality as measured by the students' performance and the overall learning environment. It includes documentation of the program's noteworthy qualities, its deficiencies, and concerns about the program's future performance.

While all this information may be overwhelming, these documents may be helpful to consider because they provide both an overview of the program from the academic unit itself and a review of the program by an outside group.

RANKING OF ARCHITECTURE PROGRAMS

While rankings are a popular method to assist you in selecting an architecture program, be cautious. Do you know what criteria the book or magazine article uses when ranking programs? Are the criteria used important to you? You should use your own set of highly subjective criteria when determining which program is best for you. Consider that none of the associations involved with architectural education attempt or advocate the rating of architecture programs, beyond their accreditation status. Qualities that make a school good for one student may not work that way for another. You should consider a variety of factors in making your choice among schools.

Although few would argue that certain programs, particularly those at the Ivy League schools, are excellent, the fact is that if a degree program is accredited by NAAB, it is valid for you to consider.

One resource, DesignIntelligence, attempts to assess the best architecture schools each year by asking practitioners to comment on how recent graduates from different schools fare in the marketplace. This report provides valuable information but also urges critical evaluation of the research results.

Application Process

When you narrow your choices and receive application materials, you must complete the applications by the stated deadlines. Be cognizant of these deadlines, as more universities set earlier and earlier deadlines within the academic calendar.

Also, remember that the purpose of the admissions process is to select highly talented, diverse individuals who will succeed in that program. Institutions use the application materials — application, test scores, transcripts, portfolio, and recommendations — to measure performance to date and project future performance. Schools also want to know about you as a person; contact the school for more insight on what you can do to maximize your application for admission.

APPLICATION

At first, you might think that applications are designed to be complex and difficult, but if you simply read the instructions and review what is being asked, completing the application is easy. In most cases, the application is a series of questions related to you and your background. Do not make it hard! If you do not understand an aspect of the application, contact the admissions office for clarification. More and more universities are using online applications. Do not be intimidated by this trend; instead, just print out such applications and complete them by hand to ensure accuracy when you submit them online.

PERSONAL STATEMENT

As part of the application, you may be asked to write a personal statement. Undergraduate applicants may have a choice of topics. For example, applicants to Carnegie Mellon University may write on one of these topics:

Evaluate a significant experience or achievement that has special meaning to you.

Discuss some issue of personal, local, or national concern and its importance and relevance to you.

Indicate a person who has had significant influence on you, and describe the influence.

For graduate students, the personal statement is an integral part of the application file. Rather than a topic, most graduate programs request a personal statement describing the applicant's interest in architecture and how the institution will assist in fulfilling the goal of becoming an architect.

TEST SCORES

SAT/ACT: Without question, you must take the standardized SAT or ACT. Which test you take depends on the region of the country you live in. Some students perform better on one than the other; for this reason, consider taking both. Many institutions use these test scores as an indicator of your probable success in college, so you will want to do your absolute best. Some people, however, are not good test-takers. If your results are not at the level required for a particular institution, discuss them with the admissions office.

GRE: If you are applying as a graduate candidate, you may be required to submit Graduate Record Examination (GRE) scores with your graduate program application. Institutions vary in how much weight they give to these scores. Study hard and take the practice test. You may consider taking the GRE while you are still an undergraduate in anticipation of pursuing graduate studies. Most schools accept scores even if they are a few years old.

TRANSCRIPTS

All institutions to which you apply will require that transcripts be submitted. The admissions reviewers will, of course, look at your overall grade point average; however, just as important are trends in your academic record. If there is something in your academic background that is less than flattering, do not hesitate to include a letter explaining the situation.

Royal Library — Danish Ministry of Culture, Copenhagen, Denmark. Architect: Schmidt, Hammer & Lassen. Photographer: Grace H. Kim, AIA.

PORTFOLIO

Unlike most other majors, architecture programs may require a portfolio; this is especially true for bachelor of architecture degree programs. Requiring a portfolio does not mean you have to be a talented architect prior to admission. Rather, the portfolio demonstrates your level of creativity and commitment to architecture.

What is a portfolio? For admission purposes, it is a compilation of creative work you have done on your own or as part of a class. It may include freehand drawings, poetry, photographs, or photographs of three-dimensional models or work. A portfolio is a means used by the admissions office to determine technical skills, creative ability, motivation, and originality. To gain a better understanding of what to include, question the admissions office. Despite the temptation, it is typically recommended not to include any drafting or CAD work; again, check with the individual school.

RECOMMENDATIONS

All admissions offices require evaluations from counselors or teachers (high school students) and faculty or employers (graduate students) to aid them in making their decision.

Counselor or teacher: The application package typically includes an evaluation form for counselors or teachers to complete. For many high schools, this is the last step, and the counselor will forward your application, high school transcripts, and the evaluation form to the college or university.

Faculty or employer: Applicants to graduate programs must supply letters of recommendation as part of the application file. While most programs allow current or former employers to submit a letter on your behalf, you are far better off obtaining letters from your undergraduate professors. This may be difficult if you have been out of school for a few years, but it is worth the time to track them down. In all cases, the individuals should know you fairly well, particularly your academic abilities.

Most schools enclose a checklist with the application materials asking for an evaluation on specific personal qualities such as:

Clarity of Goals for Graduate Study

Potential for Graduate Study

Intellectual Ability

Analytical Ability

Ability to Work Independently

Ability to Work with Others

Oral Expression in English

Written Expression in English

Teaching Potential

Research Potential

Most programs also accept letters written on the letterhead of the recommender.

Now you know all there is to know about selecting an architecture program. From the degree programs to the resources available, you have the information you need to make an informed choice.

Citizen Architect

JACOB R. DAY

President, 2004–2005
American Institute of Architecture Students
Washington, D.C.

Why and how did you become an architect?

I was inspired by several extracurricular activities early in my life. Ultimately, the credit goes to those who taught me. Two programs and their respective teachers deserve the credit for introducing me to the profession: TAD (Thinking and Doing), a Wicomico County (Maryland) primary education advanced education program; and Odyssey of the Mind, an international creative problem-solving program.

Why and how did you choose which school to attend for your architecture degree? What degree(s) do you possess?

I have a bachelor of science in architecture from the University of Maryland. To be honest, I chose the school for the wrong reasons — friends and proximity to home. But fortunately the University of Maryland was perfect for me. I enjoyed the faculty, leading my peers in student service, and the body of knowledge presented to me.

What has been your greatest challenge as an intern thus far?

My internship experience thus far can be catalogued in two distinct categories. First, I was an intern for a large architecture and engineering firm, Becker Morgan Group, in Salisbury, Maryland. I faced relatively few challenges in this position. For the most part, I simply did not know what challenges to seek.

The second experience is as president of AIAS. The most challenging part is grasping an agenda of national proportions that has grown in recent years to have a sizable impact on architectural education and the profession.

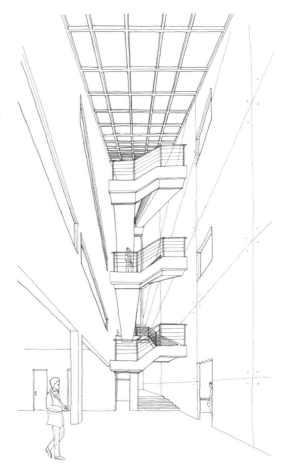

Art Gallery for Purist Art, by Jacob R. Day at University of Maryland.

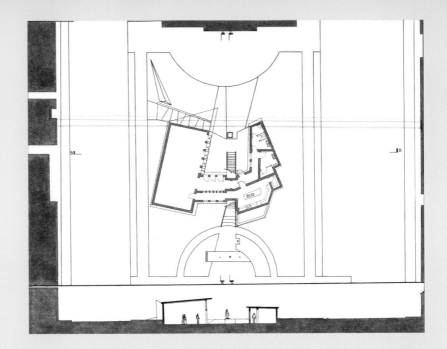

Town Hall, Centreville, Maryland, by Jacob R. Day at University of Maryland.

Immediately after graduation, you had the opportunity to serve as president of AIAS. Describe this experience.

This has been at once a thrilling and a daunting experience. The first year out of school, I entered the workforce, just like my peers, but as president and chairman of the board of a nonprofit organization.

I feel the thrill every single day. As president, I serve as national student director of the American Institute of Architects (AIA), member of the National Council of Architectural Registration Boards (NCARB) Education Committee, member of the AIA Membership Committee, Topaz Medallion Jury, AIA Community Discussion Group, and countless other committees, task forces, and appointments.

The ability to promote the AIAS agenda and enact change is tangible each and every day. The Studio Culture Summit reignited the discussion of the cultural environment in the studio model of architectural education. Freedom by Design, the AIAS's national community service initiative, is showing immense success in its first year as a pilot program. Forum, the AIAS annual convention, attracts around 1,000 architecture and design students year after year as the programming and speaker quality continue to be the best in the world. With two new competitions rolling out, the AIAS has more students involved than ever.

Daunting? Yes. Thrilling? Could not be more so.

How will this experience inform your future as an architect?

It will greatly impact my future as an architecture student. I have spent the last seven months at the forefront of the argument that the studio environment in architecture school can and must be improved. As a graduate student of architecture, I will advocate for the integration of studio into other academic realms, more effective systems of student and teacher assessment, engagement of real clients and communities in projects, and, ultimately, a culture of respect and optimism.

Moreover, this experience has drastically shifted my future as an architect. First of all, I question whether I am still interested in practice. I miss design, and I would love to build and be involved in impacting the built environment in that way. However, I am more interested now in impacting the built environment and the profession of architecture through advocacy. I would like to be involved with shaping the profession and teaching architects to be citizens, to serve their communities. I would enjoy this much more than the act of building.

Perhaps this will lead to my exiting the profession. Perhaps I will practice and continue to be involved with the professional organizations and societies associated with architecture. However, I probably won't continue on the path to design that I began in architecture school. I will never again look at a building as less than a statement of its designer's convictions and values relative to his fellow man.

What are your five-year and ten-year career goals relative to architecture?
In five years, I will have a graduate degree in architecture and, possibly, a degree in sociology or public policy. I also plan to work in local politics. Finally, I would like to have grants for research into the effects of Western architecture and design in Eastern culture on foreign diplomacy.

In ten years, I would like start a nonprofit organization advocating and honoring architects and designers in service to their community, country, and society. I would also like to serve in at least one community organization in a leadership position or in a local or state government in an elected position. I believe architects can understand community in a way that many who are taught differently cannot understand.

Silver Spring Public Library, by Jacob R. Day at University of Maryland.

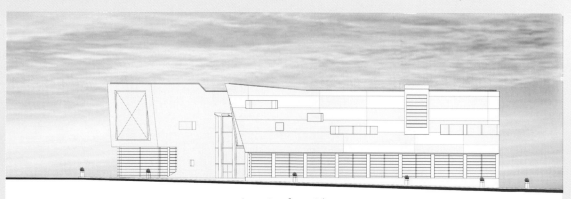

wayne street elevation

What is the most/least satisfying part of your job?

Most satisfying is the realization that AIAS actually makes a difference on the issues its members care about. I am again and again pleased with our ability to maintain a clear, knowledgeable, and respected voice.

The least satisfying part of my position is the constant awareness that it will end. You build an immense set of priorities and plans — and before you know it, you are handing the organization over to its next leaders. Fortunately, we have a history of great leaders and are building a history of strong and stable governance. So my worries are minor.

Who or what experience has been a major influence on your career?

Many people have influenced my career and will continue to influence my career. My parents have influenced my morals and values. My childhood teachers motivated me to be the best that I could. My bosses at Becker Morgan Group always treated me as invaluable to the company.

Two individuals influencing my career are my predecessors, Lawrence J. (Larry) Fabbroni, AIAS president, 2002–2003, and Wayne A. Mortensen, AIAS president, 2003–2004. They have both taught me valuable lessons.

Another major influence on my career was a difficult time during my sophomore year in college when I became quite ill. Rather than handling the situation professionally, I wallowed in my illness and told almost no one I was sick. I realized as my condition improved that my education had suffered due to my failure to communicate. The concern and compassion of my father and my academic adviser saved me from my own demise. I have worked hard and occasionally struggled to overcome this setback and learn valuable lessons from it, including the importance of communicating in every situation.

Exploring the World of Architecture

MARGARET DELEEUW

Graduate, B.S. in Architecture
University of Maryland
Chester, Connecticut

Why did you decide to choose the school you did — University of Maryland?

I chose the University of Maryland because I wanted to be near a major city (Washington, D.C.) while still living on a college campus. I wanted to attend a large university with a number of other majors to explore in case I decided not to pursue architecture. The school summer study abroad program also influenced my decision to choose Maryland.

Why did you choose to pursue the four-year pre-professional bachelor of science degree?

I appreciate the structure of the coursework of the four-year pre-professional degree at Maryland. For the first two years, I took primarily courses in mathematics, science, humanities, social sciences, and English. In addition, I took introductory architecture courses, which helped me affirm my decision to apply to enter the studio sequence. The last two years of my undergraduate studies were focused on architecture, during which I concentrated on design, technology, history, and digital modeling courses. At the culmination of my four-year undergraduate experience, I have the opportunity to decide whether to pursue graduate studies at Maryland, at a different school that offers a masters program, or to take time off to gain work experience before making my next career decision. I find the four-plus-two route more flexible than the five-year professional degree program.

What has been your greatest challenge as an architecture student?

My greatest challenge as an architecture student is handling the workload. Architecture is a highly demanding major, which I realized quickly during the first few weeks of design studio my junior year. I sacrificed my other courses, my personal life, and my sleep to countless hours at my studio desk, and I still could not get all the work done! Now that I have two years of experience under my belt, I have managed this challenge by prioritizing, reserving time for other aspects of my life, and learning to be more efficient.

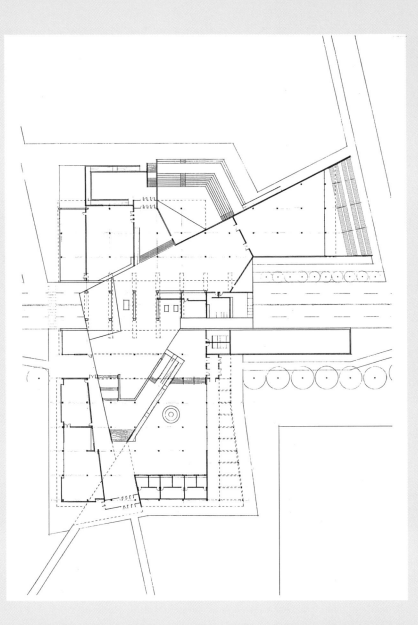

Student Center,
University of Maryland,
by Margaret DeLeeuw
at University of
Maryland.

You have had the opportunity to study abroad to Italy twice during your undergraduate studies. How were these experiences valuable to your education?
Study abroad opened my eyes and mind to the world. Both experiences exposed me to different cultures, languages, people, and places. This sparked my passion to learn and to travel, which will be lifelong pursuits. Studying buildings by sketching and analyzing them on site brought lessons I had learned in architec-

tural history courses full circle and helped me link design with the reality of forms, space, and construction.

What has been the most/least satisfying part of your education?

The most satisfying part of my education is the collegial relationship I have established with my faculty and fellow students. As I approach graduation, I doubt my level of preparedness to enter into the architectural profession, which is the least satisfying component of my education. I do not doubt my problem-solving and critical thinking skills, but I wish I felt more confident selling myself to firms. In retrospect, I think I would have benefited from an internship with a firm during school.

What do you hope to be doing five to ten years after graduation with regard to your career?

I am interested in the academic world, so to build up my credentials, I would like to get a few years of practical design experience as well as teach as an adjunct professor at a university.

Who or what experience has been a major influence on your education/career?

My fellow students in design studio most strongly influenced my education and career decisions. My peers and I mutually support each other, and we mutually celebrate the rewards of our hard work. They are the people I relate to best when making career decisions. I love the range of perspectives I get from students who all have different and specific plans for their future.

Lightbox Study—Charcoal Rendering by Margaret DeLeeuw at University of Maryland.

Irish and Catholic

JOSEPH J. NICKOL
Graduate, Bachelor of Architecture
University of Notre Dame
Coeur D'Alene, Idaho

Northeast Town Commons, by Joseph J. Nickol at University of Notre Dame.

Why and how did you become an architect?
I never really ever wanted to be anything else. Since I was young, I was interested in building. From wooden forts to Legos, my passion for architecture was clear from a young age. In high school, I took what I felt were the necessary steps to advance that pursuit and prepare me for formal education at the collegiate level.

Why and how did you choose which school to attend for your architecture degree? What degree(s) do you possess?

My selection process for college was twofold. First, I wanted an institution that contributed to the formation of a complete person. Second, the architectural pedagogy had to be of a caliber that best contributed to the profession and the study of architecture in general. I found Notre Dame a perfect fit in both regards. I will graduate with my B.Arch. in spring 2005.

Why did you decide to choose the school you did — University of Notre Dame?

The short answer: I'm Irish and I'm Catholic. I determined that the university's architecture program and the school as a whole would best contribute to my formation as a person and offer an education that would provide me with the greatest number of choices.

Why did you choose to pursue the five-year bachelor of architecture degree?

I felt it would be the quickest way to get through college. The five-year approach is an intense experience that I would recommend to anyone who is confident that architecture or one of its related fields is right for him.

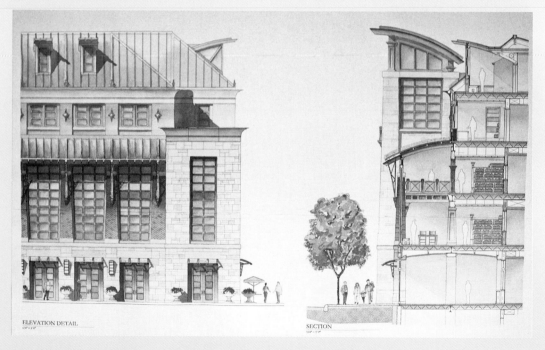

ELEVATION DETAIL

SECTION

Harvard University Knafel Center for International Studies, by Joseph J. Nickol at University of Notre Dame.

As a student, what are your primary tasks?

As far as class goes, studio dominates our time. It is the hub around which the spokes that are our other classes revolve.

What has been the most satisfying part of your education?

Having that fire lit inside me that makes me passionate about what I do.

What has been the least satisfying part of your education?

Living in South Bend, Indiana. *Sports Illustrated* ranked it the worst college town in the nation.

What do you hope to be doing five to ten years after graduation with regard to your career?

I hope to be licensed and contributing to a company. I want to be involved in a firm dedicated to the creation of places worth caring about. I also want to take part in developing urban centers.

Who or what experience has been a major influence on your education/career?

Living and studying in Rome, Italy, as is required by our program.

Extension to Parliament, by Joseph J. Nickol at University of Notre Dame.

You Are an Architecture Student

Congratulations! You are now an architecture student and embarking on the first important phase of becoming an architect. To truly understand your education, you should become familiar with the Student Performance Criteria set by NAAB (see below).

NAAB Student Performance Criteria

The accredited degree program must ensure that each graduate possesses the knowledge and skills defined by the criteria set out below. The knowledge and skills are the minimum for meeting the demands of an internship leading to registration for practice.

The criteria encompass two levels of accomplishment:

Understanding: means the assimilation and comprehension of information without necessarily being able to see its fullest implications.
Ability: means the skill in using specific information to accomplish a task, in correctly selecting the appropriate information, and in applying it to the solution of a specific problem.

For purposes of accreditation, graduating students must demonstrate understanding or ability in the following areas:

1. *Speaking and writing skills:* the ability to speak and write effectively on subject matter contained in the professional curriculum.
2. *Critical thinking skills:* The ability to raise clear and precise questions, use abstract ideas to interpret information, consider diverse points of view, reach well-reasoned conclusions, and test them against relevant criteria and standards.
3. *Graphic skills:* The ability to use appropriate representational media, including freehand drawing and computer technology, to convey essential formal elements at each stage of the programming and design process
4. *Research skills:* The ability to gather, assess, and record, and apply relevant information in architectural coursework.
5. *Formal ordering systems:* Understanding of the fundamentals of visual perception and the principles and systems of order that inform two- and three-dimensional design, architectural composition, and urban design.
6. *Fundamental design skills:* The ability to use basic architectural principles in the design of buildings, interior spaces, and sites.

(continued)

7. *Collaborative skills:* The ability to recognize the varied talent found in interdisciplinary design project teams in professional practice and work in collaboration with other students as members of a design team.

8. *Western traditions:* Understanding of the Western architectural canon and traditions in architecture, landscape, and urban design as well as the climatic, technological, socioeconomic, and other cultural factors that have shaped and sustained them.

9. *Non-Western traditions:* Awareness of the parallel and divergent canons and traditions of architecture and urban design in the non-Western world.

10. *National and regional traditions:* Understanding of national traditions and the local regional heritage in architecture, landscape design, and urban design, including vernacular traditions.

11. *Use of precedents:* The ability to incorporate relevant precedents into architecture and urban design projects.

12. *Human behavior:* Understanding of the theories and methods of inquiry that seek to clarify the relationship between human behavior and the physical environment.

13. *Human diversity:* Understanding of the diverse needs, values, behavioral norms, physical ability, and social and spatial patterns that characterize different cultures and individuals, and of the implication of this diversity for the societal roles and responsibilities of architects.

14. *Accessibility:* The ability to design both site and building to accommodate individuals with varying physical abilities.

15. *Sustainable design:* Understanding of the principles of sustainability in making architecture and urban design decisions that conserve natural and built resources, including culturally important buildings and sites, and in the creation of healthful buildings and communities.

16. *Program preparation:* The ability to prepare a comprehensive program for an architectural project, including assessment of client and user needs, a critical review of appropriate precedents, an inventory of space and equipment requirements, an analysis of site conditions, a review of the relevant laws and standards and assessment of their implications for the project, and a definition of site selection and design assessment criteria.

17. *Site conditions:* The ability to respond to natural and built site characteristics in the development of a program and design of a project.

18. *Structural systems:* Understanding of the principles of structural behavior in withstanding gravity and lateral forces, and the evolution, range, and appropriate applications of contemporary structural systems.

19. *Environmental systems:* Understanding of the basic principles and appropriate application and performance of environmental systems, including acoustical, lighting and climate modification systems, and energy use, integrated with the building envelope.

20. *Life safety systems:* Understanding of the basic principles of life safety systems in buildings, with an emphasis on egress.

21. *Building envelope systems:* Understanding of the basic principles and appropriate application and performance of building envelope materials and assemblies.

22. *Building service systems:* Understanding of the basic principles and appropriate application and performance of plumbing, electrical, vertical transportation, communication, security, and fire protection systems.

23. *Building systems integration:* The ability to assess, select, and conceptually integrate structural systems, building envelope systems, environmental systems, life safety systems, and building service systems into building design.

24. *Building materials and assemblies:* Understanding of the basic principles and appropriate application and performance of construction materials, products, components, and assemblies, including their environmental impact and reuse.

25. *Construction cost control:* Understanding of the fundamentals of building cost, life-cycle cost, and construction estimating.

26. *Technical documentation:* The ability to make technically precise drawings and write outline specifications for a proposed design.

27. *Client role in architecture:* Understanding of the responsibility of the architect to elicit, understand, and resolve the needs of the client, owner, and user.

28. *Comprehensive design:* The ability to produce a comprehensive architectural project based on a building program and site. This includes development of programmed spaces demonstrating an understanding of structural and environmental systems, building envelope systems life safety provisions, wall section and building assemblies, and the principles of sustainability.

29. *Architect's administrative roles:* Understanding of obtaining commissions and negotiating contracts, managing personnel and selecting consultants, recommending project delivery methods, and forms of service contracts.

30. *Architectural practice:* Understanding of the basic principles and legal aspects of practice organization, financial management, business planning, time and project management, risk mitigation, and mediation and arbitration as well as an understanding of trends that affect practice, such as globalization, outsourcing, project delivery, expanding practice settings, diversity, and others.

(continued)

31. *Professional development:* Understanding of the role of internship in obtaining licensure and registration and the mutual rights and responsibilities of interns and employers.
32. *Leadership:* Understanding of the need for architects to provide leadership in the building design and construction process and on issues of growth, development, and aesthetics in their communities.
33. *Legal responsibilities:* Understanding of architects' responsibility as determined by registration law, building codes and regulations, professional service contracts, zoning and subdivision ordinances, environmental regulation, historic preservation laws, and accessibility laws.
34. *Ethics and professional judgment:* Understanding of the ethical issues involved in the formation of professional judgments in architecture design and practice.

National Architectural Accrediting Board, Inc.
Washington, D.C.[1]

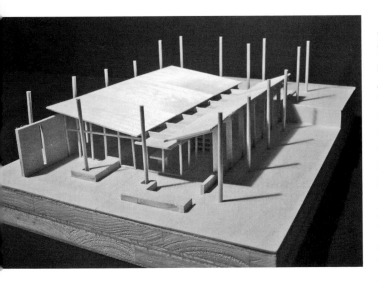

Map Library, by Brad Zuger at University of Nebraska —Lincoln.

Remember that most states require you to obtain a professional degree accredited by NAAB if you desire to become a licensed architect. What does *accreditation* mean? As stated in NAAB accreditation materials, "The program must ensure that all its graduates possess the skills and knowledge defined by the performance criteria, which constitute the minimum requirements for meeting the demands of an internship leading to registration for practice."

Through the accreditation process, NAAB dictates to the architecture programs what must be taught, but it does not dictate *how* they are to be taught. This is why not all architecture programs have the same curriculum. The differences among them can be confusing, but they also allow you to find the program that will suit you best.

COURSES

Regardless of which program you select to pursue your architecture degree, the courses you take will have similarities. A typical sequence includes the following: general education, design, history and theory, technology, professional practice, and electives.

Each architecture program requires courses in general education — humanities, mathematics and science, and social sciences. While you may not initially enjoy these required courses, realize that they will connect to your architectural studies. To the extent you can, choose courses that are of interest to you.

As you will quickly learn, design is the heart of every architecture curriculum. Once you are in the studio sequence of a degree program, you will be taking design studio each semester, usually four to six credits. Design studio may meet between eight and twelve hours contact hours with the designated faculty and countless hours outside of class. Projects may begin in the abstract and deal with basic skill development, but they quickly progress in scale and complexity. Faculty members provide the program or space requirements of a given building project. From there, students individually develop solutions to the problem and present the results to faculty and classmates. This final presentation, called a *review* or *jury*, is the culmination of hours of hard work. Comments are provided to the student on the finished project. Just as important as the product is the process. You will learn not only from the studio faculty but also your fellow students.

Design courses are central to an architectural education, but what is *studio*? More than simply a place to work, studio is where design happens. A central aspect of an architectural education, the studio is the place to work and more. The studio becomes an extension of the curriculum as you combine what you learn from your architecture courses and apply them to your design work.

As part of your studio course, you will learn architecture in varying methods as described below. At the beginning of a studio project, you, along with your classmates, may do research on the project and site, and perform a precedent analysis. You may take a field trip to the proposed site. The professor may lecture on aspects of the project as you begin the design process. You will work on design during class time and participate in desk critiques, or individual time with the professor to discuss your design and ideas. Depending the length of the project, there may be pin-ups or interim critiques with your entire studio and professor or subsets of your studio classmates. Eventually, at the end, you participate in the charrette, an intensive burst of energy to complete the project before the stated deadline. Finally, there is the final review or critique, which involves outside faculty or visitors from off-campus.

A vital aspect of the design studio and an architectural education is learning through criticism. Consider the following description offered by Associate Professor Brian Kelly, director of the architecture program at the University of Maryland:

The development of a rigorous design process governed by critical thinking is a central component of architectural education and an essential tool for successful professional practice. Design studios utilize critical review, debate, and consultation with faculty and professional guests to engage a wide range of issues central to the making of architecture. This engagement between students and their critics takes place in a public arena where students can learn from discussions of their own work and that of their peers. For some, the public nature of critique is challenging. Beginning students have been known to mistake comments about their design work as praise of their individual character. "Professor Smith likes me and therefore is always enthusiastic about my work." Likewise, others have confused critical comments focused on the work with evaluation of personal attributes. "Professor Jones has it in for me and always trashes my work." Both of these positions are naïve appraisals of the role of criticism. Criticism is not personal. The role of criticism is to improve students' design processes and thereby lead the way to a higher quality of architecture. Criticism is not simply a matter of "I like it" or "I dislike it." Criticism involves illuminating the principles on which design work is based and evaluating the rational application of those principles. Simply put, criticism is about the work and the process by which the work was conceptualized. It is not about the individual. The goal of criticism is to enable the student to become a competent critic. Both self-criticism and critique of others is an essential tool for architects in practice.

BRIAN KELLY, UNIVERSITY OF MARYLAND

All architecture programs require courses in history and theory to address values, concepts, and methods. Most offer courses that provide an understanding of both Western and non-Western traditions across the ages, from ancient Greek architecture to the modern day. In addition, more focused history courses may be required or offered as electives.

Technology covers structures and environmental systems. Each program teaches these courses somewhat differently, but structures always involve basic statics and strength of materials — wood, steel, timber, and masonry. Courses in environmental systems cover HVAC (heating, ventilation, and air conditioning), plumbing, lighting, and acoustics. As well, some programs have courses in construction materials and methods. All of these courses, required by most programs, are taught with the idea that you will connect what you learn in them to your work in the design studio.

As required by accreditation, all programs offer coursework in professional practice. This addresses the legal aspects of architecture, contracts, ethics, leadership roles, and business issues.

As well, all programs provide a wide array of electives (see sidebar at right). These may include courses in computer applications, advanced technology, history and theory, urban design, and so on. Some programs permit or require students to take elective courses outside the major in areas such as art, business, or engineering.

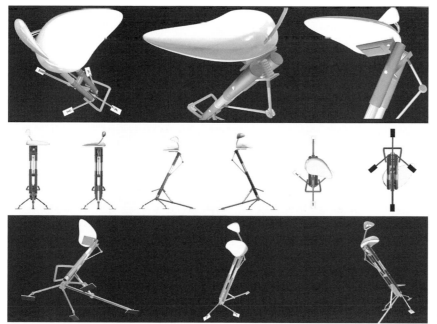

Motorcycle Fork Tubes Stool, by Chris Talbott at California Polytechnic State University — San Luis Obispo. Faculty: Thomas Fowler IV.

Architecture Electives: A Sample

Architect as Developer
Methods in Architectural Design
   Computation
History of the City
Daylighting Design
Advanced Freehand Perspective Drawing
The Ideologies of Architecture Theory:
   The Situations of Theory and the
   Syntax of History
Beyond Postmodern Urbanism
The Cultural Landscape: The Grand
   Canyon
Finding Purpose: Survival in Design
International Boulevard: The Analysis
   of Everything Else
Architecture and Corporate Culture

Qualitative and Experimental Structures
Introduction to Crime Prevention through
   Environmental Design
Understanding Clients and Users: Methods
   for Programming and Evaluation
Traditions of Architectural Practice
Psychology of Environmental Design
Critical Positions in Architectural Design
The Bone Studio 2: Experimental Concrete
   Architecture
Interactive Spaces
Legal Aspects of Design Practice
Methods of Presentation, Representation,
   and Re-Presentation
Seminar in Architectural Philosophy
Issues in Sustainability

Academic Enrichment

Beyond the required coursework outlined above for a particular degree in architecture, you can enrich your academic experience in many other ways, if you choose.

INDEPENDENT STUDY

Most programs have a mechanism that allows you to develop an independent study under the direction of a faculty member. (This is rarely undertaken before the upper years of a curriculum.)

The independent study allows you to focus on a chosen topic not typically offered at your school.

Throughout my architectural education, I realized I also had a strong interest in marketing and business in the context of architecture. Maryland did not offer a course that addressed this interest, so I developed an independent study to understand marketing as a discipline and how it relates to architecture. The course consisted of researching marketing and marketing in architecture by visiting and interviewing two architecture firms of different sizes. Pursuing the independent study was one of my most rewarding experiences in college. It allowed me to work closely with a faculty member, focus on my interests relating to architecture, and start to understand potential career opportunities for my future.

JESSICA LEONARD,
UNIVERSITY OF MARYLAND

MINORS/CERTIFICATES

If you have an interest other than architecture, consider completing a minor. An academic minor typically requires no fewer than fifteen credits (five courses) of coursework, shows structure and coherence, and contains some upper-level courses. Also, students who declare and complete an approved academic minor may receive a notation on their transcript. At the graduate level, certificate programs exist. Parallel in concept to academic minors, certificate programs allow you to gain specific knowledge in an area outside of but still related to your degree program.

DOUBLE MAJOR/DEGREES/ DUAL DEGREES

For some, a double major/degree/dual degree may be an option. Depending on the institution, you may be able to pursue a double major or degree at the undergraduate level or a dual degree at the graduate level. Because of the time demands of an architectural curriculum, this choice may be difficult at the undergraduate level. A second major or degree would typically require you to complete the academic requirements of two degree programs. If interested, consult your undergraduate catalogue. At the graduate level, many institutions have established dual degree options with the master of architecture. For example, the School of Architecture at the University of Illinois at Urbana-Champaign offers a dual master of architecture/master of business administration, allowing you to graduate with both degrees in less time than if you were to pursue each on its own.

OFF-CAMPUS PROGRAMS (SEMESTER ABROAD/ EXCHANGE PROGRAM)

Most architecture programs offer the opportunity to study abroad. Some programs, including the University of Notre Dame and Syracuse University, actually require study abroad. Other programs offer foreign study as an option. Such programs may be for a summer or an entire semester. Some students may also choose to study at another institution abroad for a full academic year. Regardless, you are strongly encouraged to study abroad during your academic tenure. In fact, faculty will say you should make it mandatory for yourself. Money is typically a burden for some students, but most programs offer scholarships. Remember, once you graduate and enter the workforce, you may not have the same opportunity to travel.

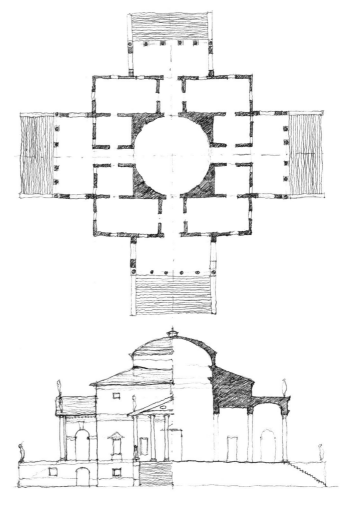

Villa Rotunda — Study Abroad Program Sketch, by Margaret DeLeeuw at University of Maryland. Faculty: Brian Kelly.

Villa Rotunda, Vicenza, Italy. Architect: Palladio. Photographer: R. Lindley Vann.

LECTURE SERIES

Almost every architecture program sponsors a lecture series. This is typically a series of lectures given by practitioners, faculty from other programs, or other professionals, designed to increase the discourse within the school. On occasion, invited lecturers include well-known architects. You should make every effort to attend these lectures to expand your architectural experience. As well, many programs sponsor more informal brown-bag lectures at lunchtime that feature faculty and, sometimes, students. In addition, attend lectures sponsored by nearby schools and chapters of the American Institute of Architects or other institutions. For example, students in schools in the Washington, D.C., region frequently attend lectures at the National Building Museum.

COMMUNITY SERVICE

A recent opportunity provided by many architecture schools is community service programs. Many institutions participate in Habitat for Humanity, an organization that works to build or renovate homes for the inadequately sheltered in the United States and in twenty countries around the world, while others assist area schoolchildren through tutoring programs. These programs provide you with an opportunity to give back to the community while developing skills.

MENTORING

Throughout the history of the architecture profession, mentoring has played a role. Architects mentor and guide their apprentices on the path to becoming an architect. Some schools have both formal and informal mentoring programs to connect you with mentors. One such program is the Mentoring Program at the College of Architecture and Landscape Architecture at the University of Minnesota, the self-proclaimed largest in the nation, which matches students with area architects. Whether or not your school sponsors a program, consider seeking out a mentor from whom you can gain insight and wisdom. Your mentor could be a student further along in the program than you, a faculty member, or a local architect. Also, consider serving as a mentor to someone earlier in the process.

Through its website, the American Institute of Architects[2] has extensive information on the topic of mentors, from defining the term to helping you locate one. Note that mentoring does not end when you finish your formal education; in fact, it should continue through your career.

STUDENT ORGANIZATIONS

Become involved with your architectural education by joining one of the student organizations within your university. First, membership in any student organization is a way to develop friendships and leadership abilities, and to have fun. Second, seek involvement with one of the architectural student organizations, the largest of which is the American Institute of Architecture Students (AIAS).

The AIAS (see appendix) operates at both the national and local levels. Located in Washington, D.C., the national office sponsors student design competitions, an annual meeting (Forum), and leadership training for chapter presidents. It publishes a magazine, *Crit,* and serves as one of the collateral organizations representing architecture students to the profession. Most programs in architecture have a local chapter of AIAS that provides varied opportunities including social, networking, and connections to the profession.

The National Organization of Minority Architects (NOMA) is a national professional association of minority architects that has chapters at over twenty architecture schools. Like AIAS, student chapters of NOMA organize to connect architecture students with each other as well as architects in the profession. In addition, NOMA has as its mission "the building of a strong national organization, strong chapters, and strong members for the purpose of minimizing the effect of racism in our profession."

Other student organizations include Arquitectos (for Latino students) and Students for Congress for New Urbanism (CNU). You will also find others unique to your institution. Also, investigate the value of involvement with student government or the academic units' faculty committees.

Conclusion

Now that you know how to prepare for an architectural education, select an architecture program suitable to your criteria, and the life of an architect, consider the following ways of getting the most out of your education, as described by Brian Kelly, associate professor and director of the architecture program at the University of Maryland:

1. Take charge of your time; you are responsible for your educational experience.
2. Work in the studio.
3. Get to know your peers and faculty.
4. Study abroad; step outside the box.
5. Take time for yourself; your health is paramount.

Retiring Optimist

ROBERT M. BECKLEY, FAIA

Professor and Dean Emeritus
Taubman College of Architecture and Urban Planning
University of Michigan
Ann Arbor, Michigan

Why and how did you become an architect?

My father recommended architecture as a career when I was in junior high school because I liked math and drawing. After that, I never considered another option, though my career has taken me to the farther reaches of what one might consider a traditional architectural career.

Why and how did you choose which school to attend for your architecture degree? What degree(s) do you possess?

I have a bachelor of architecture from the University of Cincinnati (1959) and a master of architecture from the Harvard Graduate School of Design (1961).

I was born in Cleveland, Ohio. My father had a very modest income, and I knew I would have to provide the majority of my support in school. The University of Cincinnati had a cooperative education program in architecture that combined school with work after the second year. This program required an additional year to complete the bachelor degree, six rather than five years, but the benefit of earning employment income from my chosen profession while I was still studying was attractive as I struggled with paying for my education. As it turned out, the professional experience I gained through the co-op program was a formative part of my education and directly contributed to my attending graduate school.

One of my first co-op jobs was working for a trio of faculty who had recently graduated from Harvard and were teaching as they were establishing their own architectural practice. They became my mentors, and their encour-

Bellevue Downtown Park, Bellevue, Washington. Architect: Beckley Myers, Architects with MacLeod Reckord Landscape Architects. Photographer: Robert M. Beckley.

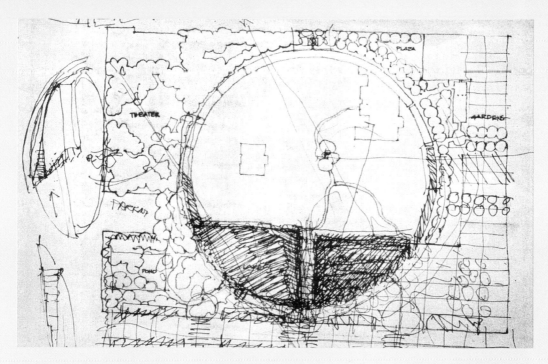

Bellevue Downtown Park —
Concept Sketch, Bellevue,
Washington. Architect: Beckley
Myers, Architects with MacLeod
Reckord Landscape Architects.
Photographer: Beckley Myers,
Architects.

agement led me to consider furthering my education so I myself might teach as well as practice.

What has been your greatest challenge as an architect?
The greatest challenge for an architect is getting the vision for a project realized. I have tried to produce projects with a strong conceptual basis. Starting with a strong concept provides a reference point from which decisions can be made. Those decisions relate to programmatic adjustments, budget, construction, time, and so on. I try not to lose sight of the vision for a project and try to vest everyone connected to it with that same vision. Without a clear vision, you seldom end up with your original idea.

Our design for the Bellevue Washington Downtown Park was conceived as a circular "great lawn" defined by a canal, walkway, and alley of trees, with other park activities located between the circle and surrounding streets. The project has had four construction phases over nearly two decades, but this simple concept has endured through each phase.

Another example is our master plan for the Milwaukee Theater District (now called the Milwaukee Center). The concept was to create a linear galleria that connected elements of the project to each other and the surrounding streets and river. The master plan was changed several times in response to new economic mandates, but each variation respected our original concept of a public galleria connecting buildings and activities.

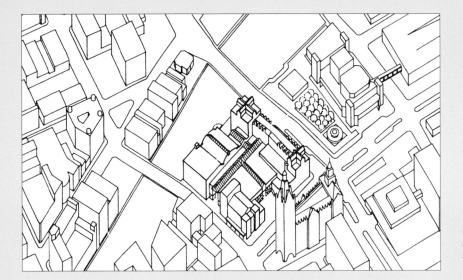

Milwaukee Theater District, Milwaukee, Wisconsin. Architect: Beckley Myers, Architects. Photographer: Beckley Myers, Architects.

I have taken the liberty of using the title *retiring optimist* from the University of Michigan Taubman College newsletter. How are you a retiring optimist?
The term *retiring optimist* came from the journalist who interviewed me for an article on my retirement from the university. I guess she saw in me a tendency to put a positive spin on my answers to difficult questions. I think that comes from my personal conviction that we can, we must, learn from our mistakes.

In other words, mistakes are okay as long as you learn from them. That is why I have enjoyed teaching so much. Teaching has provided me with the opportunity to work with students in asking questions. Even though we don't always come up with the correct answers, we learn in the process of conducting our patient search.

One of my favorite stories is from a biography of Leonardo da Vinci. The book described an event when he and his assistants were in a town being besieged by an army. One of his staff ran to Leonardo and told him soldiers were using his equestrian statue located in the public square for target practice. Leonardo picked up his sketch pad and went outside to sketch the soldiers in the act of destroying one of his works. Leonardo turned what others considered a disaster into a creative opportunity. Leonardo was an optimist.

As a professor of both architecture and urban planning, can you describe the differences between the two?
I don't see much difference between them because I have always thought of architecture within its (urban) context and planning as it affects architectural decision making. I think the two are closely related. However, as these two professions developed over the latter part of the twentieth century, they grew further apart.

Planning and planning education are more concerned with policy and sociopolitical issues and less with the built environment. My teaching and professional endeavors have tried to present planning and architecture as part of a larger whole that considers aesthetic, human, natural, ecological, and behavioral issues as one regardless of scale.

How do you balance your two primary career roles — faculty member and architect?

In a large research university, faculty are expected to make a creative contribution to their chosen field. This means scholarship or research through writing and presentation of scholarship (the commonly accepted form of dissemination of knowledge in higher education). It also means built work, competition entries, funded and nonfunded research, and theoretical projects. Peer review is critical when the work of faculty is evaluated. Simply producing work is not enough.

In this way, teaching and practice are closely related. The qualifier is that the educator/architect is expected to make a creative contribution to the field at a high level and to show evidence that his or her work is considered a contribution to the profession of architecture. Thus, built and unbuilt work must be published and reviewed, or entered into competitions, or presented at conferences. I think those standards should apply to any teacher.

Who or what experience has been a major influence on your career?

My faculty mentors in undergraduate school were terribly influential in my professional life. They opened my eyes to aesthetic possibilities I had not imagined before. They served as role models, combining teaching with an active and exploratory practice, and they inspired and encouraged me to raise expectations for my own career.

Finally, I have been influenced and inspired by many others — students, who always teach teachers as much as they are taught, colleagues, and collaborators. Architecture is a team sport, both as it is taught and as it is practiced. One's success must be measured by the success of the team. You have to know how to block as well as run.

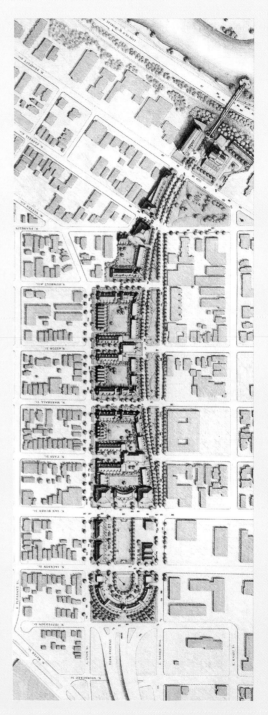

Park East Development Plan, Milwaukee, Wisconsin. Architect: Beckley Myers Flad, Architects. Unbuilt. Photographer: Beckley Myers Flad, Architects.

Creative Dual Careers

W. STEPHEN SAUNDERS, AIA

Principal, Eckenhoff Saunders
Architects, Inc.
Chicago

Westell Corporation Headquarters, Aurora, Illinois. Architect: Eckenhoff Saunders Architects. Photographer: Don Du Broff.

Why and how did you become an architect?

I started learning to be an architect when I was eleven years old. I'm now fifty-four, and I'm still learning. I have always been fascinated by how things look and how they are built. Becoming an architect was an opportunity to spend my life exploring both.

Why and how did you choose which school to attend for your architecture degree? What degree(s) do you possess?

I hold a bachelor of arts in architecture from Washington University, which was my first choice among the four schools I applied to when graduating from high school. My school counselor recommended all of my college selections.

What has been your greatest challenge as an architect/principal?

The greatest challenge any architect faces is getting his or her best design effort built. All designs must stand the tests of the client's budget, the contractor's expediency, and public scrutiny. Coming in with a good idea is not the hard part; the hard part is having the confidence and belief in the idea to defend and sell it without being emotional, possessive, or combative.

As a principal, my greatest challenge is keeping my firm moving in a direction that motivates and fulfills staff expectations while maintaining client confidence.

What are your primary responsibilities and duties?

As one of three principals in a thirty-person firm, I am involved in all aspects of the business except production. I

Private Residence, River Forest, Illinois.
Architect: Eckenhoff Saunders Architects.
Photographer: W. Stephen Saunders, AIA.

Private Residence, River Forest, Illinois.
Architect: Eckenhoff Saunders Architects.
Photographer: W. Stephen Saunders, AIA.

spend about 30 percent of my time on business administration (i.e., contracts, proposals, invoicing, insurance) and the remainder on architecture (business development, design, project administration, and client relations).

I spend more time on firm business than the other principals. This includes paying bills, signing agreements, and human resources. I am responsible for establishing the design direction on all projects and overseeing project development from programming through construction.

What is the most/least satisfying part of your job?

Unquestionably, the most satisfying aspect of practicing architecture is seeing a design come to life. The transformation of lines on a sheet of paper to steel, concrete, and glass is an experience few professions offer. I am fortunate that as I have matured as a professional, the design projects I undertake have become more complex and demanding.

On the other hand, confronting the disparity between the amount of talent, personal will, and technical knowledge required to design a building and the public perception of what an architect does is frustrating. The public is unaware of how complex and unpredictable the process of producing buildings is. This perception gap permeates the entire building process: It undermines fee negotiations with clients; it denigrates the architect in the public review process; and it weakens our effectiveness on the job site, where we are charged with protecting the owner's interests.

Since graduating from college, you have worked for five firms prior to establishing Eckenhoff Saunders Architects, Inc. Did you know you eventually wanted to establish your own firm, or did it just happen?

The idea of branching out on my own evolved over time. In my late twenties (around six to eight years out of school), I felt my career was stagnating. I think this is common in architecture: You know the basics of how to put a building together and are ready to take on your own project, but your firm has pigeon-holed you as a producer, not a designer.

The opportunity to open my own firm arose when a friend and former college classmate reached the same point in his career. We both felt it was time to try. What started as an experiment has become a successful thirty-person firm with a mature portfolio of work in five market sectors. We own our own building in downtown Chicago and have started to transition to the next generation of ownership. If I had not established my own firm twenty-one years ago, I would not have stayed in architecture as a profession.

Besides being an architect, you list yourself as an architectural and landscape photographer. How do the two disciplines — architecture and photography — complement each other?

Architecture and photography both require a technical response to a predetermined set of conditions. I strive for mastery of that technical response — a creation that, while precise and calculated, is inspired by creativity and vision. Architecture is an expression of craft and materials and structural purpose derived from an owner's programmatic requirements. Photography synchronizes camera and lens, film, paper, and chemistry to form a two-dimensional print that captures the three-dimensional: light, motion, and texture. In the end, both architecture and photography produce simple objective products from subtle subjective information. They oppose each other, moving back and forth from two- to three-dimensional forms of vision.

Jay Pritzker Pavilion — Millennium Park, Chicago. Architect: Frank Gehry. Photographer: W. Stephen Saunders, AIA.

Who or what experience has been a major influence on your career?

Looking back over the past thirty-five years, my professional belief system has been shaped by one or two college professors, one or two bosses/mentors, and a couple of clients who trusted me before I trusted myself. No pivotal event or person ignited a life-long passion. Instead, my commitment to a goal and recognition of opportunity paid off in the long run.

Making a Positive Impact

KATHRYN T. PRIGMORE, FAIA

Project Manager,
HDR Architecture, Inc.
Alexandria, Virginia

Why and how did you become an architect?
Architecture allows me to make a living doing everything I like and everything I am good at. These are not necessarily the same thing!

My interest in architecture began when I was in middle school. The City of Alexandria Public Library had an extensive collection of architecture books and journals. After I had read all of them I ventured out to the Fairfax County library and the library at the AIA headquarters. Living in the Washington, D.C., area is a great thing!

Architecture is a dynamic discipline. In all phases of education and as a practitioner and educator it has allowed me to utilize multiple abilities and skills to expand my knowledge base or that pique my interest in other ways. I have been able to find satisfying career paths through architecture as I have matured or as life situations created challenges and opportunities — often unexpected.

2001 M Street, Washington, D.C. Architect: Segreti Tepper Architects, PC. Photographer: Kathryn T. Prigmore, FAIA.

Why and how did you choose which school to attend for your architecture degree? What degree(s) do you possess?

My physics teacher suggested I apply to Rensselaer Polytechnic Institute (RPI), partly because at least a dozen of my classmates were applying to my first-choice school and he knew the program was just as good, although not as well known. I visited Rensselaer and immediately became intrigued with studying architecture there. The university was smaller than most of the other programs I had applied to, and it was in the heart of a small, very walkable city. I also liked that the School of Architecture was relatively self-contained and that the entire faculty had active professional practices. Although located in a technical university, the creative aspects of architecture were clearly fundamental to the pedagogical approach.

Another reason I decided to attend RPI was that I would be able to obtain two degrees in five years — a bachelor of science in building science and an accredited bachelor of architecture degree. After I began to take courses, I found out it was easy to receive minors, and my adviser did not prevent me from taking overloads as long as I did well in my courses. I also took courses during the summer at universities in Washington, D.C. I ended up graduating four and a half years after I matriculated with both degrees, with a minor in architectural history and another in anthropology/sociology, plus a few extra credits related to technology and the industrial revolution.

Pentagon Renovation — Wedge 2, Arlington, Virginia. Architect: HDR Architecture. Photographer: HDR Architecture.

What has been your greatest challenge as an architect?

I am sure I have lost opportunities because I am both African American and female, but the most blatant discrimination I have faced seems to be looking ten to twenty years younger (on a good day) than I am. Invariably when I show up for an interview or to a first job meeting, it is clear the participants do not believe that a person my apparent age could have my credentials.

What are your primary responsibilities and duties as an architect?

For one project, I am the project manager for the tenant fit-out of Wedge 2, Phase 3, for the Pentagon Renovation Project. We ran tenant programming meetings and produced documents for over 140 tenants, including the secretary of defense, the chairman of the Joint Chiefs of Staff, and the secretary of the Navy over the course of a year.

I developed a process for working with the design-build contractors, the Pentagon client representatives, and tenant representatives and training staff to do the work. Key to the success of the project was the Process Manual, a multilevel tracking schedule, and HDR network folder and paper files systems customized to suit the needs of the project.

Pentagon project challenges included managing client expectations, which evolved as they could see we were able to be more responsive to the schedule and client requirements than the previous consultant; creating and documenting a process that could be easily followed as the composition of the team expanded or evolved; and maintaining the morale of a team that worked for months under a relentless schedule.

What is the least/most satisfying part of your position?
The most satisfying aspect of architecture is the ability to make a positive impact on others through my work. On a daily basis, it is building teams or helping a designer and an engineer resolve a problem. In the long term, the satisfaction comes from the glow on a client's face as he enters a completed building for the first time, or when a former student says she just got licensed.

I sometimes feel internal conflicts because I like what I do so much that I often work too many hours, sometimes to the detriment of maintaining good relationships outside of the workplace.

Previously, you taught at Howard University. Why did you choose to teach?
I spent thirteen years at Howard University teaching and nurturing the students. About half of these years, I also served as associate dean. Teaching is the most rewarding task I have undertaken, with the exception of being a parent. To teach, you have to learn, especially when you teach technology-based topics, as I did.

The ideal career situation for me would be to teach and practice. I started and finished my teaching career doing both, and I plan to return to doing both at some point. In the interim, I have found opportunities at HDR and other firms to satisfy some of the yearnings that draw me to teaching. We have created a professional development team to encourage interns to get licensed, and I am on the faculty for the Architecture Section's monthly educational sessions.

The reward of teaching, however, surpasses everything else I have done as an architect. I do not have the words to adequately express the satisfaction I feel for the gift of inspiring others to learn.

What was your role in serving on the board of Architects, Professional Engineers, Land Surveyors, and Certified Interior Designers and Landscape Architects (APELSCIDLA) in the state of Virginia? What does a state board do?

State board members are responsible for upholding laws and regulations related to the practice of architecture. This includes approving candidates for examination and accepting individuals for licensure. The board also hears and decides disciplinary cases brought against individuals and entities with professional credentials. During my tenure on the board we reviewed and updated the regulations and assessed the need for continuing education.

1001 Pennsylvania Avenue NW, Washington, D.C. Architect: Segreti Tepper Architects, PC — Architect of Record; Hartman Cox — Design Architect. Photographer: Kathryn T. Prigmore, FAIA.

I found an article that talked about you mentoring students. Do you still mentor students? Why do you feel mentoring is important?

I have been mentoring students since I was in college. A few years ago, I found out that a young lady I started mentoring when she was in eighth grade eventually did graduate from architecture school. I continue to mentor many of my former students.

Mentoring is important because it makes a better world for all of us and can change people's lives. I have two primary mentors, one for over twenty years and the other for almost thirty years, who have helped me plan my destiny. They have supported my decisions, whether they would have chosen the same path or not. Therein lies their legacy to me. Mentors do not dictate; they do not impose their will on their protégés. They listen, offer options and support, and open doors when they can. Like your parents, mentors support you no matter what.

You were one of the first African American women licensed to practice architecture. Why do you think that was the case?

I first became licensed in 1981. To the best of my knowledge, I was the fourteenth African American woman licensed to practice architecture in the United States. As of today, about 170 of the 1,480 African American architects are women. I was the fifth of six African American women elevated to fellowship in 2003.

As the legend goes, architecture is a rich, white, male profession. Even as opportunities opened up, we were often relegated to the back rooms of offices. This persisted well into the 1970s in many firms for both women and minorities. Rather than face discrimination, many opened their own firms, some married partners who were the face of the office, but unfortunately many were driven away. Today the hearts of many are in the right place, and we are taking our places in the front offices of many firms. For some firms, however, the risk is still perceived as too great.

Architect Specialty/ Consultant

GAINES HALL, FAIA

Vice President
Kirkegaard Associates
Chicago

Why and how did you become an architect?

In an eighth-grade art class, something clicked inside that told me being an architect was my destiny and where I needed to focus my studies, so I did. My high school elective curriculum was formulated by courses that seemed important to the pursuit of my future design studies and career in architecture.

Why and how did you choose which school to attend for your architecture degree? What degree(s) do you possess?

With limited monetary resources for college, I chose the only state-funded school of architecture, Auburn University, which was a five-year bachelor program. In addition, I pursued a parallel career in the U.S. Army Reserve, Corps of Engineers; I completed the Command and General Staff College, the Air War College, and the Army War College. The leadership training that came with those extended studies had a lasting and positive impact on my career.

What has been your greatest challenge as an architect?

School taught me the basics of good design, building systems fundamentals, architectural history, site planning, etc. It did not emphasize adequately the elements one must know in order to practice architecture — that is, the business of architecture. Learning how to survive as a business while practicing architecture took many years. I did more than my share of blindly working through the complicated and tangled web of the business of architecture and construction.

What are your primary responsibilities and duties?

I am vice president of a thirty-six-person firm that specializes in architectural acoustics, and my primary duty is as managing principal. With that title goes the responsibility for most of the firm's operational decisions, and I often find myself involved in fee negotiations, contract review, and business development and marketing, plus I offer a bit of design advice along the way. I also oversee fiscal and personnel matters.

What is the most/least satisfying part of your job?

Most satisfying is receiving the first call that invites you to be part of the design and construction team for a new project and then attending opening night of that project after living through all of the complicated design and construction process. Contributing to the reality that began as a dream or an idea in some-body's mind is the pinnacle of satisfaction.

Haggling over contract language, most of which revolves around who will pay in the event of a problem, is what I most like to avoid.

You served in the U.S. Army Corps of Engineers during Desert Shield/Desert Storm in 1990–1991. What did this experience mean to you?

That period was the most focused of my life and will likely always be. We were too far from home and unable to communicate enough to keep things at home going smoothly. We had no time to think about anything except what we were there for. We worked twelve to sixteen hours a day toward fulfilling a mission whose dangers were unknown at the time, we ate, we slept, and we exercised. That was all of life in the theater of war. Looking back, I realize it is the kind of life most of us yearn for but can never truly experience because too many diver-gent forces pull at us constantly. I saw the behavior of people in a life-or-death environment. I understand more clearly the true blessing of freedom, and as a result I want to continue to contribute wherever and however I can for as long as I can.

Who or what experience has been a major influence on your career?

I cannot specify a single individual or experience, but certainly the dual paths of architecture and military are the major influences on my career. The military taught me leadership early, as well as an understanding of leading and decision making that points in the direction of the next appropriate step. Members of the American Institute of Architects (AIA), among all the people I have met and served the profession with, had a major influence on my career and the direction it took. Being willing to serve and take leadership roles in my practice and in my professional organization broadened my horizons beyond anything I could have ever imagined. The experience made me an advocate of Burnham's challenge: "Make no little plans; they have no magic to stir people's blood and probably themselves will not be realized."

Environmental Design Excellence

NATHAN KIPNIS, AIA

Principal
Nathan Kipnis Architects, Inc.
Evanston, Illinois

Why and how did you become an architect?
Near where I grew up, along the North Shore of Chicago, were amazing homes designed by everyone from David Adler to Frank Lloyd Wright. The area was built starting in the late 1800s, with a peak of homes constructed between 1910 and the late 1920s. Many of the ones located right along the lake, on Sheridan Road, are textbook examples of great European homes mixed in with the first Prairie homes designed by Wright. Although less numerous, contemporary designs are also built in the area.

My parents would drive into Chicago, and we would occasionally travel along Sheridan Road to get there. I would be glued to the window watching these great homes.

Later, the 1973 Arab-Israeli war and ensuing Middle East oil embargo opened everyone's eyes to America's dependence on foreign oil. I felt that designing energy-efficient buildings would help decrease our reliance on that volatile energy source.

Why and how did you choose which school to attend for your architecture degree? What degree(s) do you possess?
I applied to four schools: the universities of Colorado, Arizona, Michigan, and Illinois. Originally, I wanted to attend a small university, smaller than 5,000 students. This turned out to be nearly impossible, as the number of architecture schools is limited, and they tend to be at large universities. I considered these four schools because Illinois was local, my mother had gone to Michigan, and Colorado and Arizona were closer to the scale of school I was looking for.

I attended Colorado, even though it was the only school with a pre-architecture program, meaning that the degree I received, a bachelor of environmental design, was not a professional degree and would require that I obtain a master of architecture to complete my studies. My career counselor in high school told me this was the same as either a bachelor of architecture or a bachelor of arts in architectural studies, but this was not the case.

I also chose Colorado because of its very good program in solar architecture. Located in Boulder, the university is a natural center of interest in solar design. The climate is nearly perfect for it, being 5,000 feet above sea level and having more than 300 sunny days a year. Boulder is also a university town known for its liberal thinking; that helped too.

For my graduate studies, I was able to do more research on where to attend. Arizona State University (ASU) in Tempe is recognized internationally for its solar and energy-conscious architectural design. I felt that ASU, along with University of California, Berkeley, and Massachusetts Institute of Technology (MIT), was one of the best schools for this field of study in the country. I was provided a partial scholarship, which made the decision simple. I enrolled at ASU and graduated with a master of architecture with an emphasis in energy-conscious design.

What has been your greatest challenge as an architect/principal?
The greatest challenge is convincing clients to let me push the envelope with what I want to do with green design. I have to see what the client's limits are and then try to nudge that to a higher level.

Moldan Corporation, Evanston, Illinois. Architect: Nathan Kipnis Architects. Photographer: Nathan Kipnis, AIA.

Another major challenge is to be constantly bringing in high-quality projects. I am fortunate to have had a nearly constant increase while rarely running slow periods or periods of too much work. It also seems that every year I obtain commissions that allow me to do design that generates positive publicity, which in turn helps me bring in work of the same caliber or higher. This kind of cycle feeds on itself in a positive manner.

What are your primary responsibilities and duties as an architect?
My specific responsibilities are threefold. Clients come first and foremost. It is important that I carefully listen to their requests and make sure we achieve them, even reading between the lines occasionally. I tell them the project is theirs, but my name is also associated with it, which means I want to be sure certain standards are upheld.

The next responsibility revolves around my office. I have to make sure we are properly compensated for the work we do, make sure the contracts are correctly set up, and be smart about how we market ourselves. Marketing is an ongoing commitment that requires constant attention to make sure we have new and ongoing material in the pipeline.

Finally, I have significant responsibilities to the people in the office. They must feel they are part of the team and that their input is important to me. I have them attend green seminars or events to further their education. I also try to get them to sample a wide range of experiences in the office, from CAD work, client meetings, and field administration to public presentations. This effort is mutually beneficial.

Evanston Paper, Evanston, Illinois. Architect: Nathan Kipnis Architects. Photographer: Nathan Kipnis, AIA.

What is the most/least satisfying part of being an architect?

For me, the most rewarding part of being an architect is when I have finished a custom home, after spending many months doing design work and the better part of a year or more having it built, and then having the owners invite me over to give me a personal tour. This happens unsolicited on almost every project, and I get a deep sense of personal satisfaction when they do that. I know every square inch of the project has a story, but the clients achieve a sense of euphoria when the project is complete that puts them in a different place mentally. Sometimes they have my wife and me over for dinner and, again, they revel in showing me exactly how the house is working, from the kitchen to the entertainment center to the mechanical system.

The least satisfying part is dealing with design review boards and the general permit review process. Having to justify a design to a review board, especially one composed of nonprofessionals, is tough. They sometimes do not understand the nuances of a design, and I have found that some board members fall back on a limited palette of "expert knowledge."

Ford Calumet Competition, Chicago. Architect: Nathan Kipnis Architects. Photographer: Nathan Kipnis, AIA.

Your firm is strongly committed to integrating excellence in design with environmental awareness. Can you provide more detail to this statement and describe how it is accomplished?

What my firm attempts to do with as many projects as possible is to incorporate green principles at as many stages as possible, and the earlier in the process, the better. We try to do this in an integrated way rather than just tacking on a green technology or material.

At the beginning of the project I try to see what design decisions make the most sense in terms of green design and in response to the project's specific goals. If a solution works to satisfy both, I pursue it in detail. Usually, a single overall theme unifies a design. Finding it is the real challenge. If I can get that one big idea to solve the project's key problem and make it work green, it usually can be done economically and the client supports it. Just because I am doing a project green, however, does not excuse it from being a great design.

Can you describe more about your work with the Green Bungalow Initiative?

Begun at the request of Mayor Daley, the Green Bungalow Initiative (GBI) was a program to provide green design guidelines for people purchasing bungalows in the city of Chicago. Mayor Daley grew up in a bungalow and has a natural affinity for them. The city had already established Bungalow Design Guidelines for people renovating bungalows. The Green Bungalow Initiative was established to provide a green aspect to renovations and additions.

The GBI had four primary consultants—one was for architectural design, another for technical issues (ranging from mechanical systems to the physics of insulation's systems), one for green materials and methods, and one for health issues.

I was chosen to work on the green materials and methods, principally because I had recently completed the Green Homes for Chicago program, an international design competition in which my firm was one of five selected to have their designs built. The house I was involved with was the least expensive to build and used many green methods and materials.

The four consultants provided written information that was collated into a pamphlet intended for use by owners of bungalows or those about to purchase them as a guideline for green principles specific to bungalows. The information could be applied to any home style, but the presentation was geared toward bungalows.

Who or what experience has been a major influence on your career?

As I mentioned, I think the single biggest influence in my career was the 1973 oil embargo and how I thought I could contribute to a solution to it. This event started my career in energy efficiency, which has grown into green design in all its forms.

Professors Philip Tabb at the University of Colorado and John Yellot and Jeffery Look at Arizona State University influenced the way I practice environmental design. Amery Lovins, who taught a summer school class at Colorado, made a huge impression on me with respect to the relationships among architecture, energy, and national security.

I was also fortunate to have worked in two good, though very different firms. At Porter Pang Deardorff and Weymiller in Mesa, Arizona, the design principal, Marley Porter, had a great outlook on how fun design should be. This infectious quality spread through the office. The other partners also shared their skills generously. It was a great work environment.

PHL of Chicago was much more production based and very serious. Once you were at the project manager level, you ran a project like it was your own firm. They really taught me how to run an office.

Belmont Development, Lake Bluff, Illinois. Architect: Nathan Kipnis Architects. Photographer: Nathan Kipnis, AIA.

More Than I Ever Dreamed

DIANNE BLAIR BLACK, AIA

Vice President
RTKL Associates, Inc.
Baltimore

Architects at Work with Model. Photographer: Dave Whitcomb.

Why and how did you become an architect?

I knew at an early age that I wanted to be an architect. My parents hired an architect to design two family homes, so I was introduced to this inspiring profession when I was five years old. My mother always encouraged creativity and found a summer camp across the street from Taliesin at the home of an architect who apprenticed with Frank Lloyd Wright. I had several teachers who inspired me: Mr. Godding, my art teacher from first through sixth grade, and my high school physics teacher, Mr. Ellenbecker. They gave me the confidence to pursue architecture even though I was intimidated by the challenges of school.

Why and how did you choose which school to attend for your architecture degree? What degree(s) do you possess?

When I graduated from high school, Wisconsin had no accredited architecture schools, so I attended the University of Minnesota in Minneapolis. The great Ralph Rapson was dean of the School of Architecture, and it was an exciting time to be there. In those days, the professors were all practicing architects, and every student held a part-time job in a Twin Cities firm. In fact, an internship was a prerequisite to thesis. I earned a bachelor of arts in urban studies and a bachelor of environmental design on the way to my bachelor of architecture. After passing my architectural registration exam, I studied business at Johns Hopkins University and earned a masters degree and the Stegman Award for Excellence in the Study of Administrative Science. Even now I'm thinking about a pursuing a couple more degrees.

What has been your greatest challenge as an architect?

Our greatest challenge is dependence on the economy and our clients' ability to undertake inspiring projects.

Lobby, RTKL Offices — Bond Street Wharf, Baltimore. Architect: RTKL Associates. Photographer: Dave Whitcomb.

Within your firm, RTKL Associates, you are a vice president. What are your primary responsibilities and duties?

At RTKL, a vice president's essential responsibilities include pursuing project excellence, providing leadership, supporting cultural behavior, financial management, and revenue generation. Each vice president has expertise in a particular market or service; my passion is for public and corporate work in the earliest phases of project development, programming, and pre-design. I work closely with clients to understand project objectives, to communicate their vision, and to develop a shared mission with the design team. As vice presidents, we manage project teams and are responsible for design, budgets, profitability, and production quality. We are expected to contribute to the firm's vision and uphold that vision in daily practice. We are also expected to lead beyond project responsibilities in our professional organizations and communities.

Interior Stair, RTKL Offices — Bond Street Wharf, Baltimore. Architect: RTKL Associates. Photographer: Dave Whitcomb.

Briefly, how did you become a vice president of a well-respected firm?

First off, my interests and education gave me the right foundation for success at RTKL. I not only had a degree in architecture but also in urban studies — a fundamental tenet of all of the projects of RTKL. I spent my early years getting a broad range of experience so I could become a licensed architect. Then, I found the project phase I excel at: programming and pre-design. Developing an area of excellence is important at RTKL because each vice president is responsible for bringing work into the firm, and our clients look for expertise. Eventually I earned a master in business and consequently directed one of the largest offices of RTKL. Currently, I'm completing a three-year term as a member of the board of directors at RTKL.

What is the most/least satisfying part of your job?

The best part is the opportunity to work with clients who have the vision to pursue exciting projects and to collaborate with the unbelievably talented experts in our office to make those dreams reality. Some of the professionals in our firm are so impressive that it is a privilege to accomplish things together.

The worst part of my job is facing the harsh realities of staff reductions when the economy fails. Losing wonderfully talented people who have contributed to our work and firm is excruciating.

Who or what experience has been a major influence on your career?

One of my studio professors, James Stageberg, had a significant influence on my career. He offered me an internship at Hodne/Stageberg Partners, where he was a principal; I was honored to work with both great professionals and some of the most talented students at the university. James is always full of encouragement —a true mentor with zeal for life and architecture. He always had confidence in me, and he convinced me to take the position with RTKL and to go on to graduate school.

Conference Room, RTKL Offices — Bond Street Wharf, Baltimore. Architect: RTKL Associates. Photographer: Dave Whitcomb.

Multiple Paths: Architect, Author, Professor

ANDREW PRESSMAN, FAIA

Professor, School of Architecture and Planning
University of New Mexico
Albuquerque

Editor-in-Chief, *Architectural Graphic Standards*
The American Institute of Architects
Washington, D.C.

What has been your greatest challenge as an architect?

During the evolution of my career as a design professional, I have always taken time to reflect on the relevance or ultimate significance of what I do. The process I invoke has to do with defining the impact of the work: What are the specific effects, and what is the maximum potential? Prioritizing, obviously, is critically important — determining the dimensions on which I can have the greatest impact. For me, these dimensions have shifted with time. The biggest challenge has been fulfilling the prophecy — after determining what I want to achieve, then going out and doing it.

You have written five books on the profession. How and why did you begin writing as part of your professional pursuits?

I would like to say it was intellectual curiosity as well as the noble idea to give something back and help students. The real reason was that I needed extra cash to augment income from my fledgling firm. But amazingly, in spite of myself, I have been extremely fortunate to structure a situation in which writing is directly related to doing architecture. Writing is sometimes quite satisfying, always difficult, and provocative.

One of your books is entitled *Architecture 101: A Guide to the Design Studio.* Please describe the design studio for the reader who has not experienced it.

Educational traditions such as basic training in the military, gross anatomy lab in medical school, and moot court in law school have an importance far beyond that of simple course material. The design studio in architecture programs is no different; it is perhaps the most intense and multidimensional classroom experience in all of higher education. In what is really a short span of time, the studio becomes the matrix within which the student develops the habit of thinking and talking, both as a design professional and as a member of a team. The routines, the beliefs, and the standards associated with the studio all help form a professional self-image. This occurs at personal and collective levels — how the individual sees himself or herself as a distinctive member of a profession, and how the emerging group begins to see the nature and value of the profession in which they are being trained. Thus, in the studio, a student begins to absorb and respond to the culture of the architectural profession.

Then, of course, there is the manifest content — the more obvious and concrete things that are done in studio. Through assigned projects, students develop considerable skill in identifying and solving problems. Their ability to assess a creative challenge, integrate and synthesize available data, conduct research, apply material from other courses, and respond to an array of forces and constraints with a three-dimensional solution becomes quite amazing. Their ability to communicate verbally as well as graphically grows enormously. Their capacity to listen and observe grows in equally profound fashion. Their personal resources for absorbing and reacting to the inevitable criticism of colleagues, teachers, critics — and, above all, clients — matures.

Another book you have written, *Professional Practice 101: A Compendium of Business and Management Strategies in Architecture,* explores professional practice issues based on case studies and stories. Why is professional practice so important to architecture students?
Practice in the real word is often exciting and fascinating in many dimensions, and issues of professional practice help inform and enrich design solutions. Practice is central to doing architectural design. Design solutions must become more creative and innovative (in response to real-world constraints) to be considered architecture. And design decisions are a lot less arbitrary when guided by principles of architectural practice.

What do you like/dislike about practice, teaching, and writing?
First and foremost, I am an architect, and passionate about doing design. I discovered that teaching was incredibly stimulating and that the academic environment provided a venue for the discussion of ideas. It was difficult for me to find time to reflect and think while working exclusively in an office context. Writing presents an extraordinary challenge, with the possibility of failing miserably and making a great fool of myself. But, as the cliché goes, without risk, without failure, there is no growth, professional or otherwise. Writing has become another mode of creative expression, similar to other artistic endeavors, that helps me

discover and communicate meaning in design. So, all of these activities — practice, teaching, and writing — are synergistic, inform each other, and infuse my work with excitement, energy, and passion for engaging new architectural challenges or examining mundane architectural projects in new ways.

Who or what experience has been a major influence on your career?
Travel, to both exotic and not-so-exotic locations, is an architectural tradition, and for good reason. During periods when it may not be so easy to find work, traveling is a reliable and fascinating way to keep growing and learning professionally. As an aside: To get the most out of your travels, consider selective advanced preparation to maximize benefit: research plans, photos, and contexts of buildings you anticipate visiting. Slides (or the digital equivalent) — and, of course, the famous travel sketch — are wonderful ways to record what you see on the road; they are a personal resource that can be treasured and referred to often. As an added perk, you can bore insufferable relatives with them upon your return.

Integrating Practice with the Academy

CLARK E. LLEWELLYN, AIA, NCARB
Director, School of Architecture
Montana State University
Bozeman, Montana

Why and how did you become an architect?
For an unknown reason, I wanted to be an architect from the time I was ten years old. However, when I was in high school I was counseled to take coursework in the sciences and mathematics and nothing in the visual arts. As I neared graduation, the high school counselor suggested I become an engineer because of my high school preparation. I attended my first year of college as engineering major and became disillusioned with college. In the spring of my first year I called my uncle, who is an architect in Montana, and asked him whether or not I could major in architecture without an art background. With his encouragement, I made the best decision of my life!

Why and how did you choose which school to attend for your architecture degree? What degree(s) do you possess?
My father was in the United States Air Force, and I graduated from an American military high school near Tokyo. Before going to Japan, we were stationed in the state of Washington. Therefore, I attended Washington State University because I was a Washington resident and it was affordable. After entering the program, I was pleasantly rewarded to discover it was an outstanding undergraduate program with exceptional faculty and students. I graduated with a five-year bachelor of architecture in 1972.

During my fourth year of design studio I became suddenly inspired about learning versus producing. I began asking *why* instead of *how*. Wanting this to continue, I decided to apply to a graduate program.

I looked at numerous programs, both internationally and within the United States. With much more forethought about my education than five years earlier, I applied and was accepted to the Graduate School of Design at Harvard University. The education I received was everything I had hoped for. In 1973, I received my master of architecture from Harvard. Because of the education I received, I have not stopped learning.

Why did you choose Harvard University to pursue your post-professional master of architecture? What was your focus or interest?

I chose Harvard because it did *not* have a particular focus or interest. It provided the world's most outstanding resources for learning. With the combined resources of Harvard and MIT (two miles away), not one program could complete for quality of faculty, library, or breadth of programs. Gund Hall was a new building in 1972, and it was an exciting place to learn. It seemed to be a place where the student rather than the school or faculty could set the direction. I had already been through a structured undergraduate program and sought a resource. I was not disappointed. I tried to take advantage of the resources available. I took courses in development, structures, theory, and design at Harvard. I also took courses in building materials, construction law, and planning (with Kevin Lynch) at MIT. Werner Seligman and Shadrack Woods taught me the why of architecture that I had missed so much as an undergraduate.

In retrospect, receiving my first professional degree from Washington State and my masters degree from Harvard was ideal for my needs. I could not have asked for a better and more appropriate education.

What has been your greatest challenge as an architect/faculty member?

As an architect, my greatest challenge is the ability to create and build work I feel capable of producing.

As a faculty member, my greatest challenge is to eliminate student biases.

As an administrator, my greatest challenge is to provide support for our faculty, staff, and students.

How does teaching architecture differ from practicing architecture?

Teaching is inspiring or guiding others to value learning. Therefore, I often do not consider myself a teacher. The knowledge I impart, in general, is past knowledge. It may exist within a journal or book, but it is still within our past. As an educator (versus teacher), I am responsible for inspiring students to look toward an unknown future. They must take risks that cannot be taken in practice. They must imagine beyond what is historically possible.

My practice, on the other hand, must make the future part of our history. What I imagine must be built through construction means and tools that are usually historically based. Though I may attempt to create new techniques, forms, construction processes, and so on, they are all based on historical realms of possibility.

Whipple Ridge — Private Residence, Big Sky, Montana. Architect: Llewellyn Architects. Photographer: Clark E. Llewellyn, AIA.

Whipple Ridge — Private Residence, Big Sky, Montana. Architect: Llewellyn Architects. Photographer: Clark E. Llewellyn, AIA.

What is your primary responsibility as director of an architecture program?

When I assumed directorship of the School of Architecture at Montana State University in 1995, my primary responsibility was to provide leadership and direction. I needed to build cohesiveness within the school and to expand our vision. In 1997, Montana State was one of three schools to first initiate the five-year master of architecture programs. Two years later, the program expanded in size, budget and technologies.

Ten years later, in 2005, my primary responsibility has changed from leadership and direction to supporting the existing program. I am confident in our faculty, staff, students, and program. However, to build an even stronger program and meet the ever-increasing demands placed on the school, we require outside support. Therefore, I find my primary responsibility has changed to building stronger relationships with university administration, alumni, the profession, and others. As expectations have increased, the school has expanded its horizons to include national and international arenas.

Because of my administrative responsibilities, I rarely find time to teach more than Basic Design in the first summer session. I miss teaching, but I also believe that is why I may be a good administrator. I support those I serve: the students and faculty.

Why did you make this career choice for your professional career?

I became involved in education through a series of events that were not fully planned. After becoming a licensed architect in 1975 while practicing in Portland, Oregon, I decided to open my own firm. Because I had grown up in a military household and moved throughout my life, I did not have many connections from which to establish a client base. Therefore, I believed that if I returned to Washington State University and taught for a few years, I could move to an urban center, practice architecture, and teach part-time to provide income while establishing an office. My mistake was underestimating how much I would like teaching. However, because I also enjoyed practice, I did both. Doing both full time requires much more than forty hours a week.

My heart tells me I am first an architect, second a university professor, and third an administrator. I may be a better administrator than either of the other two, but that may be because I value those two so highly.

Throughout your career, you have been involved with AIA. Why is this important for you as an architect?

I have been an active member of the AIA for about as long as I can remember. As a student, I was active in the AIAS. After graduation I was an associate member, and I became a full AIA member after gaining licensure in 1975.

I have stayed involved over the decades for a number of reasons. The first is that I believe the profession should have a stronger and more effective voice. As much as professional organizations may be frustrating because of their tendency to promote the status quo, I believe the way to make effective and long-range change is through the AIA, which is a place people can actually make a difference if they get involved. Therefore, I am.

The second reason I am a member of the AIA is because of the people I have met there over the years. I served seven years on the board of directors in Montana, driving almost 1,000 miles to meetings, so I met people who share a similar commitment to vision. They are valued allies and valued friends.

Llewellyn Residence, Three Forks, Montana. Architect: Llewellyn Architects. Photographer: Clark E. Llewellyn, AIA.

The third reason is because I am an architect, educator, and administrator. Therefore, I work with students, faculty, and architects in training daily. These groups are part of our profession but are historically underrepresented within the AIA community. Because I also practice architecture, I hope to help bridge the gap that exists between the constituent groups.

The final reason I belong is because I feel a responsibility to be a member. I have used AIA contracts for decades; benefited from their national and state lobbying efforts; handed AIA scholarships to students; benefited from their educational programs; and seen national advertising supporting the need for architects. Even if I had done nothing as an AIA member, I feel as though I have benefited from the organization and its volunteer membership. I have a sense of debt and obligation that must be paid in order for me to practice and teach within the profession I so much enjoy.

Who or what experience has been a major influence on your career?
Robert M. Ford III, FAIA, has had the greatest influence on my career. I first met him as a professor at Washington State, where we had many discussions that lasted well into the night. We later taught together at Washington State, Mississippi State University, and at a private architecture program in Portland, Oregon. He mentored me through learning, teaching, and much of life. One other person who had a major influence on my career is my wife, Beverly. She encouraged me to apply for tenure when I did not believe in such appointments and then to apply for director when I thought otherwise. She has supported my practice, both in times of growth and recession. These people have had, by far, the greatest influence on my career.

However, I cannot leave this section without noting the influences of places. I remember the first time I walked into the Pantheon in Rome. I was awestruck. Since then, other particular places have influenced me. These include the Alhambra, the ruins in Tikal, the Great Pyramids, and indigenous villages in Greece, Italy, Portugal, Turkey, Ecuador, the Middle East, and Asia. I have also been influenced and inspired by the rural West, by the power of its landscape and the architecture that attempts to respond.

Endnotes

1. NAAB (2004). *NAAB Conditions for Accreditation for Professional Degree Programs in Architecture.* Washington, DC: National Architectural Accrediting Board, pp. 11–18.
2. American Institute of Architects Mentoring Website, http://www.aia.org/mentoring

Armada Housing, s'Hertogenbosch, Netherlands. Architect: Building Design Partnership (BDP). Photographer: Grace H. Kim, AIA.

Chapter Three

The Experience of an Architect

The second major requirement for becoming an architect is experience. In most states, candidates satisfy the formal requirement for experience by participating in and completing the Intern Development Program (IDP). However, the important part is early exposure to the profession through the experiential programs often offered through your institution. These programs may consist of shadowing an architect before you begin your formal education, a credit-bearing internship while in school, a career-related summer position, or your first full-time position in an architecture firm. In all cases, you should seek opportunities for experience.

The authors of *Building Community: A New Future for Architecture Education and Practice*[1] recommend that schools, practitioners, and local and national architecture organizations collaborate to increase the availability, information about, and incentives for students to gain work experience during school. Clearly, because this report and study of architectural education was commissioned by the five collateral organizations, there is substantial consensus within the profession that gaining experience while a student is valuable. But the question is *how*? How do you, as a student of architecture, obtain a work position when you have no experience? This is a classic catch-22; you need experience to gain a position and a position to gain experience.

What is experience? The dictionary defines *experience* as follows:

n. 1: the accumulation of knowledge or skill that results from direct participation in events or activities; 2: the content of direct observation or participation in an event[2]

Thus, to become an architect, it is important for you to participate directly in the profession — to observe or participate in architecture, an architectural firm, or your education. As you begin your studies, check with your school to determine if they have programs to assist you in gaining experience. Even if it does not, you still gain experience as you work in the design studio and other courses.

Gaining Experience as a Student

SHADOW

One way to learn about the profession is to shadow an architect through a typical day of activities. Obviously, this is a short-lived experience, but it should be easy to accomplish. Many architects are more than willing to help the next generation in this way. Also, some high schools have a career program involving shadowing to expose their students to career fields. Any opportunity to interact with an architect, however briefly, can help you understand the profession.

VOLUNTEER

Volunteering is a common way to gain experience. After shadowing an architect, you could request an opportunity to volunteer in the firm for a limited period. A number of nonprofit organizations have formal programs that can help you find a firm at which to volunteer.

RESEARCH WITH FACULTY

A wonderful opportunity for college students is a research experience with a faculty member. As for volunteering, approach a faculty member with teaching or research interests parallel to yours. Specifically ask if you may assist in some manner with his or her research or writing efforts. This kind of experience may lead to further opportunities, both during college and after.

EXTERNSHIP

Sometimes considered a mini-internship, an externship provides students the opportunity to explore a specific career path, gain marketable experience, and make professional connections by working with professional alumni for an abbreviated period, usually a week during the winter or spring break. In many cases, schools match students with alumni, but they may also make connections with other area professionals.

The School of Architecture at the University of Virginia sponsors one of the largest externship programs in the country. Held during the winter break, the program provides students an opportunity to shadow an architect — typically an alumnus — in their workplace for a week. More than 125 students have this professional experience each year.

INTERNSHIP

The formal training required for licensure as an architect is typically referred to as an *internship,* but some institutions sponsor an internship program for students. The purpose of an internship is to provide the student with work experience for an extended period, usually a semester. In many cases, the internship bears academic credit. The position is unpaid because it involves a large learning component.

At Massachusetts Institute of Technology (MIT), the internship program helps students gain experience, improve practical skills, and be involved with real projects and practice during their Independent Activities Period, typically three weeks in January. Interns work full time for 3½ weeks in small, medium, and large firms or in public and nonprofit agencies, and they receive six units of academic credit. In preparation for the program, students are expected to attend three meetings during the semester before the experience.

At the University of Texas at Austin, the Professional Residency Program allows students at the advanced levels of architectural design to serve an internship under the supervision of a registered architect in a selected architectural firm. The seven-month internship spans a semester and the preceding or following summer. Students can earn academic credit for the experience by extensive documentation of their work and may receive a modest stipend while in residency. Each year, the program involves approximately fifty students, both undergraduate and graduate students, in two sessions, January–July and June–December. Students are placed in firms in Texas and throughout the United States and other countries.

COOPERATIVE EDUCATION

This educational strategy combines classroom learning with productive work experience in a field related to a student's academic or career goals, achieved through a partnership of students, educational insti-

Getty Center, Los Angeles. Architect: Richard Meier. Photographer: R. Lindley Vann

tutions, and employers. While details differ from school to school, some have established programs based on the idea of cooperative education. Because typical cooperative education programs rely on the student alternating between school and work, establishing a program is difficult with an architectural curriculum.

The Boston Architectural Center (BAC) has one of the most distinctive approaches to educating future architects in the entire country.

The professional degree programs feature the BAC's model of concurrent learning: working in approved, paid, supervised positions in design firms during the day—the "practice"

component of the curriculum—while studying several evenings a week at the BAC—the "academic" component of the curriculum. Although each component has a sequence of its own, the two are designed to be concurrent, allowing progress in one to facilitate learning in the other.

BAC CATALOG[3]

Required for all students in the School of Architecture and Interior Design at the University of Cincinnati, the Professional Practice Program gives students selected practical experience purposefully mingled with a gradually expanding academic background. The program consists of three months of carefully planned professional practice assignments alternating with three-month study periods. For students in architecture, the year-round schedule allows for eight quarters of experience while obtaining a six-year bachelor of architecture degree. Through the Professional Practice Program, students obtain firsthand knowledge of professional practices, expectancies, and opportunities. At the same time, they benefit from a realistic test of their career interests and aptitudes. Finally, as graduates, their experience makes them valuable to employers and increases their qualifications for responsible career opportunities.

Established in 1994, the cooperative education program for students in the School of Architecture at the University of Arkansas is designed to allow students to work for a full academic year (nine to fifteen months) in an architecture firm after the third year. Initiated by the faculty, the program presently has students working throughout the state and the country.

CAREER-RELATED EXPERIENCE (PART-TIME/SUMMER)

Perhaps the most popular way to gain experience while in school is simply obtaining a position in a firm. While not a formal program like an internship or cooperative education, a career-related experience can be just as valuable, although perhaps more difficult to set up. Most schools post positions with area firms, sponsor career fairs to connect students with firms, or host firms to interview on campus, but securing a position requires fulfilling a need of the employer.

Regardless of the type of program, gaining experience while in school makes you more marketable to prospective employers upon graduation. In addition, the experience may count toward IDP if it meets certain requirements (these have to do with the timing and length of the experience). For graduates of the BAC, completing the degree usually coincides with taking the exam because students work full-time while attending school. Note that in a recent survey of interns and young architects, almost half indicated that they had gotten practical experience while in school.

FULL-TIME POSITIONS

Of course, the true challenge is securing your first full-time position with an employer. Searching for full-time work on your path to becoming an architect is important, but not easy.

When you graduate, you are *not* an architect. Remember, you must continue working under the supervision of an architect before being eligible to take the Architect Registration Examination (ARE).

What Do You Look for in Hiring a New Designer?

I look for passion and problem-solving ability.

> **Carol Ross Barney, FAIA**
> **Principal, Ross Barney + Jankowski, Inc.**

I look for an excellent listener who has experience designing and planning buildings for the environment I work in.

> **H. Alan Brangman, AIA**
> **University Architect, Georgetown University**

Our firm looks for graduate architects who have an inspiring portfolio, solid experience, and excellent references. We want to see an interest in the urban scale and the project types on which we thrive — large, complex, and important. We want to meet an engaging professional who can become part of our culture of creativity, collaboration, and communication.

> **Dianne Blair Black, AIA**
> **Vice President, RTKL Associates, Inc.**

For me, all professional staff members must be designers. Therefore, all must be able to work together in a constructive and positive manner. Because of the size of my office and my inability to meet with everyone every day, all designers must be self-motivated and confident in making decisions and communicating with clients, contractors, public agencies, and suppliers. They should also know what they do not know — that is, they must know when to ask questions, do research, or seek an answer. Finally, designers must think creatively, responsibly, and with vision.

> **Clark Llewellyn, AIA**
> **Director, Montana State University**

Borneo Island, Amsterdam, Netherlands. Photographer: Michael R. Mariano, AIA.

I look for incredible talent and ambition.

> **William Carpenter, Ph.D.,** FAIA
> **Associate Professor, Southern Polytechnic State University**
> **President, Lightroom**

First, and foremost, I look for people who think like an architect—that is, can solve problems architecturally. By this I mean they can look for unexpected solutions and solve them poetically. Many pragmatic concerns must be resolved in the design of a building.

In addition, I look for a good work ethic, good people and leadership skills, commitment to excellence in architecture, creative problem-solving capabilities, and the potential to develop technical skills.

> **Edward Shannon,** AIA
> **Assistant Professor, Judson College**

A designer's communication skills—the ability to listen, speak, write, and represent ideas—provide insights into how well he or she can function within a professional practice. The last, representing ideas, is what distinguishes architects from others. In the final analysis, architecture is our ability to turn ideas into representations. Whether the representation is in the form of a diagram, sketch, rendering, or physical or digital model, the architect's ability to represent precedes the construction of reality. A young designer who impressed me the most and became a leader in our firm was expert at taking notes at meetings. This rapid method of communicating design ideas made him valuable as a designer and leader in our firm.

> **Robert M. Beckley,** FAIA
> **Professor and Dean Emeritus, University of Michigan**

Basic intelligence and a willingness to learn are all aspects of the craft. Can the individual logically explain his or her work? I look for people to whom I can be an effective teacher and mentor and who will be engaging students. I also looked to build a team rather than hire a lone talent. Chemistry is always an important ingredient of accomplishment.

> **Richard A. Eribes, Ph.D.,** AIA
> **Professor and Dean Emeritus**

The best first impression is made with a good, well-organized, well-presented portfolio that exhibits creative work. Next, we seek communication in all of its forms, including graphic images and verbal skills. In addition, we look for good work habits, strong character, and people skills, including the ability to work with others and with clients.

> **Jack Kremers,** AIA
> **Professor, Judson College**

I look for people who communicate well, think broadly and deeply, display freehand drawing skills, and have a true passion for being an architect.

> **Gaines Hall,** FAIA
> **Vice President, Kirkegaard & Associates**

From a practical perspective, I look for someone who cares, who is interested in the world around him or her—someone who is aware and sensitive, who listens and asks questions, who moves forward with initiative even if backtracking is required to get it right. I look for someone who tunes into people, places, and things. From a philosophical perspective, a portfolio is not enough. I want people who speak of places they have visited that moved them in some way, and why. I want to know of specific life experiences that have shaped them personally and informed their design work.

> **Barbara Crisp**
> **Principal, Underwood + Crisp**

I look for self-confidence, preparation, and a sense of humor. I look for people who know their strengths and weaknesses. I look for people who can be themselves.

> **F. Michael Ayles,** AIA
> **Director of Operations, Antinozzi Associates**

I look for a candidate who is different from the rest of my team — someone who will add an aspect of the profession we do not have. I look for a candidate who has the basic skills but will also help us question the future from a different perspective. The best team is a diverse and collaborative team.

> **Roy Abernathy,** AIA
> **President, Jova/Daniels/Busby**

Because young practitioners often have a considerable wealth of knowledge in technology that can be useful to the development of a practice, I recruit individuals with expertise in a range of digital tools who also have excellent visual, oral, and written communication skills because they add value to the firm.

> **Kathryn T. Prigmore,** FAIA
> **Project Manager, HDR Architecture, Inc.**

I look for people who can communicate graphically with their hand and a pen. They must be able to analyze problems and have a natural curiosity to find solutions. I want people who are self-motivated and not intimidated by risk. They also must enjoy people, because we work as teams with our consultants or as a design and construction team.

> **Katherine S. Proctor,** FCSI, CDT, AIA
> **Director of Facilities, Jewelry Television**

First, I look for the ability to conceptualize a problem, and second (immediately after the first), the ability to translate concepts into the physical world in the form of space, object, detail, etc.

> **Doug Garofalo,** FAIA
> **Professor, University of Illinois at Chicago**
> **President, Garofalo Architects, Inc.**

Bibliothèque Nationale, Paris, France. Architect: Dominque Perrault. Photographer: Isabelle Gournay.

In interns, including those just out of school, we look for strong hand drawing and sketching skills, strong computer aptitude, a spark of design inspiration and understanding in the portfolio, and an eager enthusiasm and openness to a variety of experiences.

The ability to solve design problems through sketching solutions in real time with the client is a key differentiator in our services. Also, critically, our designers must have an aptitude for and willingness to use a computer.

Carolyn Jones, AIA
Associate Principal, Callison Architecture, Inc.

I generally look for skills not represented in a portfolio. We focus on evidence of basic technical capabilities and skill sets. I emphasize the basics, especially for entry-level staff, because we know people need time to develop more advanced skills. If someone has strong basic skills, we can add to and develop them over time.

I look for people who can learn and are willing to take on new challenges. Communication skills are also vitally important, including writing, speaking, sketching, drawing, and listening. Professional attitude and appearance, evidence of commitment or loyalty, and dedication also make a strong impression on me. I have always said that I can train for a lack of technical skills but I cannot correct character flaws of disloyalty, indifference, laziness, or untrustworthiness.

Randall J. Tharp, RA
Senior Vice President, A. Epstein and Sons International, Inc.

I look for passion and commitment to the profession when I interview young graduates. Their portfolios provide insight into their underlying talent, which is an essential ingredient, but architecture requires tenacity and perseverance, which can be just as important.

W. Stephen Saunders, AIA
Principal, Eckenhoff Saunders Architects, Inc.

I look for communication skills, both verbal and graphic. I look for confidence, a broad range of skills, and team spirit. I look for evidence of volunteerism.

Grace Kim, AIA
Principal, Schemata Workshop, Inc.

We do not hire talent or seek out conscious individuals and nurture their talents. Instead, in our practice we seek out designers who are committed and passionate about becoming fully conscious of their world, humanity, and themselves rather than individuals who possess only narrowly focused disciplinary knowledge and skills. We nurture and develop designers who are alert, curious, question what they see, willing to collaborate, take risks, and provoke change within us.

Max Underwood, AIA
Professor, Arizona State University
Architect and Principal, Underwood + Crisp

I look for great optimism. Most important, I look for people who are inquisitive and appear to possess a quest for analyzing, theorizing, and implementing their ideas regardless of obstacles or barriers.

Patricia Saldana Natke, AIA
Principal and President, Urban Works Ltd.

I look for a strong portfolio of work.

Thomas Fowler IV
Associate Professor and Associate Head
California Polytechnic State University — San Luis Obispo

A Dialog with Design

MONICA PASCATORE
Freelance Designer, P Inc.
Baltimore

Thesis: Abstract Expressions of Life, by Monica Pascatore at University of Maryland.

Why and how did you become an architect?

As a child, I was always making adjustments to Barbie's house — it just was not well thought out — and I had a grandfather who was always building things. For as long as I can remember I have always loved designing and building things, getting my hands in the dirt or on paper and letting my imagination take over. As for becoming an architect, I am still on that expedition. I am addicted to creativity and asking myself to see things in different ways.

Why and how did you choose which school to attend for your architecture degree? What degree(s) do you possess?

My mother knew I wanted to go to school for architecture but she wanted me to get a liberal arts education, so she picked three schools to apply to, all in our home state so I could receive in-state funding and not be too far from home. I graduated from a small liberal arts school with a bachelor of arts; I double-majored in pre-architecture and studio art. While there I took advantage of an abroad program, the Denmark International Study (DIS), a joint program with accredited architecture schools. After graduation I worked for a year in an architecture firm while I applied to master of architecture programs. I was accepted at several schools and made my decision based on three factors: the location, the diversity of the faculty, and the financial aid offered. I received my master of architecture from the University of Maryland School of Architecture.

You have had the opportunity to work in firms of different sizes, from three people up to seven hundred. What are the pros and cons with different firm sizes?

In a large firm, you have all the resources you need and the opportunity to work daily with individuals in multiple disciplines. Depending on the firm, you may be able to travel to other offices including abroad. On the other hand, you may not be heard, and loyalty may be nonexistent. Your responsibilities on a project may be narrow, and you may not be able to see a project throughout the process.

Baltimore City Convention Center and Hilton Hotel, Baltimore. Architect: RTKL Associates.

In a small firm, you may see a high level of responsibility and range of opportunities in all aspects of the firm. As projects are typically smaller, you have a greater chance of seeing a project through from beginning to end. The downside may be lower compensation, limited resources, and a narrower range of projects.

You are working full time on the renovation of a turn-of-the-century row house in South Baltimore, including design and coordination of all disciplines, demolition, phasing, and reconstruction. Please describe the project —and its challenges—in more detail.

Maryland Institute College of Art Residence Hall Competition, Baltimore. Architect: RTKL Associates.

The project involves the conversion of a chopped-up, multi-room single-family town house (11 feet wide by 55 long) into a gracious, open space more appropriate for a couple. The challenges include finding ways to open up the house to increase the sense of space, creating ways to get light deep into the house, realizing storage opportunities within such a small area, and resolving structural issues. The biggest challenge to date has been figuring out how to live in it during the renovation. The phasing of the project has allowed the demolition of 75 percent of the existing interior systems, the construction of the new design, and then the finale of the remaining 25 percent. The design allows for a new kitchen and bath to be completed before shutting down the existing kitchen and bath, which is an obvious concern, as we are living in the house.

While challenging, the project is a fantastic learning opportunity. All architects should have to build something they have designed.

In September 2004, you became Leadership in Energy and Environmental Design (LEED) accredited. Can you describe LEED and what it means to architects?
LEED is a system by which buildings are rated on how well they integrate/respond to the environment. It includes all processes of design, construction, and post-occupancy maintenance. It is critical that architects and all designers recognize the impact of our built environment on our natural environment; for either to endure they must be designed to coexist.

What are your five-year and ten-year career goals relative to architecture?
I do not think of my future in terms of architecture but rather design. I have a number of goals, many of which relate to the betterment of the world and the balance of life through design. Architecture plays a role in some of these goals, but I do not see it as defining my career or me. With that — in five or ten years I hope to be living well and designing a lot of everything!

What is the most/least satisfying part of your career?
I am sure this will change along the way, but right now the most satisfying part has been just getting ideas out there. I love getting others excited about what I am working on and collaborating with other people and really seeing a project evolve.

Rue Hercules, Carthage, Tunisia, by Monica Pascatore at University of Maryland.

RUE HERCULE. CARTHAGE DERMECH
ZOM

The least satisfying part has been the professionals I have worked with. They have exhibited a pessimistic attitude about the possibilities of architecture and the profession and about the relationship of good design, fiscal realities, and clients.

Who or what experience has been a major influence on your career?
Two major influences are my undergraduate schooling and my subsequent travel. The first taught me to keep my eyes and mind open, and the latter continues to present the innumerable ways things have been and are done.

Introduction to Practice: From Frustration to Excitement

ELIZABETH KALIN

Architectural Intern
Studio Gang Architects
Chicago

Why and how did you become an architect?

Somewhere around fifth grade I decided I wanted to be an architect. As a child, I definitely enjoyed playing with Legos; I was prone to assembling the modular pieces in my own design.

It helped that I grew up in a sprawling suburb of Minneapolis and that my father had an interest in architecture. Our family also often participated in a real estate wonder called the Parade of Homes. I recall it took place every spring and fall to showcase new homes for sale in the metro area's newest suburbs. On these outings I first saw floor plans and began to understand how the drawing represented the built spaces in front of me.

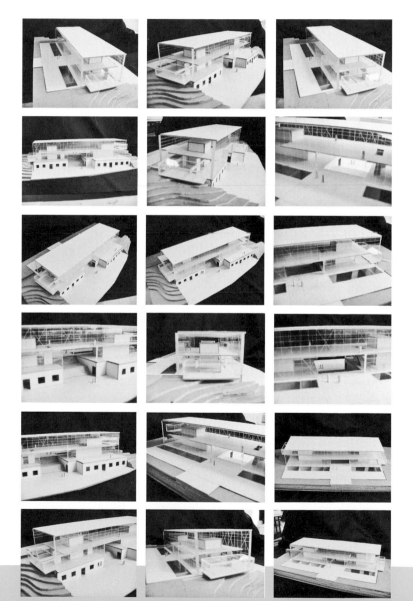

Study Model: Series of Photographs, by Elizabeth Kalin at Illinois Institute of Technology.

Sagrada Familia—Study Abroad Sketch, by Elizabeth Kalin at Illinois Institute of Technology.

Finally, shadowing real architects cemented my desires to become a professional architect. During middle school, for a morning I shadowed a friend's father who was architect and was absolutely fascinated with the scaled models and large mockups on display in his office. Later, in high school, I was paired with a woman who owned a small firm with her husband. I spent a day with her and was itching to go to college by the end of it. So many aspects of the career seemed appealing—the designing, the teamwork, the meeting new people, the variety of work, the building models.

Why and how did you choose which school to attend for your architecture degree? What degree(s) do you possess?

I decided to attend a school for architecture and began actively investigating my options in my junior year of high school. From the little I had learned of the five-year professional degree versus the four-plus-two master's degree, I was always more open to schools offering five-year programs, which seemed more suited to my interests.

After several visits and interviews, and after receiving information on scholarships at the schools I'd applied to, I decided to attend Illinois Institute of Technology (IIT) to obtain the five-year professional bachelor of architecture degree.

Why did you choose to study at IIT?

My mother and I took a long weekend to make a road trip around Midwest architecture schools in the late spring of my junior year of high school. We started off at North Dakota State, swung by Iowa State next, and finished up in Chicago with visits to both IIT and UIC.

Many factors influenced my decision to attend IIT, but the biggest draw was Crown Hall. I had never heard of Ludwig Mies van der Rohe. I had no sense of the legacy of the school. I do remember the day was cool, cloudy, and damp. But the light in that building was incredible. So many of the other facilities I had seen were dismal, dark, and cramped. I imagined myself somewhere for the next five years of my life—and there was simply no contest.

I was also drawn to Chicago itself. It was larger than I the city I had grown up in, and I was looking forward to moving away from home, but Chicago was not too far away.

Additionally, I had a wonderful interaction with the assistant dean of the College of Architecture. He gave me the tour personally, took my mother and me out to lunch, and was interested in my reasons for visiting the school and studying architecture. He was by far the most receptive and encouraging administrator I met in my college search.

Paying for higher education is daunting no matter what schools a person is considering. Scholarships, both from the school and outside sources, had a large impact on my final decision to attend IIT and obtain a five-year professional bachelor's degree. It was the best decision I have made thus far in my life.

What impact did attending a pre-college architecture program at Pratt have on your decision to pursue architecture?
Attending the pre-college program at Pratt was an amazing experience, even though it had a fairly small impact on my decision to pursue architecture. I already had such a strong desire to study architecture in college that the experience only helped fuel the existing desire.

The Pratt program was a wonderful taste of the challenges of college ahead. It was an intense time where my boundaries were pushed in both sections of the program—foundation arts and architecture. It fostered personal growth in many ways. I highly recommend the experience to people interested in pursuing an architecture education.

What has been your greatest challenge as an intern/architect thus far?
The difference between being a full-time architecture student and being a full-time architectural intern is immense. I knew this adjustment was coming, and I felt I had prepared for it with my experiences working in offices over summer and winter breaks, but I still struggle with it. Being a student is wonderful because education is so personal, selfish, and indulgent. You are the client as well as the architect. The constraints on projects are relatively small. You are absolutely free to take design ideas and run with them.

The introduction to practice can be overwhelming but still critical to one's education and preparation. I enjoyed myself more as a student, when I lived in denial, selectively ignoring the fact that architecture is a business. Certainly many components of the real world are never touched on in school, and I've felt a range of emotions dealing with them in practice, from frustration to excitement. This extension of one's education still offers learning opportunities, but the parameters are shifted, and coming to terms with this shift is critical.

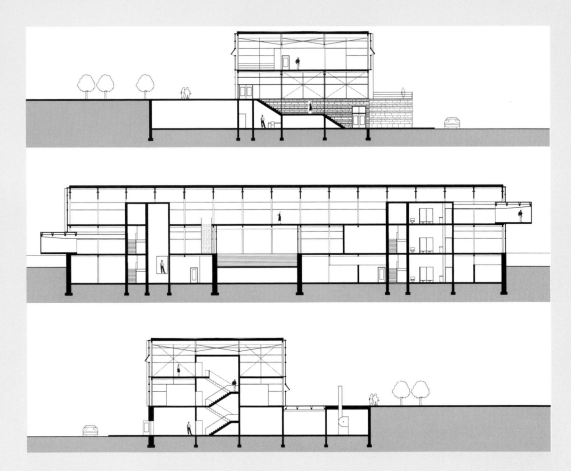

Section, by Elizabeth
Kalin at Illinois Institute
of Technology.

What are your primary responsibilities and duties?

My primary responsibility is assisting the project architect on my project team.
The majority of my time is involved with production — production of sketches,
drawings, models — that are created and used from the programming stages of a
job through the construction administration. I spend a lot of time on the computer, drawing or modeling, but such a range of tasks exists, both on the computer and away from my desk, that rarely am I plagued with boredom. I am an
involved member of the team. I am involved with the design of the project, but
often in small doses or with components of the whole.

Education Begins at Graduation

DAVID R. GROFF

Intern Architect
Dalgliesh, Gilpin, and Paxton Architects
Charlottesville, Virginia

Why and how did you become an architect?
I pursued a career in architecture because I felt it would allow me to use both
my creativity and my practical mindset in a complementary way.

Beaver Stadium Sketch, by David R. Groff at University of Maryland.

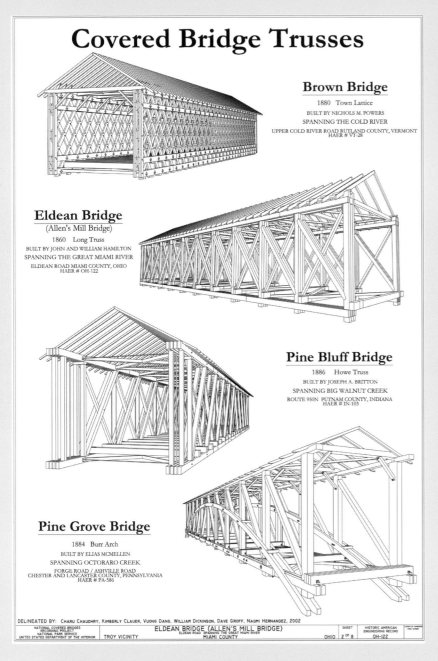

Covered Bridge Trusses

Brown Bridge
1880   Town Lattice
BUILT BY NICHOLS M. POWERS
SPANNING THE COLD RIVER
UPPER COLD RIVER ROAD RUTLAND COUNTY, VERMONT
HAER # VT-28

Eldean Bridge
(Allen's Mill Bridge)
1860   Long Truss
BUILT BY JOHN AND WILLIAM HAMILTON
SPANNING THE GREAT MIAMI RIVER
ELDEAN ROAD MIAMI COUNTY, OHIO
HAER # OH-122

Pine Bluff Bridge
1886   Howe Truss
BUILT BY JOSEPH A. BRITTON
SPANNING BIG WALNUT CREEK
ROUTE 950N PUTNAM COUNTY, INDIANA
HAER # IN-103

Pine Grove Bridge
1884   Burr Arch
BUILT BY ELIAS MCMELLEN
SPANNING OCTORARO CREEK
FORGE ROAD / ASHVILLE ROAD
CHESTER AND LANCASTER COUNTY, PENNSYLVANIA
HAER # PA-586

DELINEATED BY: CHARU CHAUDHRY, KIMBERLY CLAUER, VUONG DANG, WILLIAM DICKINSON, DAVE GROFF, NAOMI HERNANDEZ, 2002

| NATIONAL COVERED BRIDGES RECORDING PROJECT NATIONAL PARK SERVICE UNITED STATES DEPARTMENT OF THE INTERIOR | TROY VICINITY | ELDEAN BRIDGE (ALLEN'S MILL BRIDGE) ELDEAN ROAD SPANNING THE GREAT MIAMI RIVER MIAMI COUNTY | OHIO | 2 OF 8 | SHEET | HISTORIC AMERICAN ENGINEERING RECORD OH-122 |

Covered Bridge Trusses, Historic American Buildings Survey (HABS)—National Park Service. Delineators: Charu Chaudhry, Kimberly Clauer, Vuong Dong, William Dickinson, David Groff, Naomi Hernandez. Photographer: Library of Congress, Prints and Photograph Division, Historic American Buildings Survey, HABS OH-122.

Why and how did you choose which school to attend for your architecture degree? What degree(s) do you possess?

I earned a B.S. in architecture from the University of Maryland (2003). I started my college career at Mount Saint Mary's College, going back and forth between majors in studio art, business, accounting, and marketing. After realizing that none of these fields was the right fit for me, I decided to transfer to Maryland to study architecture.

What has been your greatest challenge as an intern/architect thus far?

The challenge is to make the time to learn everything about the building industry that was not taught in school and that I am not exposed to on a daily basis. So many decisions must be made during the building process, and I feel I currently have a grasp of only a tiny percentage of what is out there. From a practical standpoint, my design skills are improving every day as I inherit more and more job responsibility, but I also find myself falling behind with respect to basic construction knowledge.

Describe your experience with the Historic American Buildings Survey/Historic American Engineering Record (HABS/HAER).

My summer internship with HABS/HAER was invaluable. I worked with a team of ten people, including architects, engineers, historians, and a photographer. Our team was assigned to study and document historic wooden covered bridges in the northeastern United States.

We spent about a week in the field at each bridge, documenting, drawing, measuring, and photographing their every physical aspect. Each one we studied utilized a different type of truss system, and each was considered the best of its type. After gathering the information from the sites, we returned to Washington and spent the rest of the summer creating plans, sections details, and three-dimensional models on the computer. Along with the engineers, historians, and photographers, we created a detailed biography of each bridge that now rests in the Library of Congress.

During your senior year, you entered the Birds-I-View competition; your entry was selected and built for display. Describe the experience.

The Maryland National–Capital Parks and Planning Commission; Department of Parks and Recreation, Prince George's County, Maryland, sponsored "Birds-I-View," a public arts exhibition of over fifty fiberglass bluebirds created by artists from all over the county. The resulting designs were displayed at various sites throughout the county during the summer and fall of 2003.

We all started with a five-foot-tall fiberglass bluebird that we were to decorate in a creative and appealing way. My design incorporated lights attached to the outside of the shell; these illuminated a multicolored stained-glass exoskeleton.

I had worked with stained glass before, but I had never done anything close to this size or scale. It was particularly challenging because I had to figure out how it was going to be put together and then I actually had to build it. At many points in the process I was not sure whether it was going to work, but the project finally came together after about two months and I was pleased with the results. My creative design for the bluebird was featured in the *Washington Post*.

What are your five-year and ten-year career goals relative to architecture?

My main goal is to become licensed within the next five years. After that, I would like either to start my own design-build firm or find a position where I can both design spaces and help build them. I am hoping to avoid sitting behind a desk for the rest of my life. This is my ten-year goal. I also hope to work on socially relevant projects after gaining the practical knowledge and experience necessary to become licensed.

Bluebird—Maryland National Capital Park and Planning Commission, Prince George's County Department of Parks and Recreation Competition. Designer: David R. Groff.

What are your primary responsibilities and duties?

I am primarily a drafter, but I also take over a lot of minor design responsibilities throughout the course of the project. While I cannot take credit for designing any project in its entirety, I do contribute at least 50 percent of my projects' designs.

My main task is to put together a complete set of construction drawings for a given project. After the initial design stages are complete, I usually take over all of the drafting responsibilities and also become the main line of communication between my firm and our clients.

What is the most/least satisfying part of your job?

Working for a small firm that does not specialize in any building type is satisfying because I work on a variety of buildings, sites, and sizes. I rarely work on a single project for more than a few months; the constant change keeps my job interesting and enjoyable.

Sitting behind a computer screen for seven hours a day is probably the least satisfying aspect of my position. I enjoy drafting and coordinating a set of construction documents, but I'd rather not have to sit in the same chair, staring at the same screen, day in and day out.

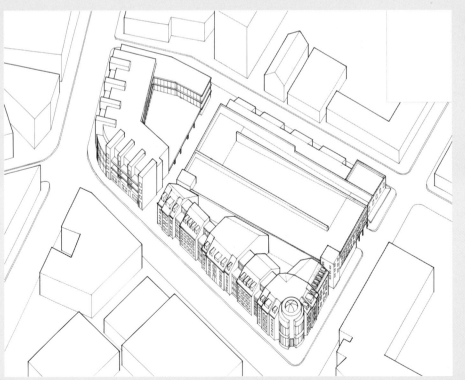

Annapolis Redevelopment Project, by David R. Groff and Aaron Zephir at University of Maryland.

From Teacher to Architect

TAMARA REBURN, ASSOCIATE AIA

Intern Architect
Fanning/Howey Associates, Inc.
Novi, Michigan

What has been your greatest challenge as an architect?
As an intern, the challenge has been learning and continuing to learn the many and varied aspects of constructing a building. I was surprised to learn that every project presents unique problems that require a custom solution. Learning how to coordinate the disciplines within a project has also been a challenge for me because it requires not only great attention to detail but also a clear understanding of all of the systems in a building and how they interact with and impact each other.

Fishing Shack, Upper Michigan, by Tamara Redburn at University of Michigan.

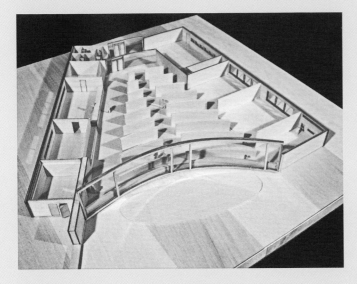

Branch Library, Ann Arbor, Michigan, by Tamara Redburn at University of Michigan.

What are your primary responsibilities and duties?

As an intern, I serve as the project coordinator, which means I work under a designer (who designs the building), a project manager (who manages the team and client), and a project architect (who is responsible for implementing the design). I produce construction documents, coordinate with other disciplines, and meet with clients. I make minor decisions involving the design of the building — for example, designing doors and choosing colors.

I also use Photoshop to show clients "before" and "after" photos of the effect renovations would have on the look of their building. I have also done extensive pre-project work, designing presentation materials to sell a client or a community on a building proposal.

My unusual background as a teacher has come into play in my work. The firm I work for designs schools; I chose to work for them in order to remain involved in education and to use my knowledge of schools and teaching in a new way. I have been fortunate to participate in interviews with prospective clients, explaining my role as faculty liaison with expertise in facilitating communication among architects and educators. Additionally, I have developed potential designs for school buildings and interacted with community members in forums to garner their input on these proposals.

What is the most/least satisfying part of your job?

Three aspects of my position are equally satisfying. One is seeing and hearing the excitement of community members when we discuss future improvements to their schools, including new buildings and renovations and additions to existing facilities. It is energizing to know my work will have a positive impact on children and the wider community for many years to come.

Another is wrapping up a set of documents, putting the finishing touches on the construction drawings, knowing that many, many hours of my time went into the project and that it is on the cusp of being built.

The third is seeing a project built. It is exhilarating to see the results of my work, to experience in three dimensions what was previously only on paper.

It is difficult for me to say what is least satisfying because I love going to work every day. I enjoy each task for its potential to teach something new. I appreciate the need for attention to detail, the problem solving required, the interaction with other people, both in my firm and outside of it.

With a degree in secondary mathematics education and sixteen years of experience as a middle school math teacher, what prompted you to become an architect?

I participated in a summer program that enabled teachers to work at a business of their choice and incorporate that experience into their lesson plans. Because of a previous house-building project, I decided to go to an architecture firm to get ideas on how to expand the project. I very much enjoyed my time there and was fascinated with all I observed.

The owner of the firm urged me to take classes at the local community college. The firm owner invited me back for the entire next summer and I took him up on it, doing basic drafting work and learning as much as I possibly could. I continued to teach during the day and took classes at night. He hired me again the following summer, when he hit me with a bombshell: When was I going to enroll in a master's degree program?

At the time I thought that was an impossible dream, but after visiting the design studio at the University of Michigan, I started to see a way to make it happen. With the generous and loving support of my husband — we had been married only two months at the time! — I quit my teaching job and went back to school full-time. I have loved every day of it, and I have never looked back.

Bus Stop, Ann Arbor, Michigan, by Tamara Redburn at University of Michigan.

How has your background in education been helpful in the transition to architecture?

In teaching, I was always learning and trying new things. I developed a hands-on, interactive curriculum for eight-grade math that did not incorporate a textbook. This background in experimentation is helpful in architecture because I'm constantly learning new things and developing new strategies and design solutions.

Because of my previous work and life experiences, I have a maturity and outlook that most new interns do not possess. I think it makes me more

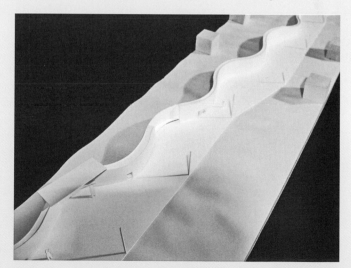

reliable, more composed, more able to deal with personalities and situations. I was active in the governance of the school where I taught; this gave me valuable speaking and organizational skills as well as experience in dealing with factions that were sometimes at odds. All of these skills are useful in architecture.

However, being a teacher made me critical of architectural education. I had many amazing professors, but I also had my share of those who, though they knew their subject matter well, were unwilling or incapable of communicating it to their students. I was also bewildered and somewhat disillusioned by studio culture. I had some wonderful studio professors and experiences, but I also experienced humiliation, anger, and frustration. Critiques were often haphazard and random, and success or failure was sometimes dependent on which reviewer you happened to draw, not on clearly defined expectations.

Who or what experience has been a major influence on your career?

Obviously, the employer at my first architecture firm, who urged me to get my master's degree, was the primary and largest influence on my career. Without this influence, I would not be where I am today. I've also enjoyed the kind support of several wonderful mentors. I had a mentor in school who encouraged me, answered my many questions about the profession, allowed me to shadow her, and generally supported me. I also have a mentor and friend who serves as my supervisor at the firm where I work, guiding me through the maze of completing a project well and on time.

Through the American Institute of Architects (AIA), I have encountered many wonderful influences, from my incredibly talented and dedicated peers on the National Associates Committee (NAC) to the amazing architects on my state board of directors to the architects on the national stage who are working for real change. I have been influenced and inspired by all of these people to various degrees.

Finding a Place in Architecture

MICHELLE HUNTER

Lead Designer
Garage Takeover — Discovery Channel
Washington, D.C.

Why and how did you become an architect?

Since the age of five, I wanted to be an architect. A close family friend who is a builder sparked my initial interest in the profession, explaining to me the role of the architect in the building process. Ever since then, I was intrigued by what an architect does and spent time as a child learning more about architecture. In school, I excelled in math and art classes, two subjects that are conveniently helpful in architectural education. The more my understanding of architecture evolved, the more interested I became in the subject and pursuing it as my career.

Mind over Media Lobby, Pittsburgh. Architect: Studio D'Arc. Photographer: Nicholas Taub.

Why and how did you choose which school to attend for your architecture degree? What degree(s) do you possess?

I currently hold a bachelor of architecture degree from Carnegie Mellon University. After months of researching programs at various universities, I decided on attending a program that awarded a five-year professional degree. Some schools I was applying to offered only a four-year bachelor degree, which requires students to obtain a master of architecture. The five-year architecture programs seemed to cover more material and prepare students better for a professional track. Additionally, after five years of undergraduate work, I could get a job at a firm, immediately participate in the Intern Development Program, and be that much closer to obtaining my license.

What has been your greatest challenge as an intern thus far?

My greatest challenge as an intern thus far is understanding the role a firm wants me to play and conforming to that ideal. While certain aspects of work are taught in school, when and where to show initiative, when to voice an opposing opinion, who to speak with when a problem arises, how severe a problem needs to be in order to call attention to it, and how to deal with office politics are not made clear. These challenges are not unique to architecture, but they are common among recent graduates struggling to begin their career.

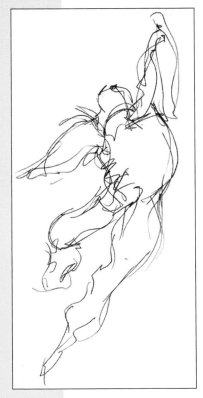

Grand Pirouette, by Michelle Hunter at Carnegie Mellon University.

Similarly, maintaining continuity on a particular project is also a challenge. Often, as a young person in a firm, you are hired to fill in holes, to jump around among projects and teams, and to adapt to expectations for various situations. While this experience allows for a breadth of exposure, it prevents one from seeing the architectural process develop from beginning to end. Without being able to follow the development of a particular project, one's exposure is limited, and often one is pigeonholed and winds up performing the same tasks on every project.

What are your five-year and ten-year career goals relative to architecture?

In five years, I hope to be a licensed architect with a position of significant responsibility in a firm. I hope this firm is one that promotes thoughtfulness in design and is constantly generating new and exciting ideas, a place where my education can continue and I can not only learn process but also design excellence.

In ten years, I hope to have my own small firm with a strong client base and to begin to address significant design issues and make a name for myself in the architecture world.

Harrison Garage—Garage Takeover, Beyond Productions, Cabin John, Maryland. Designer: Michelle Hunter. Photographer: Michelle Hunter.

Please describe your recent position with *Garage Takeover*, a new show produced by the Discovery Channel.

My most recent design job is working on a television show airing on the Discovery Channel. On this reality-based home renovation show, cluttered and damaged garages are converted into newfound habitable space. As the designer on six episodes, I met with the homeowners to get an idea of what they wanted to turn their space into. Many of these people had dreams for their garages but never had the time or resources to accomplish them. Their ideas included an art studio, a wine cellar, a home office and mudroom, a home gym, a garden center, and a lounge. I had a week or two to meet with the homeowners, design the space, research materials and pricing, and produce construction documents and presentation drawings. The actual construction and filming took place over three days, and I had to remain within a budget of under $4,000 for materials.

What were your primary responsibilities and duties?

My primary responsibilities were understanding the scope of work by meeting with the homeowners and measuring the garage, designing an exciting space that fulfilled their desires, and coming up with a set of construction documents that communicated my ideas clearly to the contractor. Additionally, I was responsible for presenting my ideas and drawings to a group of people including the executive producer, project manager, and design support staff. I did a significant amount of material research, pricing, and ordering as well.

What was the most satisfying part of the job?
The absolute most satisfying part was during the reveal of the space, seeing the reaction of the homeowners and the delight on their faces. Because they were not allowed to see any part of the construction process, nor were they allowed to see the plans, they were always genuinely surprised with the results.

Seeing the clients' satisfaction and hearing their praise for the work is indescribably wonderful. Being a part of the show and making the clients happy reminded me why I want to pursue architecture as my career.

What was the least satisfying part of your job?
The least satisfying part of my job was the constant struggle I had with the contractor. While the homeowners were always thankful for my hard work, it was quite frustrating to know that the crew, contractor, and producers took it for granted.

Who or what experience has been a major influence on your career?
With all its imperfections and frustrations, working on the show is a huge influence on my career, reaffirming why I am pursuing architecture and giving me a sense of what it is like to work with my own clients.

A few people have also significantly influenced my career:

Laura Lee, FAIA, professor and head of the architecture program at Carnegie Mellon University, is a woman who has such an innate sense of architecture that everything she says seems to make an incredible amount of sense. She has been an important role model not only in architecture but for life in general. She has devoted her life and all her time to architectural education and the advancement of young professional architects.

Gerard Damiani, AIA, a professor I had my first year of architecture school, was later my employer when he hired me at his firm. His role as my teacher carried over into the firm setting, where he was constantly challenging me and making sure I was learning something.

My most recent boss, Mark Boekenheide, AIA, ASID, a partner at BBGM, has also been an influence. I really admire him—he has an excellent business sense, and although he was always extremely busy when I worked there, he still made sure I was being taught when I was staffed on his projects.

Making an Unrelated Degree Count

LYNSEY GEMMELL

Architect II, Holabird & Root
Chicago

Why and how did you become an architect?
My undergraduate studies were in art history and psychology. My emphasis was architectural history, and my exposure to the theory and history of the practice of architecture led me to consider how I could continue my interest in the built environment. I found I didn't want to write about other people's buildings but rather to be involved in the design of buildings myself. In addition, I wish to teach in the future, and with architecture the possibility is open to teach both during and after practice.

Why and how did you choose which school to attend for your architecture degree? What degree(s) do you possess?
I chose a graduate program at an accredited school with a good international reputation located in a large metropolitan setting. My undergraduate degree is a master of arts (First Class), and my graduate degree is a master of architecture.

What has been your greatest challenge as an intern/architect thus far?
I cannot identify a single *greatest* challenge, but a big one is learning to accomplish as much as possible in the time available without working enormous amounts of overtime. I try to keep in mind the difference between professional responsibility and the goal of the task at hand rather than my ultimate design ambitions.

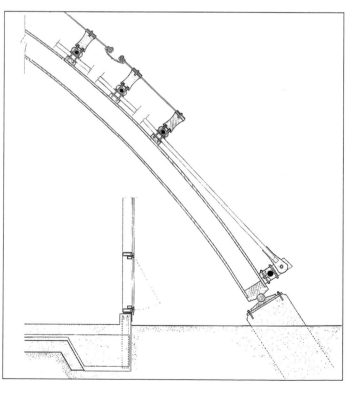

Section Detail—Second-Year Graduate Project, by Lynsey Gemmell at Illinois Institute of Technology.

What are your five-year and ten-year career goals relative to architecture?

In the short term, my goal is to become licensed. In the medium term, I want to capitalize on the experience I have had thus far and take on greater responsibility. I would like to become more involved in the design process at the outset of projects while building up my technical knowledge. In the long term, my goals are to be involved in management decisions and to teach, at least on a part-time basis.

What are your primary responsibilities and duties?

On larger projects, my responsibilities include researching products and systems, detailing, coordinating with consultants, and providing production support. On smaller projects, my responsibilities are more varied and include close client contact and construction administration.

What is the least satisfying part of your job?

Writing lengthy reports.

Temples of Paestum—Study Abroad Sketch, by Lynsey Gemmell at Illinois Institute of Technology.

Who or what experience has been a major influence on your career?

As an undergraduate, I had an art history professor, Margaretta Lovell of the University of California, Berkeley, who pressed me to talk about what I wanted to do in the future. She encouraged me not to be afraid of the mathematics and physics I thought would be involved in architecture (this has proved correct) and exposed me to the three-year master of architecture program for nonrelevant degree holders.

New Science Building, Wabash College, Crawfordsville, Indiana. Architect: Holabird & Root.

Sustainable Residential Design

LISA VAN VEEN

Architectural Designer
Design Forward
Pasadena, California

Why and how did you choose which school to attend for your architecture degree? What degree(s) do you possess?

I was always told that Chicago was the birthplace of American modern architecture and the home to the first high-rise. My initial interest in architecture was to build the tallest building in the world, so I began my search in Chicago. I happened upon the Illinois Institute of Technology (IIT) and their skyscraper studio. I spent a weekend visiting the school and was impressed with the students' work and the professors and even more impressed with the city itself. I have my bachelor's of architecture from IIT and am currently working on a master of business administration at Norwich University.

What has been your greatest challenge as an intern/architect thus far?

I have found being in the in-between stage — out of architecture school but not yet licensed — to be a challenge. Being self-employed, I find myself explaining my status to clients. I use the term *designer* to market myself; however, it does not fully explain my skills. Over the last three years, I have been mistaken for a licensed architect because I have my own business and lost potential work due my lack of licensure.

Hayes Residence, Ocotillo Wells, California. Architect: Design Forward. Photographer: Gina Van Veen.

Hayes Residence, Ocotillo Wells, California. Architect: Design Forward. Photographer: Gina Van Veen.

Out of school less than five years, you founded the company Design Forward, which focuses on sustainable residential design. What motivated you to this career decision?

I was always told that in order to be a successful architect, you obtain an architecture degree, find a job as an intern, work for five to ten years, acquire a license, and move on to open your own firm. Yet, when I found myself walking that path, I became discouraged. I did not enjoy many aspects of my day-to-day work. I imagined myself working a drafting job for five years and decided it was simply not an option. I had reached a point where I needed to either leave the profession or start challenging myself.

At the time, I had been out of school just under a year. I was living in San Diego and working in a residential architecture firm. I had a strong interest in exploring straw bale design. Only one or two firms in San Diego concentrated on sustainable architecture, and I discovered a high demand for design work. I saw an opportunity to take a chance on myself. I started Design Forward in March 2002 and began concentrating on sustainable and green architecture.

You belong to the California Straw Building Association. What is straw building?

Straw building refers to the use of straw as a building material. The typical use of straw bales is as an insulation material. A common building form is a non-load-bearing structure, a post-and-beam frame with an infill of bales of wheat or rice straw. The result is a two-foot-thick wall with substantial insulation value. Straw is gaining popularity in the green building industry, as it is a natural material in addition to an energy-efficient insulation.

What are your primary responsibilities and duties?

As a single-person firm, I am responsible for *everything*. I spend most of my time design and drafting projects; this includes client meetings, design sessions, working with engineers and consultants, developing construction documents, and creating material boards and renderings. I devote nearly ten hours a month to maintaining my website, www.designforward.net, and marketing my business to new clients. Additionally, I spend a few hours billing and maintaining accounting records.

What are your five-year and ten-year career goals relative to architecture?

My five-year goal is acquire my architecture license in the state of California. In the long-term future, I plan to take a more active role in establishing building codes for green and alternative architecture. I often find building departments uneducated about alternative material and building systems, and it is difficult to acquire building permits without a fight. I hope to make the process easier.

What is the most/least satisfying part of your job?

The most enjoyable part of my job is interacting with my clients and watching a project come together over a long conversation. The most satisfying clients and projects are the ones where the owners are involved in the process. On the flip side, it is discouraging to watch a design change due to conflict with building departments or city design requirements. Sometimes the heart of the design is lost in red tape.

Hayes Residence, Ocotillo Wells, California. Architect: Design Forward. Photographer: Gina Van Veen.

Who or what experience has been a major influence on your career?

During my fifth year of architecture school at IIT, I studied under Professor Peter Land. Our semester design project was to create an energy-efficient environment. However, before we were allowed to put pencil to paper, he required us to spend a few weeks researching sustainable systems. This is when I found straw bale construction and was instantly intrigued. The process was not appropriate for my assignment, but I filed the information away, knowing I wanted to use it later.

Hayes Residence, Ocotillo Wells, California. Architect: Design Forward. Photographer: Gina Van Veen.

A.R.C.H.I.T.E.C.T.

By applying your talents as an architecture student to gaining experience, you will be able to design your own career rather than just letting it happen. Be creative in organizing your search for prospective employers. While not guaranteed, the following ideas, spelling out the word *architect*, may assist you in gaining experience more quickly.

ASSESSMENT

The first step in gaining experience involves assessing yourself. Assess what aspect of architecture inspires you: programming, design, interior architecture, construction management, etc. What do you want to do in an architecture firm? What are you able to offer a prospective employer? Ask yourself, "Why should this firm hire me?" Constantly evaluate your interests, abilities, and values and how they match those of your current or a prospective employer.

RESEARCH

Research is critical. What positions in an architecture firm can best utilize your skills and knowledge? What employers have such positions? Do not limit your search to the architecture profession; the best employment opportunities may be with an interior design firm, a construction firm, or an engineering firm. Again, be creative in your search.

CONNECTIONS

Connections are crucial to success. Regardless of the career field, over 60 percent of all openings are obtained through networking. Consider adding five to ten names to your network monthly. Be sure to attend local AIA meetings, where you will meet architects with area firms. Listen. Learn. Talk. Remember, every conversation is a possible lead. The more ears and eyes you have looking out for the positions you want, the more likely options will materialize.

The most effective method of learning of opportunities is networking, but most people, especially students, do not know what this is. Simply put, networking is informing people around you of your intent to gain experience and asking if they know of leads for you. In a school setting, you may network with classmates, professors, and staff. You may also approach guest lecturers or architects on your juries. Ask if they hire students for the summer or for part-time positions. They may not be immediately responsive, so politely ask for a business card so you can follow up.

HELP

You can get help with your search from a variety of sources. A good place to start is the university career center; a career counselor can help you target your job search. Many local AIA chapters post positions on the website or allow you to post your resume. Public libraries are another valuable resource. As well, you should seek support from others, especially family and friends;

talking to them can be a big boost to your job search.

Most programs in architecture have a job board or notebook that announces regional employment opportunities or an online system of informing students of such openings. When seeking students to perform entry-level tasks, many firms send schools a position announcement outlining job duties and responsibilities, qualifications, and contact information.

If you determine that you either need or want to work part-time while in school, use these postings as a first step to learn of opportunities, but do not stop there. Contact the local AIA chapter to learn if they accept listings from area firms. Some local AIA chapters collect resumes from individuals seeking employment and allow firms to review them.

INTERIM POSITIONS

If you are unable to secure your ideal position for the summer or after graduation, consider an interim job. An interim job provides you with related experience, but is only a stopgap solution; you have no intention of staying permanently. Ideally, interim jobs allow you to continue your search, network with a wide variety of people, and build up your skills.

TOOLS

Your resume, portfolio, ability to write cover letters, and ability to interview are critical to the job search. They are important tools for communicating yourself to potential employers. Are your tools in top form? If not, practice your interviewing skills, rework your resume, or have someone critique your portfolio.

- *Resume/Cover Letters:* As in any discipline, a resume is essential when conducting a search for experience. Just as critical is a well-crafted cover letter. While this book cannot fully cover the rigors of resume writing or other aspects of the job search, it can convey insights to these necessary tools. Keep your resume simple and straightforward. Provide information from your background and experiences that demonstrates your abilities. Do not be afraid to include skills learned from studio or other classroom projects under a section entitled "Course Projects." If you have not worked formally in an architectural office, you can still promote your drawing, modeling or building, and design skills learned in studio.

  You can add graphics to your resume. With the ease of scanning drawings and graphic publishing software, placing an image on your resume can be powerful; however, exercise caution, as the image may make reading the resume difficult. Rather than including graphics on your resume, you could create a one-page portfolio, sometimes referred to as a "viewsheet."

  Cover letters are often treated as an afterthought, but they are in fact your introduction to the prospective employer. Most cover letters consist of three paragraphs: The first introduces you and explains the purpose of the letter; the second sells your skill set and makes the match for the employer, and the third provides the terms of follow-up. Be sure to address the letter to an individual, not "Dear Sir/Madam." If you do not know the name of an individual, take the time to contact the firm and ask. Be persistent if the firm is reluctant to provide this information.

Finally, remember that the purpose of the resume and cover letter is to obtain an interview!

- *Portfolio:* Just as important as the resume, and perhaps more important, is your portfolio. As architecture is a visual discipline, the portfolio is a direct link between the employer and your skills as an architect. For this reason, you should provide images that demonstrate all of your architectural skills — drafting, model building, drawing, design, and so on. As well, provide drawings from the beginning of one project's design process to the end. In other words, do not include only finished ink-on-Mylar drawings. The sequential drawings allow the employer to see your thought process as it relates to a design problem.

The portfolio is a creative act, showing your skills and imagination, but it is also an act of communication and a tool for self-promotion. Demonstrate originality and inventiveness, but also accept the restrictions and conventions of professionalism, and show that you can get your ideas across in terms that working architects and designers can understand.

HAROLD LINTON[4]

- *Interviewing:* Good interviewing skills can make the difference between receiving an offer and not. Prepare for an interview by researching the firm. Think what questions might be asked of you and what questions you might ask of the interviewer.

EXPERIENCE

At this point in your career, you may feel you have little experience. Keep in mind, however, that in many cases employers are hiring your *potential.* If you do not have adequate experience, consider trying one of the following to obtain it: part-time work, volunteer work, informal experiences, or temporary work.

COMMITMENT

Searching for a position that will give you experience can be a full-time task. Although you are busy with school commitments, you should devote every possible minute to your search; doing so will pay off. In fact, if you have not already done so, start your search now! Do not wait until next week or next month.

TRANSITION

Realize that you are going through a major life transition — that of entering the profession of architecture. Recognize that all aspects of your life will be affected. Summer vacations are a luxury of the past. Financial adjustments are necessary as you begin to receive a salary and acquire new expenses.

The job market may be tough; therefore, be assertive, learn the search process, and do not fear rejection. Searching for a position is a skill you will use throughout your life.

The answer, in a nutshell, is:
    Thru your research
    And then thru your contacts.
                    RICHARD N. BOLLES

Johnson Wax Building, Racine, Wisconsin. Architect: Frank Lloyd Wright. Photographer: R. Lindley Vann.

Moving toward Licensure

Transition: n. The process or an instance of changing from one form, state, activity, or place to another. Passage from one form, state, activity, or place to another.[5]

Entry into the real world should be a time of excitement, enthusiasm, and exploration. School, for the time being, is over, and it is finally time for you to apply the knowledge and insights you acquired during all those hours of studio. A yearly salary assures financial independence. All kinds of doors are opening, presenting a world of opportunities.

This transition from the world of education to your first career position is dramatic and perhaps challenging. Many college graduates are not fully prepared for the magnitude of the transitions and adjustments that must be made on virtually all fronts, and are unaware of the consequences for not making these adjustments in a mature and speedy manner.

What a shock it can be when you, a new graduate, drop to the bottom rung of the career ladder. Just as a new college student has to learn the ropes of the new environment, the recent graduate starting a career position faces a whole new world. The challenges range from maintaining a budget, dealing with your personal life, and adjusting to your first career position. The difficulty is that the real world is less tolerant of mistakes, offers less time and flexibility for adjustment, and demands performance for the pay it offers.

INTERN DEVELOPMENT PROGRAM (IDP)

How can you make the transition into the world of work easier? One program that helps is the Intern Development Program (IDP), established jointly by the American Institute of Architects (AIA) and the National Council of Architectural Registration Boards (NCARB) in the late 1970s. Not only does it assist you, it may actually be required for you to become an architect. Most state boards have adopted IDP as the training requirement necessary for licensure. It is thus in your best interest to become aware of IDP early in your progression.

Intern Development Program is a profession-wide, comprehensive program that contributes to the development of competent architects who can provide exemplary architectural services; it helps you achieve comprehensive exposure to architectural practice.

IDP GUIDELINES[6]

IDP training requirements are the program's foundation. To satisfy them, you must complete specific periods of training in four major categories:

Category A: Design and Construction Documents

Category B: Construction Administration

Category C: Management

Category D: Related Activities

Each of these training categories is subdivided into training areas (see Sidebar).

Training requirements are measured in training units equaling eight hours of accept-able experience. You earn training units for training acquired under the direct supervision of a qualified professional in one of two ways: participation or observation. Experience is gained by performing a particular task (preferred) or by observing a professional with whom you work perform the task.

An integral part of IDP is the mentorship system. Within IDP, you have access to two individuals who assist you with your work experience and career plans. The supervisor is typically your immediate supervisor in your place of employment, while your mentor is an architect outside your firm with whom you meet periodically to discuss your career path.

As a participant in IDP, you are solely responsible for maintaining a continuous record of your experience in the training categories. The record identifies areas where training is being acquired and areas where deficiencies may exist. For supervisors, it is an assessment and personnel management tool; for state registration boards, it is verified evidence of compliance with the IDP training requirements.

To ease the tracking process, NCARB developed a nationally recognized record-keeping system. You may develop your own recordkeeping resources or use your firm's time management system, which may accommodate the IDP training categories and areas. Because state registration boards may require the system developed by NCARB, you are encouraged to contact your board regarding acceptable recordkeeping procedures.

Launched in 2004 by AIA and NCARB, the Emerging Professional Companion (EPC)[7] is an online professional development tool for interns on their path to licensure. Primarily intended as a means for interns to earn IDP credit, the EPC is broken into chapters that parallel the training areas of IDP. Each chapter is structured with ten sections designed to lead the user through an in-depth look at each training area.

In a recent discussion with an intern-architect a few years out of school, she confessed that while architecture school prepared her to think and design, it did not sufficiently prepare her to work in an architectural office. She further admitted that IDP, with its training areas, simply lists out what you need to do. Asked for advice to give current students of architecture, she replied, "Take a chance, take a risk, and enroll in IDP now while you are still in school."

Regardless of your academic level, take the first step to learning about IDP by contacting NCARB and requesting an information packet. Begin the transition now; do not wait until graduation.

Intern Development Program (IDP) Training Areas

Category A: Design and Construction Documents

Programming is the process of discovering the owner's requirements and desires for a project and setting them down in written, numerical, and graphic form. For a project to be successful, all participants, including the owner, must understand and agree on a program at the outset.

Site and Environmental Analysis involves research and evaluation of a project's context and may include environmental evaluation, land planning or design, and urban planning.

Schematic Design is the development of graphic and written conceptual design solutions to the program for the client's approval.

Engineering Systems Coordination involves selecting and specifying structural, mechanical, electrical, and other systems, and integrating them into the building design. These systems are normally designed by consultants in accordance with the client's needs.

Building Cost Analysis involves estimating the probable construction cost of a project.

Code Research involves evaluating a specific project in the context of relevant local, state, and federal regulations that protect public health, safety, and welfare.

In *Design Development,* a project's schematic design is refined, including designing details and selecting materials. This step occurs after the owner approves the schematic design.

Construction Documents are the written and graphic instructions used for construction of the project. These documents must be accurate, consistent, complete, and understandable.

(continued)

Specifications and Materials Research leads to analysis and selection of building materials and systems for a project. The materials specified for a particular project communicate the requirements and quality expected during construction. Specifications are included in a project manual that is used during bidding and construction.

Document Checking and Coordination is the means by which quality assurance is established and maintained throughout the project.

Category B: Construction Contract Administration

Bidding and Contract Negotiation involves the establishment and administration of the bidding process, issuing of addenda, evaluation of proposed substitutions, review of the bidder qualifications, analysis of bids, and selection of the contractor(s).

Construction Phase — Office: Construction contract administrative tasks carried out in the architect's office include facilitating project communication, maintaining project records, reviewing and certifying amounts due contractors, and preparing change orders.

Construction Phase — Observation: Construction contract administrative tasks specifically carried out in the field include observing construction for conformity with drawings and specifications and reviewing and certifying amounts due to contractors.

Category C: Management

Project Management includes planning, organizing, and staffing; budgeting and scheduling; leading and managing the project team; documenting key project information; and monitoring quality assurance.

Office Management involves the allocation and administration of office resources to support the goals of the firm.

Category D: Related Activities

Professional and Community Service Interns find that voluntary participation in professional and community activities enhances their professional development. Such activities increase their understanding of the people and forces that shape society as well as augment professional knowledge and skills. Community service need not be limited to architecture-related activities for volunteers to accrue these benefits.

ARCHITECT REGISTRATION EXAMINATION (ARE)

The last formal step in becoming an architect is taking and passing the Architect Registration Examination (ARE), administered by NCARB. The purpose of the ARE is "to determine if an applicant has the minimum knowledge, skills, and abilities to practice architec- ture independently while safeguarding the public health, safety, and welfare."

Its purpose is not glamorous, but glamour is not the intent of the ARE. It does not measure whether or not you are a good architect but rather your ability to practice architecture.

In February 1997, a tremendous change was made in the way individuals became architects, namely, the ARE was offered exclusively by computer in all divisions. In development since the mid-1980s, the new format generates a more comprehensive and efficient exam that more accurately measures a candidate's ability in a shorter period than traditional methods. In addition, the automated exam allows for more frequent and flexible testing opportunities, a more relaxed testing environment, faster score reporting, and greater testing security.

The computerized exam consists of nine divisions:

Graphic Divisions
1. Site Planning
2. Building Planning
3. Building Technology

Multiple Choice
1. Pre-design
2. General Structures
3. Lateral Forces
4. Mechanical and Electrical Systems
5. Materials and Methods
6. Construction Documents and Services

NCARB CERTIFICATION

Once licensed as an architect, you may wish to become licensed in additional states. To do so, consider obtaining an NCARB Certificate to facilitate licensure in other states,

Wexner Center, Columbus, Ohio. Architect: Peter Eisenman. Photographer: Isabelle Gournay.

a process known as *reciprocity.* The first step is to establish an NCARB Council Record, which you would have done for initial registration. Once you complete the requirements for the NCARB Certificate — earning an NAAB-accredited or CACB-accredited degree, fulfilling the requirements of the IDP, and passing the nine divisions of the ARE — you can apply for licenses from other states as needed to practice architecture. Based on an NCARB survey of registered architects, on average, architects are registered in two jurisdictions. There are 109,757 reciprocal (out-of-state) registrants and 210,936 total registrations in the United States.

Experience is a vital step in becoming an architect. Begin to gain experience in the profession as soon as possible by shadowing an architect in high school, completing an internship, or pursuing a summer position while in college. As well, your experience after you complete your professional degree will play an important role in your future career. Choose wisely.

Creating a Framework for Collaboration

GRACE H. KIM, AIA

Principal and Co-founder
Schemata Workshop
Seattle, Washington

Why and how did you become an architect?

My path to architecture was not a deliberate one. As a high school senior, life beyond graduation was far from my mind. I listed three areas of interest on my college application, one of which was architecture. My guess is that the admissions officer chose alphabetically and I was assigned to architecture for freshman advising.

From my first day of classes, I really enjoyed the architectural courses and never looked back. The problem solving and ability to shape the built environment was fascinating and challenging.

Why and how did you choose which school to attend for you architecture degree? What degree(s) do you possess?

I have a bachelor of science in architectural studies and a bachelor of architecture from Washington State University, the only in-state school to which I applied. At the time, I did not know I wanted to study architecture, so it worked out great that I ended up starting in a five-year bachelor of architecture program. The program structure provided the fundamentals to put me on a level playing field with my classmates in terms of skills and knowledge by the end of the first quarter.

The Epicenter, Seattle, Washington. Architect: Bumgardner. Photographer: Grace H. Kim, AIA.

The Epicenter, Seattle, Washington. Architect: Bumgardner. Photographer: Grace H. Kim, AIA.

Now I am two-thirds of the way through a one-year post-professional master of architecture program at the University of Washington (UW). I chose the UW program because I am a working professional, managing a small practice, and needed a program that would be adaptable to my educational goals (research in a specific topic).

What has been your greatest challenge as an architect/principal?
Maintaining balance in work and life. Within the studio, this means balancing the time to draw, manage, and obtain new projects. This is achieved by the flat structure of the office. As the principal, it is not healthy to control everything. Our employees are privy to and accountable for the budgets of the office and projects.

In my personal life, the challenge is to balance work with friends, family, and my husband. All are equally important, and even though my husband is my business partner, we make a conscientious effort not spend all our time talking about work or the firm. We also find time to participate in the greater world through hobbies and philanthropy.

How is being a principal of Schemata Workshop different than being an intern at SOM?
As in intern at Skidmore, Owings, and Merrill (SOM), I felt like a cog in a large machine. I did my job and understood that others were also doing their part to make sure the project was successfully completed, but I never had a sense of the greater picture, not only architecturally but also from a management standpoint.

As a principal of a small firm, I have a comprehensive view of the business as well as the practice of architecture. But I also want everyone else in the studio to be as aware of this too. Open communication and a clear understanding of our business objectives ensure that we all satisfy the contractual requirements to our clients while helping the company make a profit, which ultimately translates to bonuses and profit sharing.

Sogn Residence, Bothell, Washington. Architect: Grace H. Kim, AIA—Place Architects. Photographer: Steven Meyer.

How did you arrive at the name Schemata Workshop? How does it describe the philosophy of your company?

My partner and I did not want the name of our newly incorporated firm to be our last names, to be the bosses with our names on the door. Instead, we wanted to create a collegial studio environment where everyone felt integral to the team.

A *schema* is a framework or outline. It describes the overarching ideals of the studio and our design approach — to focus the design efforts of the entire design and construction team during the schematic design phase to create a strong conceptual framework. The plural, *schemata,* is also a psychology term used to describe the way people perceive and organize environmental information. We paired *schema* with *workshop* to imply a casual work environment as well as our hands-on design approach.

Our philosophy is dedicated to a collaborative design process that provides innovative and client-specific design solutions. Schemata Workshop produces award-winning designs, but as a goal, awards are secondary to client satisfaction.

As the first recipient of the Emerging Professionals Mentorship Award, can you define *mentorship* and describe how an aspiring architect finds a suitable mentor?

Mentoring is more about leadership than it is about satisfying IDP requirements. Mentoring is about being a role model, giving others the courage and confidence to tackle the situation themselves in the future. This is the way I think leadership is integral to mentoring.

To find a suitable mentor, consider someone in your office, such as a supervisor, to serve as a mentor, but be sure to seek formal mentors outside your firm. This will help in the long term as you develop within the office and politics begin to come into play.

Here are many avenues for finding a mentor:

Ask your professors about colleagues or alumni.

Consider asking the principal of that firm where you interviewed and had a great conversation, but who had no available position to offer.

Attend AIA or other professional organization functions.

Ask a fellow young architect serving on a committee with you if he or she can recommend a supervisor or someone else from the firm who might be a good mentor.

If you work in a large firm, consider finding a mentor from another studio within the firm.

Contact your state IDP coordinator and ask for help in locating a mentor.

What are your primary responsibilities and duties?

Vision: Setting direction for the firm and helping the staff see their role in steering the boat in that direction.

Mentorship: Leadership through actions.

Marketing: Securing new projects and potential client contacts.

Design direction: Working with the project team to establish a strong design concept and provide critiques/reviews as the design progresses.

Technical oversight: Ensuring that codes are adhered to and documents satisfy permit and constructability requirements.

Client management: Guiding clients through decisions and helping them identify opportunities that add value to their project.

Ocean Retreat, Seattle, Washington. Architect: Schemata Workshop. Photographer: Steven Meyer.

What is the most/least satisfying part of your job?

Most satisfying is making a positive impact on people's lives through architecture. Least satisfying is expending countless hours on a Statement of Qualifications and an extensive public interview process, only to receive a letter from the owner stating that the project was awarded to another firm but that we were a close second.

Who or what experience has been a major influence on your career?

Donna Palicka, an interior designer at SOM, for whom I worked for eight months on the programming for General Motors Global Headquarters. From her, I learned the importance of building relationships and that as a woman architect I could be feminine and still maintain a professional presence.

Mark Simpson, AIA, and Jennie Sue Brown, FAIA, are two principals of Bumgardner, a Seattle architectural firm that has seen its fiftieth anniversary. Both were instrumental in helping me develop skills that eventually enabled me to start my own architectural practice.

Most important, my husband and business partner, Mike Mariano, AIA, has played a critical role in my career development as a classmate, fellow intern, and now as a business partner. As a husband, Mike has supported me through difficult career decisions and been patient with challenging work schedules.

Finally, I had the opportunity to attend Masonry Camp, an International Masonry Institute–sponsored event in 1997. Spending the week with apprentice tradespeople and other young architects, I realized that the adversarial relationship between architect and contractor typically seen on jobsite could easily be avoided if all parties had a place at the table to discuss problems and arrive at consensual decisions.

Three Degrees from USC

RICHARD A. ERIBES, PH.D., AIA
Professor and Dean Emeritus
College of Architecture and Landscape Architecture
University of Arizona
Tucson, Arizona

Why and how did you become an architect?

I became an architect because the idea appealed to me from a very early age. I could always draw, and several members of our family who were commercial artists and graphic designers encouraged me. One recognized my fascination with buildings, drawing, and model making and said I should become an architect. I probably thought an architect was a carpenter who got to wear a white shirt and tie. At the time, this was important to a Hispanic kid growing up in East Los Angeles.

So, from about the age of twelve, I saw myself becoming an architect. Of course, this was totally improbable, given my family's lack of resources. No one in my family had finished high school, much less gone to college. I was fortunate to walk among people who wanted to help me realize my dream. These were usually teachers, but they included neighbors, scoutmasters, family, and friends.

Upon graduation from the University of Southern California (USC), I received the thesis prize (group project) and the Henry Adams Award. I was first licensed in California and practiced in Los Angeles for several years before I thought of obtaining a graduate degree so I could teach. How fortunate can one person be? Truly, my whole career has been magical.

Why and how did you choose which school to attend for your architecture degree? What degree(s) do you possess?

For me, the choice was pretty easy, and it did not involve the critical decision-making prospective students go through now. My worldview was pretty small from East Los Angeles, so anything outside of California was not viable even in my dreams. At the time, California had only two architecture programs: USC and University of California, Berkeley.

My school must have made a big impression on me, as I earned all three of my college degrees — B.Arch., M.Arch., and Ph.D. — from USC. It has been a big part of my life, but the choice to go there for my education was not exactly planned.

Can you describe the differences between being a professor and a dean?

As a faculty member, you focus on your own scholarship and that of your students. As a dean, you continue to be responsible for the students, but now you have the added responsibility of the success of your faculty. The best deans spend most of their time establishing the conditions within which success is possible. The faculty-student relationship morphs into the dean-faculty-student relationship.

What is the most/least satisfying part of your job?

The opportunity to help faculty be successful is tremendously satisfying. On the other side, I have had the misfortune to be a dean in a period of declining university budgets. It is stressful and difficult to explain to faculty, students, and alumni why a program is subject to cuts even though it is gaining in quality.

You have served as associate dean or dean at three universities: Arizona State, New Mexico, and Arizona. What differences do you see among these three architecture programs?

The programs share more than they differ. Each has some great students and faculty. No program has a lock on student quality. Of the three, only the University of Arizona is an undergraduate professional degree program, and I admit to a great fondness for an educational opportunity where you can come right out of high school, study hard, and be able to go out and successfully pursue a professional career.

The focus and mission of each program is considerably different because of context. Arizona State is a large urban university in a large metropolitan area, so its opportunities center on the development of rapidly growing cities.

The University of New Mexico has a unique location. Its cultural history and continuity of tradition are truly amazing. The program is about New Mexico and nowhere else, but the power of its architecture has the ability to influence other places.

The architecture program at the University of Arizona is engaged in a deep conversation with the land. Its international border location drives natural collaborations with cities and universities throughout arid Latin America.

I do have a concern that accreditation standards can have the effect of creating programs characterized by their uniformity rather than their uniqueness as a response to place. This must be resisted. Let us not forget that all architecture is fundamentally about place.

Unlike many deans in the discipline of architecture, you possess a doctorate in urban studies. How does this inform your role as a dean?

My professional focus on urban studies has been tremendously useful. My first university teaching position was in a public administration program. I taught public-sector planning and urban management classes. I have been able to teach in several types of programs, holding positions in public administration, planning, and architecture. It is fascinating to see how each discipline views the world. Let me assure you, each is distinct. This experience alone has prepared me for relationships with individual faculty, department chairs, and the multiple perspectives that exist on a university campus. It has also given me insight into how architecture can be a player in the research mission of the university.

My decision to pursue the urban studies degree hinged on the feeling that I did not adequately understand the big picture. How does public policy influence affordable housing? What role does politics play? What are the consequences of tampering with market systems, and how do large, complex organizations impact communities?

Urban studies and planning are essentially social science disciplines, and my doctoral work provided me with excellent analytical and decision-making methodologies that have proven invaluable in college leadership work. I also learned to write in an academic style other members of the academy understand.

Who or what experience has been a major influence on your career?
I have been blessed to have many individuals looking out for me during my education and my professional career. Both my parents were heroes to me, but my father was especially influential and remained my best friend until his death in 1967. He was a perfectionist craftsman and fostered in me the love of building.

Two that influenced me at USC were Emmet Wemple, the landscape architect of Getty Museum fame, and the Greene and Greene authority, Randell Makinson. Frankly, I wanted to be Emmet Wemple. He became the standard for me to follow in creativity, personal demeanor, integrity, cultural awareness, and clothes!

Hal Jones, the managing architect at Adrian Wilson Associates, helped me stay in school by providing a tuition loan. This was an amazing act of kindness in an era when loans and scholarships were difficult to come by.

Finally, I was exposed to sheer academic leadership brilliance when I worked for Mary Sue Coleman, then provost at the University of New Mexico. This was my first deanship and a great learning experience. I hated to see end when she became president of the University of Iowa. Now she is president of the University of Michigan.

From Academy to Practice

KATHERINE S. PROCTOR, FCSI, CDT, AIA
Director of Facilities
Jewelry Television
Knoxville, Tennessee

Why did you become an architect?
I was artistic. I needed to draw to live. It satiated me. But I loved to solve problems also, especially math problems. So I graduated from high school and went on to major in mathematics in college at the University of Tennessee. I took art courses on the side for fun and relaxation. Mathematics and art. Mathematics and art. Right brain–left brain. The other students who were also taking both math and art classes were architecture students. I decided to take an introductory architecture class to see what they found so exciting, and I was hooked.

I chose the Tennessee School of Architecture in Knoxville in 1971. The school was just a few years old and about to graduate their first class. The excitement was contagious throughout the faculty and the students. Everything was possible because it had never been done before there. Being the only architecture school in the state brought support from across the design and construction profession. The program was rigorous but left much room for flexibility and exploration. I spent months abroad with off-campus programs, which helped craft the professional I was to become.

The school offered a wide array of off-campus study opportunities, which took me to study in a castle in Fontainebleau, France, with the École de Beaux-Arts, to the desert with Paolo Soleri, and to Central America to help reconstruct the capital city of Managua, Nicaragua. In our design-build studio I worked on a project for a Girl Scout troop in the mountains of East Tennessee. I learned that a college education is a gift that grows as you pour it out on others.

What has been my greatest challenge as an architect?
Most people would say that being a female in a male-dominated profession in the 1970s and 1980s was pretty challenging. I made it even worse because I took my bachelor of architecture degree and went into construction after college. I worked as a carpenter, a cost estimator, and then as a project manager for a general contractor for a few years. I imagine that every rookie on a construction jobsite has to prove himself or herself, and I went though my share of hazing

and practical jokes. But what I learned in that phase of my education is now priceless in my current role as an owner's representative, and I believe it brought real practicality to my teaching.

How did your work as a faculty member inform architectural practice, and vice versa?
I taught first- and second-year design. I saw young people struggle to make the perfect mark on the page. I saw the discipline they developed over time and how they applied that discipline to hone their talent. As I taught, I learned how clear communication is the key to success for both me and the students. Part of that realization came through taking the time to listen, and part was through learning to articulate my thoughts and motivate others. This ability has since taken me to national professional venues as a speaker and teacher.

After fourteen years of teaching, you are an owner's representative of a large corporation. What are your responsibilities, and how do they differ from teaching and advising? How did you come to make this decision, and why?
I was approached by a local company, Jewelry Television, which was seeking a project manager to oversee the design and construction of its first corporate headquarters, a $25 million to $35 million project. I was immediately interested because of the complexity of the project.

I started with the company as I transitioned out of my role as director of student services at Tennessee. Within weeks I was interviewing employees, analyzing and documenting the company, and developing a program for the architecture firm to use later. I have a team of employees from a wide range of backgrounds, just like a class at school. Each person brings different gifts, talents, and experiences to the group. I must motivate each person in a different way in order to capture what he or she has to offer to move the project forward. In many ways I still am a teacher, mentoring the less experienced team members, encouraging them as they develop, painting the big picture, and dividing it into parts that each person can address.

I think this is what architects do: They see the big picture and break it into discernable parts, rearrange it, and find the solutions. What a great job!

What is CSI, and why is important for an architect?
A professional organization, Construction Specification Institute (CSI), started forty-five years ago as a group of design and construction professionals who wanted to create a consistent method for organizing construction information. This quest resulted in the development of MasterFormat, which is a standard throughout the industry for organizing specifications, product information, and cost estimating.

I joined CSI as a third-year architectural student on the encouragement of my materials and methods teacher, and through his leadership started a CSI student chapter at Tennessee. CSI provides architects access to all members in the design and construction industry through its horizontal organizational structure. The membership comprises architects, engineers, contractors, material suppliers, construction lawyers, and all members of the industry. It is a wonderful resource for architectural students seeking their place in this broad profession.

I believe that active participation in our professional organizations is a vital responsibility of design professionals. These organizations provide a structure where the free exchange of ideas and experiences is encouraged. They also provide avenues for developing leadership skills in a nonthreatening environment, and then we can take these skills back to our firms and volunteer lives. The time spent in these organizations is well invested.

Who or what experience has been a major influence on your career?
I am blessed to have had wonderful teachers and mentors who influenced me both during my undergraduate experience and in my professional career. The ability to travel overseas and live in Europe and Central America helped me develop confidence and independence and understand how to serve people better. This opened the door to let me manage all the off-campus programs in our college. I will always cherish the time I spent time working with Tennessee students. I made lifelong friends with people I saw grow into young professionals.

Focused, Confident . . . and Flexible

F. MICHAEL AYLES, AIA
Director of Operations
Antinozzi Associates
Stratford, Connecticut

Webster Bank—Prototype Bank Branch, Yonkers, New York; Bridgeport, Connecticut; Norwalk, Connecticut. Architect: Antinozzi Associates Architecture and Interiors. Rendering: Kevin Matis.

Why and how did you become an architect?
Realizing both my early ability to draw exceptionally well and to build complicated structures with Legos, I intuitively knew I was to become an architect. I enjoyed drawing in high school, especially drafting, and did pretty well in my math and science courses.

In high school, my guidance counselor looked at my strengths and interests and came up with career suggestions for me: meteorology, astronomy, and architecture. None of these was going to make me rich, but the thought of becoming an architect sounded not only important but cool too. I was also told I could move into many different careers once I was an architect.

I was not a great designer in college, nor did I have a high grade point average. In fact, I nearly dropped out of architecture school until I realized that (1) my studio instructor had a theater arts degree and a master of architecture, yet had never become licensed or practiced in a firm, and (2) I had no idea what to study if I dropped architecture as my major. Thus, I graduated in 1991 and landed an internship right out of college. After one change in position, I completed the IDP process in four years and passed the last paper-and-pencil version of the ARE in June 1996 — in one try. Voilà! I was now an architect, eleven years after I first thought it might be cool.

Why and how did you choose which school to attend for your architecture degree? What degree(s) do you possess?
In order of difficulty, I applied to the University of Virginia (UVA), Virginia Tech, University of Florida, Penn State, and, finally, my safety school, Roger Williams University. I really had no shot at getting into UVA (academically) or Florida (no state residency), and Virginia Tech placed me on a waiting list. A couple of weeks later, I received my acceptance letter from Roger Williams and realized I would not be watching clouds the rest of my life!

After I started, I discovered the architecture program at Roger Williams was not NAAB-accredited. Fortunately, the program received its initial accreditation that same year, meaning my degree would be accredited.

What has been your greatest challenge as an architect?
No project, client, or individual has provided as big a challenge as myself. Without a doubt, balancing a professional career and personal life has been my greatest challenge.

What are your primary responsibilities and duties?
As director of operations, I work with the managing partners and other directors to oversee the day-to-day operations of the firm. This includes the assurance of appropriate staffing, assisting in marketing strategies, and advancing technology. Most important, my ultimate goal is to

Webster Bank—Prototype Bank Branch Interior—Entry Lobby; Darien, Connecticut. Architect: Antinozzi Associates Architecture and Interiors. Photographer: Steve Lakatos.

ensure the office maintains the highest possible standards in producing quality projects, following efficient procedures, and keeping within the project budgets —all, basically, allowing the firm to thrive in good times and in bad. I assume these responsibilities; the managing partners focus on business development strategies and client relations.

What is the most/least satisfying part of your job?
Most satisfying is hearing a client proudly state at a ribbon-cutting or grand opening that our firm produced a project that exceeded every expectation they had, not just about our firm but about the architect's role in general. As well, I find mentoring a younger or less experienced staff member hugely rewarding.

Least satisfying, without a doubt, is the combination of unrealistic demands by clients related directly to the speed at which society expects responses or a finished product.

In 2004, you chaired the Young Architects Forum (YAF). What is the YAF, and why is it important in your professional career?
The YAF is a knowledge constituency within the AIA that promotes program development and addresses issues relevant to its membership. Its overriding goals are to encourage leadership, mentorship, and fellowship.

After involvement as an intern architect on the AIA Intern/Associate Committee, I became involved with the YAF. First, I helped create a committee within AIA

Webster Bank—Prototype Bank Branch Interior—Entry Lobby and Teller Lobby, Darien, Connecticut. Architect: Antinozzi Associates Architecture and Interiors. Photographer: Steve Lakatos.

Connecticut, was appointed the YAF Regional Liaison for New England, and applied for a national YAF position on the Advisory Committee in 2002. As member of the YAF Advisory Committee, my expectation was to advance the recognition of young architects across the country.

From my involvement, I was able to learn and contribute more than I imagined possible. This has not only made me a more valuable architect and community participant but also a better person.

You became licensed five years after graduating from Roger Williams. Can you describe your internship years?
After graduation, I was fortunate to obtain an intern position with a well-known 100-person architecture firm in the Hartford area. The economy was slow, I had no practical experience working in an office, and I did not have the strongest portfolio. When I was given this opportunity, I jumped at every chance to exceed expectations. I also volunteered and participated in as many challenging project tasks as possible so I could learn from the more experienced staff.

After two years with this firm, I saw I was gaining experience, but I feared I might never be looked at as anything but an intern because of the size of the office. I started to feel a bit pigeonholed, and I could see the workload was dropping substantially due to a lagging economy. I had a chance to leave and join a smaller firm — the one I am with now.

I was hired as the only intern in the office, and I was able to work at a higher, more challenging level and on several types of projects. I was not necessarily told what to do or how to perform the tasks on these projects; I just listened to and observed as much as I could of each person in the office, looked up information if I did not know it, and asked questions when absolutely necessary.

IDP played a major part in my five years of internship. As soon as I completed my studies, I initiated my NCARB council record and began recording my experience — and I did not find it all cumbersome. Based on my experience with IDP, I urge interns to start the process immediately. The internship will not be as intimidating!

Who or what experience has been a major influence on your career?
My experiences at all levels of the AIA have by far been the largest influence on my career over the past fourteen years. The activities, travel opportunities, educational resources, networking, and, most of all, the people have had a dramatic impact in my development, and not just as an architect but also as a leader. I have learned from hands-on involvement, but I also have observed (and been impressed by) individual leaders at all levels.

The Forgotten Middle

EDWARD J. SHANNON, AIA

Assistant Professor
Department of Architecture
Judson College
Elgin, Illinois

Why and how did you become an architect?

I grew up in the Chicago suburbs of River Forest and Oak Park, so at an early age I was exposed to the work of Frank Lloyd Wright and his disciples. As well, my father's business is closely related to the construction industry. Through these influences, I developed an early appreciation and interest in the built environment. I took drafting in high school and was blessed with an inspirational teacher who happened to be trained as an architect. He taught our class the difference between architecture and building. As high school students, we were exposed to

Pearson Residence Addition, Glen Ellyn, Illinois. Architect: Edward J. Shannon, AIA. Photographer: Dennis Jourdan.

all the noted Chicago architects, past and present. My teacher instilled in me a sense of confidence. He told us that any of us could become architects if we wanted it badly enough. To a great degree, I believe this to be true.

Why and how did you choose which school to attend for your architecture degree? What degree(s) do you possess?

Although Chicago has two reputable architecture schools, I chose Iowa State University for my bachelor of arts in architecture because I wanted to experience campus life at a large Midwestern university. Leaving home enabled me to mature in many ways. I learned many valuable skills that have enhanced my career greatly.

I chose Virginia Polytechnic Institute and State University for the master of architecture because I was interested in the design-centered teaching methodologies of the school. At Virginia Tech I truly learned the difference between architecture and building. I also learned that in order for a building to be architecture, architecture must be present at the early stages.

What has been your greatest challenge as an architect?

Practicing architecture in suburbia. I consider myself a part of the "forgotten middle," the middle class/suburbia. However, enlightening the middle-class sector about good architecture and urban design, why it is worth paying for, and why it can cost more to design is quite a challenge.

Shumway Residence Addition, Palatine, Illinois. Architect: Edward J. Shannon, AIA. Photographer: Dennis Jourdan.

How does your work as a faculty member inform your architectural practice, and vice versa?

My mantra is that I teach better because I practice and practice better because I teach. More specifically, I tend to bring a sense of pragmatism and reality to my teaching. I teach design studio, professional practice, and materials and methods. In the design studio, I raise students' awareness of the forces — code, zoning, program, budget — that inform the design of a project. I share my own successes and failures in my materials and practice courses.

Because I am a faculty member, a lot of eyes are on my practice — not just in terms of the work I produce but also in terms of my practice ethics. Teaching is built-in accountability.

What are your primary responsibilities and duties as an architect and a faculty member?

Practicing architecture and teaching. More specifically, I maintain my practice as a sole practitioner. I do the marketing, client contact, design, construction documents, and construction observation. I answer the phone and carry out other office duties.

In addition to teaching, I have served as the coordinator for the architecture lecture series, faculty representative for the American Institute of Architecture Students (AIAS), and on the campus facilities committee. I have also had an active role in shaping the intern program at Judson College and helped a number of students gain internships in architecture offices.

I am also active in my local AIA chapter. Through my service as a board member and on committees I have addressed professional issues as both a practitioner and academic, helping close the gap between the profession and academy.

What is the most/least satisfying part of your positions?

As a teacher, the most satisfying thing is seeing students find their voice in architecture. In practice, it is walking through a completed building project and sharing in the joy of that project with my clients.

Preparation work is the least satisfying aspect of teaching, especially for the first three to five years. Because our program was newly established, the faculty had to design the courses from the ground up. In practice, some projects tend to drag on, with many iterations and changes; this is not satisfying either.

Who or what experience has been a major influence on your career?

My upbringing in the Chicago area, as I noted, was an influence. I am also grateful for many of my teachers, especially my drafting teacher at Oak Park–River Forest High School, Mr. Urbanick. More than a drafting teacher, Mr. U had a

Private Residence—Exterior, Sister Bay, Wisconsin. Architect: Edward J. Shannon, AIA, and Lane Allen, AIA. Photographer: Doug Snower Photography.

Private Residence, Sister Bay, Wisconsin. Architect: Edward J. Shannon, AIA, and Lane Allen, AIA. Photographer: Doug Snower Photography.

passionate love of architecture. He was trained as an architect at IIT, and he could have practiced architecture or taught at the university level. Yet he chose to teach high school and instill a passion for the art of building in many young adults.

Architect Harry Weese, among others, stands out as a model architect. Mr. Weese did not have a signature style; instead he let the client and site influence the building's form. Instead of trying to be different with his designs, he simply tried to be good. He could design simultaneously in many scales—intimate, human, and monumental. Instead of designing bold buildings that scream for attention, he made buildings humane. He had a diverse practice that included single-family homes, high-rises, schools, and subway systems. Although he was a modernist, he embraced historic structures and was a pioneer in preserving old buildings.

Empowering Environments

BARBARA CRISP

Principal, Underwood + Crisp
Tempe, Arizona

When we are fully present, we not only live well, we live well for others.

una promesa

a thought

Blessing Wall—Banner Good Samaritan Medical Center Expansion, Phoenix, Arizona. Designer: Barbara Crisp, Underwood + Crisp with Thinking Caps. Photographer: Bill Timmerman.

Why and how did you become an architect?

I never considered architecture as a profession until I enrolled in an architectural drafting class at night after receiving a degree in English. Through the course, I learned that I really loved visualizing space and had a strong desire to express myself creatively. The drafting course rekindled early desires for art and expression. Later, I secured a position in a wonderful firm that gave me a lot of opportunities to grow and learn and ultimately encouraged me to go back to school. I began slowly with the prerequisites and ultimately made application and was accepted. This decision changed my life.

Why and how did you choose which school to attend for your architecture degree? What degree(s) do you possess?

Being an older student, married, with an undergraduate degree in an unrelated area, I did not have the flexibility to go wherever I might have wanted. I would have attended a three-plus year master of architecture, but none was in close proximity. I was fortunate that there was a good nationally ranked four-plus-two program where I was living. I entered the undergraduate program and obtained a bachelor of science in design. Later I earned a master of architecture from the same institution.

What has been your greatest challenge as an architect?

The challenge of the bottom line, meaning money, as it relates to the value of design, looms larger and larger. It is a constant challenge to educate clients about the effects of quality design on our world, on their world.

In addition, I strive to imbue the work I do with meaning, no matter how small the project. If I am unable to be true to my values and beliefs, I do not want the work. I have cultivated this voice over time; I follow my intuition but speak with my intellect as well as my heart. Clients do not always understand, but over time, and with trust, it has allowed some little design gems to surface that have both delighted and surprised the client.

The focus of your design work addresses sensory experience and perceptions that support and sustain well-being. Can you elaborate on this statement and what led you to this work?

On family vacations and road trips, when we stopped to eat my father would always tell us to close our eyes and ask us questions about our surroundings—about the color of the walls, the presence and placement of windows, the number of tables, the smell. This exercise probably is the framework for how I observe the world around me. I am tuned in to the subtleties of my surroundings and sensitive to how they make me feel.

We have all been in places we just cannot wait to get out of, and it is important to know why. Look a little deeper, focus with all your senses, to understand what is going on that zaps your energy or fosters your discomfort. Such environments do not support and sustain well-being; architects and designers must make this connection. As well, environments that feel right must also be analyzed. We must develop a clear understanding of what allows both types of environments to manifest. Further, we must pursue this investigation in the larger global context as well as in our local culture.

Define "life-enhancing environments, sacred spaces."

In the book I authored in 1998, *Human Spaces,* I defined *life-enhancing environment* as a place built or created to support and sustain the well-being of a particular occupant of time, place, and culture, where the body as a whole, both inner and outer, is regarded as essential to how the space is experienced. This

Place to Pause—Banner Good Samaritan Medical Center Expansion, Phoenix, Arizona. Designer: Barbara Crisp, Underwood + Crisp with Thinking Caps. Photographer: Bill Timmerman.

definition still works, but, more important, we must recognize that everything we create—our actions, our thoughts, and the words we speak—all hold meaning and the potential to affect and change the world mentally, physically, emotionally, and spiritually, and we must be conscious of that in the work we do. All space is sacred if we do our work in a sacred manner.

What are your primary responsibilities and duties?
As our firm is small, I do almost everything. More specifically, my role seems to be working with the clients and establishing relationships, developing design concepts, and following through with the idea in the design process, with less involvement in the construction document phase. My strengths and what I like are in the front end—client relationships, programming, concept, design—yet I do enjoy working through details and fieldwork as well.

What is the most/least satisfying part of your job?
Most satisfying is helping clients envision and manifest in two and three dimensions—places, spaces, objects, surfaces—what they only have words for.

Every day, I need to consciously avoid allowing the reality of doing business to overtake my core beliefs. More practically speaking, I most dislike paperwork and billing.

Who or what experience has been a major influence on your career?
Three influences stand out:

Logos Textile Collection—Banner Good Samaritan Medical Center Expansion, Phoenix, Arizona. Designer: Barbara Crisp, Underwood + Crisp with DesignTex. Photographer: Max Underwood, AIA.

My mentor, Bob Sexton, at the first architecture firm I worked in, did me the valuable service of strongly advising that I return to school for a degree in architecture, knowing I would never be happy otherwise. He saw something in me that I could not.

I was involved in AIAS as a student, and I served on the national AIA Architects in Education committee for three years. During that time I worked alongside of a number of deans of major institutions, made lifelong friends, traveled to campuses around the country, and was part of an interesting and challenging dialog on the interface of the practice of architecture and architecture education. This experience opened other unexpected doors.

Third, I received a travel fellowship to Europe in graduate school. This was significant because through it I became aware that travel is invaluable and a must for anyone who wants to grow and evolve and understand the world as a living, breathing, nonstatic opportunity. You never see things the same way again.

Creating Positive Change

JOSEPH BILELLO, PH.D., AIA

Dean
College of Architecture and Planning
Ball State University
Muncie, Indiana

Why and how did you become an architect?

Broadly speaking, I think my family values linked a college education to becoming a professional of some kind — doctor, lawyer, priest, or engineer. I merged those expectations with strong abilities in mathematics and interests in art (primarily drawing; I have always doodled). One junior high teacher recognized strong design and artistic ability in my work. Then, in high school, I became interested specifically in architecture after seeing the work of Frank Lloyd Wright in the library.

Impressed by the campus, I chose a university with exceptional architecture, the University of Pennsylvania. I went to college as a mathematics major, took a course in art and civilization as a freshman, and had a dorm room across from the Richards Medical Center by Louis Kahn. I started drawing and architectural courses in my sophomore year (in Frank Furness's Fine Arts Building) concurrent with thoughts about a major in English literature. I decided on architecture alone mid-junior year based on relatively encouraging feedback. I met influential teachers — Ian McHarg (and his visiting scholar/friends), Peter McCleary, Louis Kahn, James O'Gorman, Stasha Novitski — and a drawing teacher, Frank, who said the words "when you are an architect," which created the possibility that I could do it.

Graduation was concurrent with the army draft during the Vietnam War. I got a graduate school deferment, attended a year of graduate school, dropped out, went to Europe and galvanized my architectural interest, and returned to the United States to practice. I returned to graduate school and concluded my studies after that formative travel/work year.

I interned in public and private practices in the Southwest and West, though the internships were not structured (read, unhelpful). I became licensed concurrent with my first attempts to have my own practice in San Francisco and other urges for independence and a fruition of professional efforts.

Why and how did you choose which school to attend for your architecture degree? What degrees do you possess?

I hold degrees from the University of Pennsylvania (B.A., major in architectural studies), Washington University (master of architecture), and the University of Maryland (Ph.D.).

I decided to attend Washington University for my professional degree for a number of reasons. First, some of the best graduate students at Penn had come from undergraduate school at Washington University. I wanted to stay at Penn, but at that time, the school made a point of taking students from other schools. Washington University also represented exploration — my first move away from the East Coast. The interesting faculty included Buckminster Fuller's former partner, James Fitzgibbons. I also had soccer colleagues at Penn who were from St. Louis, had good things to say about it as a place, and were returning there after graduation.

What has been your greatest challenge as an architect/faculty/dean?
As an architect, my greatest challenge is getting good design built. As a faculty member, it is balancing excellence in teaching with attempting to generate new knowledge (scholarly inquiry). Finally, as a dean, the challenge is creating positive change and closure. I work to stay focused on the dynamic high ground of excellence in design and planning education amid the constant challenges of administrative, paperwork, and personnel management duties that are never finished.

Can you describe the differences between being a professor and a dean?
At my present institution, architecture professors teach students primarily. Some engage in scholarly pursuits. A few are deeply committed to the production of new knowledge. Some engage in community-based service activities. Some maintain small practices. Though the faculty members have many levels of commitment, the thirty-week academic year allows for comparatively high levels of discretionary time for inquiry.

Keet Seel Ruins Stabilization—National Park Service, Navajo National Monument, Arizona. Architect: Southwest Cultural Resources Center. Photographer: Joseph Bilello, Ph.D., AIA.

In contrast, the deanship carries a comparatively minor teaching responsibility but does have a significant leadership and fundraising dimension and a huge administrative responsibility — personnel and budget management, strategic planning, implementation, and reporting to constituents of all stripes, primarily upper-level administration. It is a largely nonstop around-the-clock, seven-days-a-week, fifty-two-weeks-a-year, notwithstanding delegation of duties.

What is the most/least satisfying part of your job?
Most satisfying are the incredible moments when groups and individuals — students, faculty, staff, and visitors — are at their best, achieving breakthroughs, thinking globally, acting locally, and realizing that things larger than us are happening as a result of what we are doing.

Least satisfying is absence of closure, impossibility of completion, the futilities of public higher education administration, chronic credit deficit from those constituencies that know little of what a dean does or how higher education operates — overall, knowing what we are capable of and seeing what we do. The trouble is the distance between the vision and the reality, and yet being a guardian of the status quo.

You have served as the associate dean for research at Texas Tech University and on the board of directors for the Architectural Research Centers Consortium. In the context of that part of your background, what is the importance of research in architecture?

As defined by the Initiative for Architectural Research, research is the way in which new knowledge can most readily enter the profession and professional education.

It is also the way that all professions recharge themselves (their knowledge base) and justify their need to remain a profession in a world where knowledge can be rapidly disseminated and put to use. Regrettably, most architects and architectural educators have little knowledge or understanding of architectural research — what it is, how it is produced, how to effectively integrate it into design, and how it accelerates rates of learning/practice possibilities. This is a huge challenge ahead.

Who/what experience has been a major influence on your career?

Major influences include Buckminster Fuller, Ian McHarg, and my family. Experiences with an influence include global travel, professional failures, and conversations with remarkable people.

The Temple de la Sagrada Família, Barcelona, Spain. Architect: Antonio Gaudi. Photographer: Joseph Bilello, Ph.D., AIA.

Notes

1. Boyer, Ernest L., and Mitgang, Lee D. (1996). *Building community: A new future for architecture education and practice.* Princeton, NJ: Carnegie Foundation for the Advancement of Teaching, p. 117.
2. *The American Heritage dictionary.* (2000). Boston: Houghton Mifflin.
3. Boston Architectural Center, www.the-bac.edu, accessed June 28, 2005.
4. Linton, Harold. (2003). *Portfolio design.* New York: W. W. Norton.
5. *The American Heritage dictionary.* (2000). Boston: Houghton Mifflin.
6. NCARB. (2005). Intern Development Program Guidelines.
7. Emerging Professional Companions, www.epcompanion.org, accessed June 28, 2005.

VOB BMW, Rockville, Maryland. Architect: DNC Architects. Photographer: Eric Taylor, ASSOCIATE AIA. Photo © EricTaylorPhoto.com.

Chapter Four

The Careers of an Architect

The building of a career is quite as difficult a problem as the building of a house, yet few ever sit down with pencil and paper, with expert information and counsel, to plan a working career and deal with the life problem scientifically, as they would deal with the problem of building a house, taking the advice of an architect to help them.

FRANK PARSONS[1]

As Parsons says in the above quotation, the building of a career — the process of career development — is a difficult but important task, yet he also notes that few individuals prepare for their careers in a thoughtful, careful, and deliberate manner. Instead, many fall into a career, while others make random career choices that show little commitment to their occupation, often leading to dissatisfaction.

Career Designing

Regardless of where you are on the path to becoming an architect — completing your architectural education, gaining experience in an architecture firm, or in the process of taking the Architect Registration Examination (ARE), you should pursue deliberate career designing to maximize success.

You may argue that a career is not something you create or plan, that it just happens. However, like architectural projects, careers should be carefully planned. In many ways, designing a career is like designing a building. Programming, schematic design, design development, working drawings, and construction are replaced in the career development process with assessing, exploring, decision-making, and planning.

ASSESSING

Know thyself.

INSCRIPTION OVER THE ORACLE
AT DELPHI, GREECE

When an architect designs a project, what is typically the first step in the process? Most likely programming. As William Pena points out in *Problem Seeking,*[2] the main idea behind programming is the search for sufficient information to clarify, understand, and state the problem. In a similar manner, when designing your career, the process begins with assessing.

Assessing is learning about yourself. Assess where you want to be; analyze what is important to you, your abilities, the work you would like to do, and your strengths and weaknesses. Just as programming assists the architect in understanding a particular design problem, assessment helps determine what you want from your career. This ongoing process must be reiterated throughout your entire career. The details of assessment include your values, interests, and skills. But what exactly are values, interests, and skills, and how do you determine them?

Values

Values are feelings, attitudes, and beliefs you hold close to your heart. They reflect what is important to you; they tell you what you should or should not do. Work values are the enduring dimensions or aspects of your work that you regard as important sources of satisfaction. Values traditionally held high by architects include creativity, recognition, variety, independence, and responsibility.

As a quick inventory, circle the items on the following list you value in the work you do:

Helping others

Improving society

Creativity

Excitement

Working alone/with others

Monetary reward

Competition

Change and variety

Independence

Intellectual challenge

Physical challenge

Fast pace

Security

Responsibility

Making decisions

Power and authority

Gaining knowledge

Recognition

Interests

Interests are the ideas, events, and activities that stimulate your enthusiasm; they are reflected in choices you make about how you spend your time. In simplest terms, interests are activities you enjoy doing. Typically, architects have a breadth of interests because the field of architecture encompasses artistic, scientific, and technical aspects. Architects enjoy being involved in all phases of the creative process,- from original conceptualization to a tangible finished product.[3]

To determine your interests, for an entire month note on your desk calendar what you most and least enjoyed doing each day. At the end of the month, summarize and categorize the preferences you recorded. Here is another method: In ten minutes of continuous writing, never removing your pen from the paper or fingers from the keyboard, answer this question: What do I like to do when I am not working?

Skills

Unlike interests, skills and abilities can be learned. The three types of skills are functional, self-management, and special knowledge. Having a functional skill means you are able to perform some specific type of activity, action, or operation with a good deal of proficiency. In contrast, self-management skills are your specific behavior responses or character traits such as eagerness, initiative, or dependability. Special knowledge skills are what you have learned and what you know.

The importance of knowing your skills is noted by Richard Bolles in his book *The Quick Job-Hunting Map:* "You must know, for now and all the future, not only what skills you have, but more importantly, what skills you have and enjoy."[4] With respect to skills, think back over the past five years. What were your five most satisfying accomplishments? Next to each, list the skills or abilities that enabled you to succeed. Similarly, review your failures to identify traits or deficiencies you want to overcome.

A variety of techniques may be used to conduct an assessment. The few listed here are simply to get you started; others include writing an autobiography and undertaking empirical inventories or psychological assessments with the assistance of a career counselor. Regardless of the

HSB Twisting Torso, Malmo, Sweden. Architect: Santiago Calatrava. Photographer: Grace H. Kim, AIA.

method you choose, only you can best determine what skills you have acquired that you enjoy using, the issues, ideas, problems, organizations that interest you, and the values you care about for your life and career.

You know the story of the three brickmasons. When the first man was asked what he was building, he answered gruffly, without even raising his eyes from his work, "I am laying bricks." The second man replied, "I am building a wall." But the third man said enthusiastically and with obvious pride, "I am building a cathedral."

MARGARET STEVENS

In your career, will you lay bricks, build a wall, or build a cathedral? Regardless of your answer, designing your career is one of the most important tasks you will ever undertake. Yet if career design is so important, why do most people spend such little time on it? Think about it!

EXPLORING

Students spend four or more years learning how to dig data out of the library and other sources, but it rarely occurs to them that they should also apply some of the same new-found research skill to their own benefit — to look up information on companies, types of professions, sections of the country that might interest them.

ALBERT SHAPERO

Schematic design is the phase of the design process that follows programming. Schematic design generates alternative solutions; its goal is to establish general characteristics of the design, including scale, form, estimated costs, and the general image of the building, the size and organization of spaces. According to the AIA *Architect's Handbook of Professional Practice*,[5] the goal of schematic design is to establish general characteristics of the building design, such as the scale used to satisfy the basic program requirements and estimated costs. Additionally, schematic design identifies major issues and makes initial decisions that serve as the basis of subsequent stages.

In career development, exploring is parallel to schematic design. It develops alternatives or career choices. Career exploration is the process of accumulating information about the world of work. Its goal is to obtain career information on a plethora of careers or specializations within a particular career. Even if you already have chosen architecture as a career, exploring is still necessary. Instead of exploring careers, you can explore firms, possible career paths within architecture, and other areas that affect the direction of your architectural path.

How do you explore? In *Career Planning Today*,[6] the author describes a systematic process that includes collecting, evaluating, integrating, and deciding. Following these four steps guarantees the highest possible level of career awareness.

Where do you begin? First, you must collect career information from a variety of sources, both people and publications. With respect to people, the most popular tool is called *information interviewing*. What you do is interview someone to obtain information. You could do this with one of the senior partners in a local firm, a faculty member, a classmate or colleague, or your IDP advisor. Other ways to explore include attending lectures sponsored by the local AIA chapter or your university, volunteering your time through local AIA committees or other organizations of interest, becoming involved with a mentor program, and observing or shadowing someone for a day.

As Shapero says, you should use your research skills to access any and all information you need on a career. Visit your local library and inquire about the following publications: *The Dictionary of Occupational Titles* (DOT), *Occupational Outlook Hand-*book (OOH), *Guide to Occupational Exploration* (GOE), and *What Color Is Your Parachute?* Ask a reference librarian to identify other resources you might find valuable. In addition, investigate resources at your local AIA chapter or the library or resource center at a school of architecture. Other resources include the Internet and professional associations (see Appendix A).

After completing the exploring process, your next step is the decision-making process.

DECISION-MAKING

What most people want out of life, more than anything else, is the opportunity to make choices.

DAVID P. CAMPBELL

The heart of the design process is design development. Similarly, decision-making is the heart of the career development process. Design development describes the character and intent of the entire project; it refines the schematic design and defines the alternatives. Decision-making means selecting alternatives and evaluating them against a predetermined set of criteria.

How you make decisions? Do you let others decide for you? Do you rely on gut-level reactions? Or do you follow a planned strategy of weighing alternatives? Whatever your method of deciding, you should be aware of it. While some decisions can be made at the drop of a hat, others, including career designing, require more thought.

Decision-making

Decision-making Model	Architectural Application
Identify the decision to be made.	Need or desire for new space or building
Gather information.	Develop a building program (budget, style, size, room, specification, layout).
Identify alternatives.	Develop alternative schematic designs, incorporating the program.
Weigh evidence.	Evaluate schematic designs as they meet determined needs, preferences.
Choose among the alternatives.	Select the design that best captures ideals.
Take action.	Draw construction documents. Develop timetable. Break ground and begin construction activity. Create architectural punch list.
Review decision and consequences.	Long-range evaluation may identify need for major building renovation for reuse.

Petajavesi Old Church, Petajavesi, Finland. Photographer: Ted Shelton, AIA.

For demonstration purposes, review this architectural application of the decision-making process:

Decision-making can be difficult and time-consuming, but knowing the quality of decisions is affected by the information used to make them, we quickly realize that making informed decisions is an important skill to learn.

As you can see, both exploring and decision-making are critical steps to successful career designing. Do not wait to begin this important process; instead, take this information and build your future with career designing.

PLANNING

If you do not have plans for your life, someone else does.

ANTHONY ROBBINS

Planning is bringing the future into the present so that we can do something about it now.

ALAN LAKEIN

"Cheshire-Puss,"... said Alice, "would you tell me, please which way I ought to go from here?"

"That depends a good deal on where you want to get to," said the Cat.

"I don't much care where —" said Alice.

"Then it doesn't matter which way you go," said the Cat.

LEWIS CARROLL,
ALICE IN WONDERLAND

You may wonder why I am quoting from a popular children's book. If you look closer, you realize that half of reaching your destination is knowing the direction in which you are headed. Planning is key to fulfilling your career goals.

After the owner/client and the architect decide on a design for a potential building, the next step is the development of plans. These plans — construction documents, specifications, and construction schedules — play an important role in realizing the design. In a similar way, planning, as part of the career designing process, ensures a successful career.

In its simplest form, planning is the bridge from dreams to action; it is an intention to take an action by a certain time. At its fullest, planning is creating a mission statement, developing career goals, and preparing action plans.

But what are mission statements, goals, and action plans?

In *The Seven Habits of Highly Effective People*,[7] author Stephen Covey says a mission statement focuses on what you want to be (character), to do (contributions and achievements), and on the values or principles on which being and doing are based. To start the planning process, consider your mission statement by asking yourself: What do I want to be? What do I want to do? What are my career aspirations? Review the example below:

I want to act in a manner that brings out the best in me and those important to me, especially when it might be justifiable to act otherwise.

After you have crafted your mission statement, the next step is to develop goals that will lead to its fulfillment. Goals are future-oriented statements of purpose and direction to be accomplished within a specified time frame. They are stepping stones in achieving long-range aims and should be specific and measurable. Write down your goals. It has been said that the difference between a wish and a goal is that a goal is written down.

Once you establish your goals, you are ready to develop the action plan that will help you accomplish them. Action plans are the steps on the path toward your goals; they are stepping stones in achieving related short-range intentions. Look at your established goals. What steps must you take to accomplish them? As with career goals, write down your action plan, including specific completion dates.

The final step in career planning is to review your action plans and goals regularly. Cross out the goals you have accomplished and revise, add to, or delete others. Be honest with yourself. Are you still committed to achieving your goals? You can change them, but remember that the magic road to achievement is *persistence*. Abandon goals only if they have lost meaning for you — not because they are tough or you have had a setback.

Now you have read about the entire career/life planning process: assessing, exploring, decision-making, and planning. As you progress through your professional career, you will realize that this process is never-ending and cyclical. As soon as you secure an ideal position in a firm, assess your new life situation and make adjustments to your career design accordingly.

Career Paths

Pursuing architecture prepares you for a vast array of career possibilities. Many of these are within traditional architectural practice, but many are also in related career fields.

Within the traditional architecture firm, you may obtain a beginning position as an intern and progress to junior designer, project architect, and, eventually, associate or principal. This does not happen overnight; it can take a lifetime. You may pursue your career in a traditional firm regardless of its size — small, medium, or large — or you may choose to work in a different setting, such as a private corporation or company; a local, state, or federal government agency; or a university — or, after obtaining your architectural license, you may start your own firm. You must consider which path is best suited to you.

Nontraditional career paths tap into the creative thinking and problem-solving skills you develop during your architectural education. These opportunities also are growing in popularity; in a survey of interns and young architects, nearly one-quarter of the respondents indicated that they do not plan a traditional career in architecture although they still plan to obtain their license. Further, respondents working in nontraditional settings reported better salaries, benefits, and advancement opportunities. These results are not shared to encourage you to pursue a nontraditional career path but rather to demonstrate that your architectural education is excellent preparation for many sorts of jobs. In fact, the career possibilities for people with an architectural education are limitless.

Getty Center, Los Angeles, California. Architect: Richard Meier. Photographer: Roger Lewis, FAIA.

On the next page is a beginning list of traditional and nontraditional career paths. Katherine S. Proctor, who was director of student services at the University of Tennessee for a number of years, shares her perspective:

For people interested in an architecture career, the possibilities are endless. I have seen students graduate and become registered architects, professional photographers, lawyers, bankers, business owners, interior designers, contractors, and artists. The education is so broad and has such a strong liberal arts base that it provides a firm foundation for a wide array of exploration. This comes not only from the curriculum content but also from the methodology. The design studio, the core of the curriculum, teaches a method of applying pieces of intellectual information within the design process. The movement from thinking to doing is powerful. The ability to integrate hundreds of pieces of information, issues, influences, and forms, and to find a solution, is a skill every professional needs to solve problems, whether about building or life.

KATHERINE S. PROCTOR FCSI, CDT, ATA

The Careers of an Architect

Traditional Firm
Principal
Project Architect
Staff Architect
Senior Designer
Junior Designer
Draftsperson
Intern
Model Maker

Other Employment Settings
Architectural Illustrator
Corporate Architect
Facilities Architect
Public Architect
University Architect

Architectural Education
Professor
Architectural Historian
Academic Dean/Administrator
Researcher

Art and Design
Architectural Photographer
Art/Creative Director

Artist
Clothing Designer
Exhibit Designer
Filmmaker
Furniture Designer
Graphic Artist/Designer
Industrial/Product
   Designer
Interior Designer
Landscape Architect
Lighting Designer
Museum Curator
Set Designer
Toy Designer
Web Designer

Science and Technical
Building Pathologist
Cartographer
Civil Engineer
Computer System Analyst
Construction/Building
   Inspector
Illuminating Engineer
Marine Architect
Structural Engineer

Construction
Carpenter
Construction Manager
Construction Software
   Designer
Contractor
Estimator
Fire Protection Designer
Land Surveyor
Project Manager
Real Estate Developer

Related Professional
Architectural Critic
City Manager
Environmental Planner
Golf Course Architect
Lawyer
Preservationist
Product Manufacturer
   Representative
Property Assessor
Public Official
Real Estate Agent
Urban Planner
Writer

Design Build Teaming

RANDALL J. THARP, RA

Senior Vice President and Director of Construction
A. Epstein and Sons International, Inc.
Chicago

Why and how did you become an architect?

In my late elementary years, I took several art classes outside of school and became very interested in drawing. When I was in middle school my family moved to England, where I took technical drawing classes that I really enjoyed and excelled in. We often had projects in which we would draft plans and then build the design in our wood shop or metal shop classes.

During my time in Europe, I had the opportunity to visit and see many great buildings and places in architectural history, including the Hagia Sophia, the

Alberto Culver R&D Facility, Melrose Park, Illinois. Design-Builder: A. Epstein and Sons International.
Photographer: Jeff Guerrant, Jeff Guerrant Photography.

Parthenon, Pompeii, and ancient Roman sites in England. All of these experiences set the background for an interest in architecture that was encouraged by an architect in our neighborhood. I took all of the architectural design and drawing classes in high school and decided to pursue architecture when I went into college.

Why and how did you choose which school to attend for your architecture degree? What degree(s) do you possess?
I went to high school in suburban Detroit. In talking with neighbors and teachers, I kept hearing that the University of Michigan was one of the best schools in the country. I also learned from a neighbor architect that Michigan was the only college in the state that offered a master of architecture program. While a sophomore in high school, I decided to attend Michigan to obtain a degree in architecture and become an architect. I applied to Michigan only and earned a B.S. in architecture, master of architecture, and master of business administration degrees there.

What has been your greatest challenge as an architect?
My greatest challenge has been to bridge the gap between two sides of the building industry that are traditionally adversarial: architects and contractors. Having spent my entire career in design-build, I am both and thus break down preconceived notions about these two. Some see me as an architect who does construction, while others want to view me as a contractor who tries to do design. Although I am a licensed architect, I really am neither architect nor contractor. I view my role as an integration of both that creates a synergistic result.

Iscar/Ingersoll Manufacturing/Office Building, Cherry Valley, Illinois. Architect/ Construction Manager: A. Epstein and Sons International. Photographer: Mark Ballogg, Steinkamp/Ballogg Photography.

Why did you pursue the dual degree — master of architecture/master of business administration — during your graduate studies?
In my last year as an undergraduate in the architecture program at Michigan, I really began to understand the many facets of being an architect and that not all architects

are the same. I also realized I was not going to be a designer. I saw that if I added business skills to my strong technical skills, I could be an asset to another architect who was more focused on design. At the same time, Michigan began offering a formal joint M.Arch./MBA program. I took the necessary exam, applied to both the business and architecture graduate programs, and was accepted.

I was completely surprised to see how my architectural skills applied to business, especially in marketing and strategic planning. The problem-seeking, programming, and solution development skills I had learned in architecture school fit right in, and I soon found I was a very good designer of marketing plans and business plans. I believe my business education helped me both find my niche and gave me excellent skills that have yielded many career opportunities.

How and why did you pursue a career path more related to construction than to traditional architecture?
The salary is better. Also, I felt my skills, especially my business skills, were much more valued in a construction environment than in a traditional architectural practice. Within a construction organization, my design and architectural technical skills were more unusual, and the business orientation of the construction industry offered me greater opportunity to use these talents from day one. Compared to architecture firms, construction and development firms were much more forward-thinking and immediately saw opportunities to put me in the front line with clients and leading projects because of my unique skill set.

What is design-build teaming?
Design-build is an integration of the design and construction process that breaks away from the traditional design-bid-build process.

Design-build involves the collaboration of all parties from the onset of the project. The construction professionals, the designers, the engineers, and the architects all participate in jointly understanding the client requirements for quality, cost, and schedule, and the impact of design decisions and solution alternates are evaluated by all parties. They use their combined expertise and skills to arrive at a final solution that best meets all three of basic client requirements as well as the specific details of the project.

What are your primary responsibilities and duties?
My primary responsibility is as the leader of Epstein's Construction Group, where I work with thirty-five construction professionals in our home office and at project jobsite locations around the country. In this capacity, I work with others to secure new business, maintain client relationships, identify new talent and develop current staff; I also oversee administration for the group and review project and group financial performance on a continuing basis.

For several clients, I am the project executive or principal in charge. In these cases I assure that our project execution plans are implemented and our clients' requirements are met.

I also serve on Epstein's management committee and am a member of the corporate board of directors. In these roles, my primary responsibilities are to develop and plan strategic and tactical corporate plans to implement and manage across the firm.

Albertsons Freezer Expansion, Franklin Park, Illinois. Architect/Construction Manager: A. Epstein and Sons International. Photographer: Mark Ballogg, Steinkamp/Ballogg Photography.

What is the most/least satisfying part of your job?

I love the opportunity to hire young graduates out of architecture and engineering programs or early in their careers. It is rewarding to see them succeed and to know I played a role in teaching them, providing them opportunities, and enhancing their work experience. I also find it exciting and rewarding to be involved from the initial stages of meeting a prospective client and following the process from proposal through sale, project kickoff, design, documents completion, groundbreaking, and on through construction and occupancy.

The least satisfying part is the administrative work necessary in a large organization. All of it is critically necessary, but generating and reviewing reports, sitting in update meetings, and handling bureaucratic issues is simply not stimulating.

Who or what experience has been a major influence on your career?

When I was at the University of Michigan, I had the opportunity to have a work-study position at the University Planner and University Architect handling a variety of responsibilities. I gained a better understanding of the interaction of all the parties around the table and learned how the process of getting a project from needs assessment through program, concept, and final design was much more valuable than most of what I was learning in the classroom or studio. I was an outside observer of the process and saw it for what it was.

Succeeding in the Built Environment

H. ALAN BRANGMAN, AIA

University Architect
Georgetown University
Washington, D.C.

Why and how did you become an architect?

I became an architect because I always had a fascination with building things.

Why and how did you choose which school to attend for your architecture degree? What degree(s) do you possess?

I initially went to school at the University of New Hampshire to study civil engineering. At the beginning of my sophomore year I met an art professor who had been a former instructor at Cornell University. He suggested that I transfer to Cornell. My degree is the bachelor of architecture.

What has been your greatest challenge as an architect?

My greatest challenge as an architect has been and continues to be convincing other professionals that architects are capable of doing much more than just architecture.

How is working as a university architect different from more traditional architecture jobs?

My job responsibilities are more in line with those of a principal in a real estate

McDonough School of Business, Georgetown University, Washington, D.C. Architect: Goody, Clancy.

development firm. I am responsible not only for the hiring and oversight of design and planning consultants, providing program, planning, and design oversight for all university facilities, but also for all matters related to real estate.

McDonough School of Business, Georgetown University, Washington, D.C. Architect: Goody, Clancy.

How and why did you pursue what might be considered a nontraditional career path?

Initially, I did so because I had an interest in more than just designing buildings. I spent nine years with The Oliver T. Carr Company, a real estate development company in Washington, D.C. That opportunity opened my eyes to the breadth of the built environment and provided me with a much more global perspective on place making.

During your career, you worked in the Design Arts Program of the National Endowment for the Arts, an independent agency of the federal government. Can you describe your role in this agency?

I was the deputy director of the Design Arts Program. The program was primarily responsible for grant making and supporting initiatives to spread the word about the benefits of good design. The initiatives I enjoyed the most were the Mayors Institute on City Design, a series of national forums dedicated to improving the understanding of the design of American cities through the bringing together of Mayors and urban design professionals; Your Town — Designing Its Future, a series of national workshops teaching the importance of design to those who can influence and make decisions about the way rural communities will look and work in the future; the Design for Housing Initiative, a national workshop dedicated to bringing together representatives from the housing delivery system to spur a better understanding of good design and its application to affordable housing; and the Presidential Design Awards, an honor awards program, administered in conjunction with the White House, wherein every four years the president gives awards to projects that came about as a result of federal involvement.

The first three initiatives were partnered with universities that had schools of design, such as Massachusetts Institute of Technology, Tulane University, Georgia Institute of Technology, and the universities of Virginia, Minnesota, California, Berkeley, and Maryland. These initiatives were typically run as three-day seminars and involved not only decision makers like mayors, in the case of the Mayors Institute, but also nationally acclaimed design professionals, planners, landscape architects, real estate developers, economists, sociologists, and educators.

Why did you pursue the additional credentials of a Real Estate Development Primer Certificate at Harvard Graduate School of Design and Wharton School of Business?

When I started my career in real estate development, I was counseled to consider obtaining an MBA. At the time, I did not want to commit the time required to return to graduate school. Besides, the president of my firm did not have a business degree and seemed to be doing quite fine. I decided to pursue the path of learning through experience. Besides, I had been schooled as an architect, and architects are taught to solve problems. I was able to manage the problems that were part of my job responsibilities quite well. After a few years, I took the primer courses as a way of confirming what I had learned. It worked.

What is the most/least satisfying part of your job?

The least satisfying aspect of my current job is the pace at which things are accomplished in an academic environment—very slow. Entrepreneurship is not typically associated with academia.

Multi-Sports Facility, Georgetown University, Washington, D.C. Architect: Hughes Group Architects.

SW Quadrangle, Georgetown University, Washington, D.C. Architect: Robert A.M. Stern/EYP. Photographer: H. Alan Brangman, AIA.

Who or what experience has been a major influence on your career?

Bob Smith, AIA, an associate principal of RTKL, was influential in encouraging me in 1979 to look to real estate development as a possible career. Oliver T. Carr, Jr., of The Oliver T. Carr Company, was a mentor in my early years; through my employment at Carr he provided me with the opportunity to preside over 5,000,000 gross square feet of commercial development in downtown Washington, D.C.

A Creative Career Transformation

ERIC TAYLOR, ASSOCIATE AIA

Photographer
Taylor Design & Photography, Inc.
Fairfax Station, Virginia

Corporate Interior, Fairfax, Virginia. Photographer: Eric Taylor, ASSO-CIATE AIA. Photo © EricTaylorPhoto.com.

Why and how did you become an architect?

I decided on an architectural career to combine my visual/creative side with technical aptitudes. I went to college and worked in intern positions in high school and college to learn about the work world of architecture; during my architectural career I worked in variety of firms ranging from a three-person design firm to a 150-person architecture and engineering (A&E) firm.

Why and how did you choose which school to attend for your architecture degree? What degree(s) do you possess?

I looked for a school that combined a strong design direction with the practical side. I wanted to graduate with practical skills along with design sensibilities. I chose Syracuse University and earned a bachelor of architecture degree. I also studied photography as a sideline.

Why and how did you transition from architect to architectural photographer?

I had seventeen successful years in architecture, many as a senior project architect and designer. My work included office buildings, commercial, municipal and educational buildings, and interior design. But I came to a crossroads in my career—I could join another firm, start my own firm, or try something new. I chose something new.

I had always loved photography and had coordinated the photo programs at the firms I had worked at. I realized I could bring something to architectural photography that was unique: a true understanding of architecture from inside the profession. So my new direction was set. Because I lacked some of the technical expertise, I attended photography school to learn about professional lighting and camera systems. I built a photo portfolio by shooting projects on specification and by photographing the projects of architect friends. Then I got serious about marketing and launched my new career.

How are the two disciplines the same? Different?
The skills needed for success in architecture are parallel to those needed for success in architectural photography: ability to communicate visually and verbally; ability to visualize three-dimensionally; ability to distill a set of requirements to their essence; ability to arrive at solutions that answer these requirements; ability to entertain others.

Both disciplines require attention to detail and the ability to visualize what does not yet exist. The goal of architecture is to arrive at a three-dimensional solution to a complex set of criteria. The goal of

Potomac Tower, Fairfax, Virginia. Architect: I.M. Pei. Photographer: Eric Taylor, ASSOCIATE AIA. Photo © EricTaylorPhoto.com.

architectural photography is to analyze that three-dimensional solution and find a compelling two-dimensional representation of it that explains the three-dimensional reality. While architectural design deals with form, volume, color, texture, perspective, and so on, the essence of photography is light and its effect on the rendering of those design elements. I believe architectural photography is enhanced by an understanding of design concepts, design elements, and construction methods.

When offered a commission, how do you approach the assignment?
First, I meet with the client to discuss the scope of assignment—exteriors, interiors, aerials, quantity of images expected, and so on. Next, we discuss the

Fredericksburg Academy, Fredericksburg, Virginia.
Architect: Cooper Carry & Associates. Photographer:
Eric Taylor, ASSOCIATE AIA. Photo ©
EricTaylorPhoto.com.

intended uses of the photography — display prints, award submissions, in-house newsletters, website. We discuss the design concept the designer wants to be sure is expressed in the photos, the logistics of access to the space, scheduling, and budget. From there, I scout the location to assess equipment needs. Finally, I schedule assistants and do the photography.

What has been your greatest challenge as a photographer?

Predicting the weather! It is difficult to schedule exterior shoots far in the future because they are dependent on weather. Other than that, I have faced the same challenge as anyone starting any new business: developing a client base. On the technical side, photographing interiors under mixed lighting — daylighting, fluorescent, incandescent — was a new challenge. But on the creative side, I feel I have been preparing for this my whole life.

What is most/least satisfying about your work as a photographer?

Most satisfying is creating dynamic images and having clients be excited about them, and being involved with a wide diversity of building types, design, and construction. In addition, I no longer have to wait a year or two to see the results of my efforts!

I do miss the complexity of the design problem-solving process, but this loss is outweighed by the satisfaction I get from photography.

Do you still consider yourself as an architect?

Yes, but as it influences my photography and my understanding of the buildings and construction I photograph.

Who or what experience has been a major influence on your career?

In college, I became aware of the value of strong visual presentation. Good design professors required it, and I learned that dynamic graphics and photography were essential tools for explaining to others and for gaining their support for a design solution. As an architectural photographer, I see myself as helping others in their marketing efforts by providing dynamic images of their design work.

Why still photography rather than video or interactive images?

While video allows a broad-sweep understanding of a building or space, I see architectural still photography as visual editing. In this way, still compositions present the built environment in an edited version so others can see the inherent concept, form, composition, texture, color, balance, and beauty that I see.

Ronald Reagan Washington National Airport, Washington, D.C. Architect: Cesar Pelli & Associates. Photographer: Eric Taylor, ASSOCIATE AIA. Photo © EricTaylorPhoto.com.

More Than Just Architecture

CASIUS PEALER, J.D.

Associate
Reno & Cavanaugh, PLLC
Washington, D.C.
Co-founder/Co-editor, ArchVoices

Why and how did you become an architect?

I chose to go to architecture school because it was the most challenging, mind-expanding, and creative experience I could find as an undergraduate. When I graduated from school, I used those same criteria to select a variety of jobs and experiences — representing architecture students nationally, driving a taxi, working construction, volunteering for the Peace Corp, going to law school, and helping develop mixed-income communities. All of those positions allowed me to be creative, and some actually required it. They were all challenging, and I learned a great deal about myself and the world around me. As long as I can continue in those situations, I will always be becoming an architect.

Why and how did you choose which school to attend for your architecture degree? What degree(s) do you possess?

I received a five-year bachelor of architecture from Tulane University, meaning I started my professional degree program as a seventeen-year-old, right out of high school. While I treasure the intensity of the five-year programs, I think a great many individuals would be better served by obtaining a liberal arts undergraduate degree followed by a true professional masters degree.

Typical Street in the Capital City, Kingstown, St. Vincent, West Indies. Photographer: Casius Pealer, J.D.

I was fortunate in that I pursued a double major in philosophy, which gave me more experience reading and writing than my architectural education. As for my school choice, I was fortunate to get a scholarship to attend what was otherwise my last-choice school. Tulane University and the city of New Orleans were both excellent places to study architecture and life; I could not have chosen a better place to study.

What has been your greatest challenge since graduating from Tulane?

Finding purpose and community in an entirely different culture and in unfamiliar surroundings has been my greatest challenge since (and before) my graduation. Living in a rural agricultural village in a developing country as a volunteer with the Peace Corps, I often felt the people needed so much that *anything* I did would be helpful. Other times, I felt they needed so much that nothing I could do would matter at all.

Typical Street in the Capital City, Kingstown, St. Vincent, West Indies. Photographer: Casius Pealer, J.D.

In 1999–2001, you volunteered with the Peace Corps in the West Indies. Why did you choose to perform this service? Can you provide details of what you did?

I volunteered for the Peace Corps and was assigned to an island in the West Indies to teach carpentry to teenagers who did not get into the equivalent of high school. I also worked teaching small business skills to a group of artists and craftspeople, forming a professional association of sorts. We helped this association create the first e-commerce website on the island, selling products directly to consumers as far away as Japan. Additionally,

Vincentian Family, Mesopotamia, St. Vincent, West Indies. Photographer: Casius Pealer, J.D.

I helped coordinate an SAT prep class for students hoping to attend colleges in the United States, the United Kingdom, and Canada. Finally, I made a number of good friends in, and learned a lot from, the Rastafarian community on the island. I continue to perform Peace Corps service here at home by sharing my experiences and deepening Americans' understanding of the Caribbean islands.

I feel that service to your country is important; whether you do it abroad through the military or Peace Corps or in the United States through AmeriCorps, Teach for America, or some other organization. I wanted to learn a lot about another culture and to have to question — and thus solidify — my own values and personality. Also, I wanted to make lifelong friends of people with different interests and perspectives but a similar commitment to and faith in the world.

You recently completed a law degree at the University of Michigan. Why law? How will you combine your law degree with your architecture degree?
After serving in the Peace Corps, completing IDP would have meant I still had to do the same jobs as students just graduating from college. So becoming licensed did not make sense, and I felt a need to understand more about the public policy choices that determine much of the design and layout of our built environment. I wanted to obtain a masters in public policy (MPP), but many MPP graduates with whom I spoke said they wished they had gone to law school instead. So I enrolled in a joint degree program, never intending to work in a law firm. However, I found a unique law firm where I could combine my interests in architecture and public policy, so I dropped the MPP part of the degree and started work.

Reno & Cavanaugh is a small law firm in Washington, D.C., that specializes in representing public housing authorities in the creation of mixed-income communities. In many instances, we help the housing authorities destroy and rebuild some architectural abominations, like the infamous Cabrini Green housing project in Chicago. In other cases, we help housing authorities partner with private developers to create mixed-income and mixed-use communities from the ground up. In addition to this work, Reno & Cavanaugh created the Council of Large Public Housing Authorities (CLPHA), which advocates on Capitol Hill and within the Department of Housing and Urban Development (HUD) for more flexible and effective housing policies.

What is the most/least satisfying part of your career?
The most satisfying part of my career was the year I worked as a taxi driver in New Orleans. While cab driver might sound like a ridiculous job, I was interested in understanding more about how the general public talks about architecture, the built environment, and cities in general. This position allowed me access to a wide variety of people. I spent all day driving through the city with my windows down, I had a company car, and I frankly made more money than any of my classmates were making at the time.

It turns out that people of all types and backgrounds really do talk about architecture and the built environment all the time. It took me a while to understand this, because I was used to hearing architects talk about architecture. I had thought I might need to ask specific questions, or to have a questionnaire perhaps, but I finally realized all I needed to do was to learn to listen.

What I learned was that people most appreciate things like material and color and symbolism, and usually in quite sophisticated ways—although architects are often uncomfortable with symbolism, color, and material, in approximately that order. My cab fares' appreciation of the built environment was also much more holistic than many architects', simply because architects have learned to work within defined professional boundaries and to focus on a client's project at the inevitable expense of context. But the people I talked with didn't make a distinction between the street and the street lighting and the landscaping and the handrail and the building itself.

Bamboo Carver at Yoroumei Cultural, Orange Hill, St. Vincent, West Indies. Photographer: Casius Pealer, J.D.

Who or what experience has been a major influence on your career?
Working full time for ten months in an architecture firm while taking a semester off early in my professional education was quite influential. Because the firm experienced remarkable growth while I was there, I participated in more meaningful roles than a typical second-year student. When I went back to school, I looked at architecture and at my education differently. In some ways, I realized how much we were not being taught or even told about. I became involved in AIAS as a means of seeking more direct professional contact for my classmates and me. I also realized that school was a unique opportunity to explore the full boundaries of design, and my design work became much less constrained.

The primary focus of architecture education is on the work done in the design studio, but that work least resembles the kind of work practicing architects spend most of their time doing. Like many people, I encourage students to integrate practical knowledge with their educational experience. However, I do not think the design studio is the most valuable place to learn about the actual profession.

Conscientious Real Estate Developer

AHKILAH Z. JOHNSON

Senior Analyst
Cherokee Northeast, LLC
East Rutherford, New Jersey

Why and how did you become an architect?

I thought I wanted to be an engineer for most of my adolescent years, a result of my strong mathematical skills and my mother's lobbying. My polytechnic high school emphasized engineering, calculus, and differential equations. However, my creative side grew tired of math. I stumbled on architecture in an elective Auto-CAD class, and immediately I fell in love. I can honestly say architecture was my high school and college sweetheart.

Camden Redevelopment Project, Camden, New Jersey. Developer: Cherokee Northeast, LLC. Illustration courtesy of Ernest Burden III, Ossining, New York.

Why and how did you choose which school to attend for your architecture degree? What degree(s) do you possess?

When I graduated from high school, I wanted to attend a historically black college and university (HBCU). There are very few architecture schools in the United States, let alone architecture schools at an HBCU. I really did not have many options.

I chose the bachelor of architecture at Howard University because of its strong reputation for excellence, its location in a major city, and for graduating black architects. I also relished its proximity to my mother's house in Baltimore.

I chose to attend pursue a master of science in real estate development and finance because I felt developers had more control over the built environment than architects. I wanted the control the developers had so I could create conscientious developments that respected social and environmental communities. I selected Columbia University because of its location in the great laboratory known as New York City and because of its superior masters program.

What has been your greatest challenge during your professional career?

The biggest challenge in my professional career is my being. As a double-minority in a white male–dominated profession, I am constantly subject to challenges and difficulties. The absence of role models and mentors who look like me and understand my background has adversely affected my career development.

Certainly, many of my challenges are not direct derivatives of my gender and racial composite. However, professional careers are cultivated by three distinct functions: skill, knowledge, and relationships. It is my opinion that of these three functions, the relationships component has a significant and disproportionate affect on career development. As the saying goes, "It's not what you know, it's who you know."

Nonetheless, I think I have and will continue to adapt to the absence of role

Meadowlands Golf Redevelopment Project, Bergen County, New Jersey. Developer: Cherokee Northeast, LLC. Illustration courtesy of Tom Shaller, Robert A.M. Stern Architects.

models and mentors as I continue my career. As I have in the past, I will encounter individuals who will positively influence my career. I will continue to learn and strive for excellence. I hope one day to fill the void in my own career by mentoring a young African American female who aspires to a career in architecture or finance.

Why did you pursue the additional degree — the M.S. in real estate development?

I enjoyed my career as an architect, but I did not feel I knew how to put together a building from a construction standpoint. I understood construction documents and building systems, but I did not truly understand how buildings are put together. I chose to pursue a career in construction management because I thought it would make me a better architect. I enjoyed my time in construction management, and I certainly feel it helped me hone my skill set in the built environment. Yet I wanted more.

As a real estate developer, I am able to address all of my passions for creating built environments. I now can have a commanding impact on the type of developments that are created while being true to the idealistic architect in my soul. I can create environments that are examples of sensitive and good design and planning. In this case, "good" equates to architecture and planning that works to strike a balance between green design, sound material usage, functionality, and, of course, maximum monetary value and return.

How and why did you pursue a career path more related to development than to traditional architecture?

As an architect, I felt like developers and development companies had control of and ultimate say about what was to be built. However, I did not think these individuals understood or appreciated the impact development has on our society.

What is real estate development?

Real estate development is the creation of communities and the repositioning of land or buildings for a higher or better use. Real estate development intends to capitalize on underutilized land by developing new land uses that are marketable and profitable. Real estate development is a long process that commingles multiple disciplines (engineering, architecture, planning finance, marketing, law, and environmental impact) to create an end product.

What are your primary responsibilities and duties? What is "deal analysis, due diligence, and asset management?"

Cherokee Northeast is the capital disbursement arm for a major private equity firm called Cherokee Investment Partners. Cherokee Investment Partners raises funds

Meadowlands Golf Redevelopment Project, Bergen County, New Jersey. Developer: Cherokee Northeast, LLC. Illustration courtesy of Tom Shaller, Robert A.M. Stern Architects.

from large groups, mainly pension and insurance funds, to invest in the redevelopment of brownfield sites throughout the United States and Western Europe.

As an employee of Cherokee Northeast, my primary focuses are deal analysis, due diligence, and asset management. A *deal* is a development project in the conceptual or schematic stage. *Deal analysis* is the process of reviewing deals in the pipeline. As developers, we are constantly chasing new deals and preparing for placement of capital investments. Thus, we are constantly reviewing the feasibility and positioning of prospective deals.

Due diligence is the internal review process for a site or a potential deal prior to the act of acquiring land and developing it as a project.

Asset management consists of managing the ongoing development of projects currently in our portfolio.

What is the most/least satisfying part of your job?
The least satisfying part of my job is having to sacrifice ideals for budget purposes. It seems there is always a case for value engineering in the building industry. As an architect, I notice that designs and building materials are constantly changed to accommodate needs and wants for

Meadowlands Golf Redevelopment
Project, Bergen County, New Jersey.
Developer: Cherokee Northeast, LLC.
Illustration courtesy of Tom Shaller,
Robert A.M. Stern Architects.

smaller budgets. It seems we cut and skim all kinds of important elements, functional and aesthetic, to save a buck or two.

Nonetheless, when faced with the reason I choose a career in development over a career in architecture, I remember that the practice of architecture differs greatly from the study of architecture. Architecture, when studied, is a mixture of practical and theoretical ideals; the emphasis is on design and function as a couple. In contrast, the practice of architecture is dictated by money and a developer's pro forma bottom line.

Who or what experience has been a major influence on your career?
Of course, the experience of attending undergraduate school and graduate school had a major influence on my career. The influence came from the many professors and professionals I encountered. However, I think the majority of the influence on my career came from my peers in the different university settings. The abundance and wealth of knowledge available to me while I was in university was key in my career development.

Effecting Policy Rather Than Design

LOIS THIBAULT, RA

Coordinator of Research
U.S. Architectural and Transportation Barriers Compliance
Board (Access Board)
Washington, D.C.

Why and how did you become an architect?

I started in anthropology, moved to pre-Colombian archaeology, and then transferred into art history. A great teacher on the history of architecture opened my eyes to the built environment and its history as expressed in the city of Boston and environs. As I began to appreciate good design, I began to wonder if I could produce it myself. When my children entered grade school, I decided to try. The experience was terribly difficult for all of us, but somehow it worked out.

Why and how did you choose which school to attend for your architecture degree? What degree(s) do you possess?

I have a bachelor of architecture; it was the only degree possible at the time and the school. Maryland's architecture program was new and seemed interesting and innovative, and it was affordable.

What has been your greatest challenge as an architect?

Dealing with the realization that I am not a very good designer.

How and why did you pursue a career path in the federal government after a career in private practice? How are the two career paths the same? Different?

I spent almost fifteen years in commercial and residential practices and found I liked the subspecialties: historic preservation, accessibility, code compliance. These are undervalued in many offices, which limited my ability to progress, succeed, and advocate for what I believe is important. Administrative and regulatory skills are more useful in government. Additionally, government benefits and security beat those in practice.

Earlier in your career, you were on the staff of the AIA. What did you do for the AIA? How did this experience contribute to your career?

I worked on education issues, both professional development and architecture education, and spent some fascinating time in support of our convention planning (where I met the famous and future-famous). I am proudest of the library of career advisement materials I developed for students considering architecture and of my work — with many others — polishing the IDP. I also did a brief stint with the AIA's long-range planning initiative.

All of this exposure enabled me to develop a big-picture view of the profession and its members; this, in turn, helped me focus on my own strengths and interests and led me to an opportunity opened up by the passage of the Americans with Disabilities Act (ADA) in 1990.

What are your primary responsibilities and duties with the Access Board?

I oversee my agency's research activities, planning, developing, and commissioning the work that underpins our development of design standards for buildings and facilities. I am also responsible for our rulemaking work on pedestrian facilities in the public right-of-way, and an early interest in acoustics fed by an adjunct professor in the School of Architecture at Maryland led to an agency initiative aimed at improving listening conditions in classrooms for kids who have hearing loss and related disabilities.

What is the most/least satisfying part of your position?

Most satisfying is having a substantial effect on my own profession's ability to design accessible buildings and facilities. Least satisfying is coping with the effects of political change.

Who or what experience has been a major influence on your career?

Opportunity knocking. I must say, I never planned any of it, but I was lucky enough to have been prepared so I could take advantage of opportunities when they arose. I have had a career of great range and satisfaction, with lots of autonomy. International travel has also influenced my thinking in many ways.

Associate Executive

CHRISTOPHER J. GRIBBS, ASSOCIATE AIA

Senior Director, Convention
The American Institute of Architects
Washington, D.C.

Why and how did you become an architect?
Why? It was a natural outcome of my interests and skills in art, building, and problem solving. How? By going to school, traveling, taking summer jobs related to construction and historic building documentation, and interning for a small firm.

Why and how did you choose which school to attend for your architecture degree? What degree(s) do you possess?
After floundering for a few years following high school, I went to an architecture school with a strong design-focused program. One of several architecture schools

College of Fellows, Salk Institute Laboratory Complex—2003 AIA Convention, La Jolla, California. Architect: Louis I Kahn. Photographer: Rebecca Lawson Photography.

in my area, the University of Detroit — Mercy offered small classes, solid academics, and extensive studio work. I especially enjoyed the learning opportunity afforded each semester to travel and tour architecture in other cities — a short trip each fall to nearby cities, and longer spring trips to more distant locations, including exploration of ancient ruins in Central America. I have a bachelor of architecture, a five-year degree.

Why and how did you transition from working in architecture to working in an association?
My progression from traditional architectural practice to documentation of historic buildings to association management was natural; I simply followed opportunities as they were presented. I moved out of the practice of architecture when I was in Washington, D.C., between jobs for a one-day educational seminar on historic preservation. I was an active volunteer in the AIA Detroit Chapter as the associate member director, and I had heard about a position at AIA national headquarters prior to my trip to Washington for the seminar.

I inquired about the position and was offered a quick interview that very day. They apparently liked what I had to say and asked if I could return the next day for a more extensive interview. I did, then returned to Detroit and started a new job in a small, upbeat firm. On my third day on the job, I received a call from the AIA offering me the position. To say the least, this was clumsy, as I had just started the new job and had to immediately tell them I was leaving. Yikes. Of course, they completely understood the value of the opportunity and wished me the very best of luck.

After graduation, you worked as an architectural technician and supervisory architect with Historic American Buildings Survey (HABS). Can you provide details on these experiences and what skills they developed?
The absolute best experiences in my early years were two summers spent working for HABS. It was a thrill and a tremendous challenge to travel for the summer (and get paid) to measure and draw cool historic buildings. I had the opportunity to travel to San Antonio, Texas, and San Juan, Puerto Rico, to pursue the mission of HABS: preservation through documentation. I feel this was a terrific way to contribute to the lasting memory of America's built environment. Even today, the thrill is to know the product of those summers is part of the permanent collection in the Library of Congress (LOC); the information is open freely to the public. The drawings my teams produced are now free to download in high-resolution formats from the LOC website. Search on "Mission San Jose y San Miguel De Aguayo, San Antonio Texas" and "Castillo de San Cristobal, San Carlos Ravelin, San Juan, Puerto Rico" at http://memory.loc.gov/ammem/collections/habs_haer/.

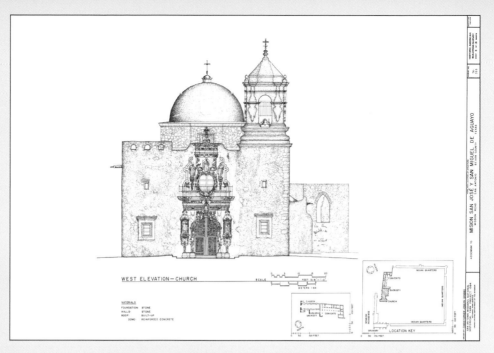

Mission San Jose y San Miguel de Aguayo, Historic American Buildings Survey (HABS)—National Park Service, San Antonio, Texas. Photographer: Christopher J. Gribbs, Library of Congress, Prints and Photograph Division, Historic American Buildings Survey, HABS TX-333.

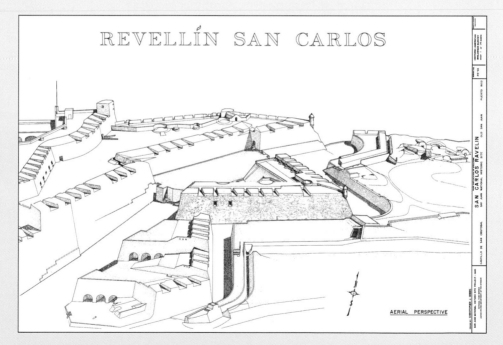

Castillo de San Cristobal, San Carlos Ravelin, Historic American Buildings Survey (HABS)—National Park Service, San Juan, Puerto Rico. Photographer: Christopher J. Gribbs, Library of Congress, Prints and Photograph Division, Historic American Buildings Survey, HABS TX-333.

During your tenure with the AIA, you have held a several positions. Please detail the projects that have been most worthwhile.

First and foremost, the various positions have afforded me the opportunity to constantly be challenged and to grow. I would not have stayed at the Institute if the work had not been both challenging and rewarding. I have had the great fortune to advance, position to position, within a large organization that affords many opportunities.

Currently I serve as the senior director with chief responsibility for the annual AIA national convention, driving the vision, development, and leadership for all convention initiatives.

For five years I was a director in the Professional Practice Department. I managed partnerships with over twenty-five allied organizations to develop design tools and award programs, disseminate information, and identify subject matter experts.

For nearly two years I was the managing director of the Professional Practice Department, responsible for eighteen staff operating the twenty-three national committees, the organization's principal source of practice information, expertise, research, and education in architectural practice fields.

What is most/least satisfying about your position?

Actually, in my role today — convention planning for a very large annual event — much of what I do is like live television. Creating all from scratch, we are given a budget and a convention center in which to hold a performance. A date is set, and we have eighteen months to assemble a live four-day show for 20,000 people. The difference from live television is that we organize nearly 480 events ranging in size from twenty-five people to as many as 3,500. The joy comes when I watch the people walk in, the lights go down, and the speaker takes the stage on cue and delivers a strong and valuable presentation. Even more gratifying is to hear the concluding remarks and applause, and then to see the audience depart in earnest stride to get to their next event.

Do you consider yourself as an architect?

Yes, in an indirect way. Somehow people seem to understand I do not design anything — until I tell them about the convention.

Each year the event is held in a different city, so the problem is renewed, the challenge is altered, and the solution unique.

Who or what experience has been a major influence on your career?

Supportive mentors have been the key to my professional success. Seeking and retaining a strong mentor has been absolutely critical to giving me the confidence to continue and succeed, even in the most difficult of times.

Notes

1. Parsons, Frank. (1909). *Choosing a vocation.* Boston, MA: Houghton Mifflin.
2. Pena, William. (1987). *Problem seeking: An architectural programming primer.* Washington, DC: AIA Press.
3. Berry, Richard. (1984). "Profile of the architect: A psychologist's view." *Review.* Summer 1984, p. 5.
4. Bolles, Richard. (1991). *The quick job-hunting map.* Berkeley, Calif.: Ten Speed Press.
5. The American Institute of Architects (2003). *Architect's handbook of professional practice.* Washington, D.C.: The American Institute of Architects.
6. Powell, C. Randall. (1990). *Career planning today.* Dubuque, Iowa: Kendall/Hunt, p. 42.
7. Covey, Stephen. (1989). *The seven habits of highly effective people.* New York: Fireside.

Beyeler Foundation Museum, Riehen (Basel), Switzerland. Architect: Renzo Piano. Photographer: Grace H. Kim, AIA.

Chapter Five

The Future of the Architecture Profession

What Do You See as the Future for the Architecture Profession?

I see a strong future for the profession of architecture as long as architects listen to the needs of clients and to the voices of people trained in architecture who do not necessarily practice architecture.

H. Alan Brangman, AIA
University Architect,
Georgetown University

The architecture profession is being challenged in ways similar to other professions. The role of the professional is being questioned in modern society because the public has much greater access to information than before.

To maintain their role as professionals, architects must maintain their role as experts. This challenge grows as buildings and the activities that buildings house become more and more complex. Even in residential construction, new materials and technologies emerge every day. Architects must master the skills necessary to stay abreast of societal, cultural, and technological changes that are part of everyday contemporary life. This is the biggest challenge for architects and the profession today and in the future.

Robert Beckley, FAIA
Professor and Dean Emeritus,
University of Michigan

Optimistically, I hope that design gains currency in certain areas, such as housing and urban planning; these areas now seem quite formulaic and static.

Doug Garofalo, FAIA
Associate Professor, University of Illinois at Chicago
President, Garofalo Architects, Inc.

The computer is the single most important development in architecture since the widespread use of steel in construction. The ability to quickly modify plans, model them in accurate three-dimensional settings, and produce a highly integrated set of construction documents is a boon to architectural design and to the construction field.

The global pressures that are pushing green design to the forefront will increase, creating high demand for architects who base their practice on green principles. I feel that green design is not a passing style but essential for all design. There is no other choice.

Nathan Kipnis, AIA
Principal, Nathan Kipnis Architects, Inc.

The role of the architect is expanding because of the amazing explosion in the number of new materials available to build with. This makes the architect the person with the most knowledge on a project. Building information modeling (BIM) systems are part of the change. Ethically, though, the architect's role remains unchanged: improving the built environment.

Carol Ross Barney, FAIA
Principal, Ross Barney + Jankowski, Inc.

In broad terms, there are two possible futures for architecture: one where the profession is radically different than it is today and one where the profession does not exist at all. What this means is that this traditionally old man's profession desperately needs creative, articulate, and passionate young people. As a result, I think this is an exciting time to enter the profession, especially for creative, big-picture problem solvers with a serious work ethic.

In the future, the profession of architecture will formally encourage graduates to seek a variety of roles in society, much as the legal profession has done for over fifty years.

Casius Pealer, J.D.
Associate, Reno & Cavanaugh, PLLC
Co-founder, ARCHVoices

I see a mixed future for the profession, but also the potential for great opportunity. The profession as a whole recognizes that architects at one time had a much greater role in leading and directing the process of conceiving, planning, designing, and constructing the built environment than today and that they ceded much of that leadership to other professionals affiliated with the industry — such as developers, contractors, design-builders, real estate professionals, even business consultants and accounting firms. Most of these are not as well trained and well equipped as architects are with the skill set to lead effectively. Individual architects, firms, and the profession as a whole must be willing to promote their strengths as problem identifiers and problem

solvers. If they focus on the products of what they do (drawings, specifications, and, ultimately, buildings) rather than the benefits their solutions provide to clients, then they will be viewed as a commodity. The willingness to take responsibility for the solutions and promoting the benefits of architectural skills can gain back leadership in the process. Architects must take professional responsibility for understanding and creating complete solutions that meet their customers' goals and objectives. For architects that do so, I think the future holds endless opportunity and greater financial rewards than for those who simply want to produce designs and drawings.

Randall J. Tharp, RA
Senior Vice President, A. Epstein and Sons International, Inc.

The future of the profession will be the insertion of architects into a range of hybrid forms of practice. We are starting to see a return of architects' direct involvement with the craft of building architecture, compared to the period in which they were mainly responsible for designing the drawings and models that a third party built. A number of emerging firms are directly involved in design

through construction. The direct link of the computer to the manufacturing process will have dramatic effects on the profession in the future.

Thomas Fowler IV
Associate Professor and Associate Head
California Polytechnic State University — San Luis Obispo

For decades, architects have been giving away their responsibilities to create other new professions — elevator, kitchen, code, and color consultants as well as owner's representatives and construction managers. This has whittled away at their role in the process and caused them to become highly specialized in fields such as health care or education. Some may argue that this is a result of our litigious society, but I think it also reflects the desire of some architects to create architecture with a capital *A*. Those architects relinquish their responsibilities for writing specifications and following through with construction documents. In some cases, foreign-based production firms are hired to crank out drawings overnight, allowing large firms to further relinquish this responsibility and deliver new buildings to their clients at breakneck speed. While these trends may yield greater profit for large architectural firms and their corporate clients, they seem to diminish the value and integrity architects can bring to a project by questioning the moral and ethical values of the triple bottom line.

I see young architects coming out of school with a renewed interest in craft and the tectonics of construction and with an ever-increasing interest in design-build as well as commercial development. I hope the architectural profession will realize the importance of being generalists and take back the roles and responsibilities that were once integral to doing good architecture.

Grace Kim, AIA
Principal, Schemata Workshop, Inc.

We need a revolution. We need to overhaul the drab, blasé office profession and redefine it. We need to inspire and excite each other within the field and strike a chord with people outside of it.

Monica Pascatore
Freelance Designer, P Inc.

The profession will grow more interdisciplinary. The architecture profession has come to encompass the need for greater knowledge of building technology with emphasis on the inter-connectedness of building systems throughout the design process.

Ethics relates to the study of thought, reasoning, and judgment. Architects must look more closely at choices that affect their own well being and that of others. The most recent accolades to the Auburn Rural Studio set the path for a more technical, sustainable, yet humane design process. This has infiltrated into many architecture schools and minds of practicing architects.

Patricia Saldana Natke, AIA
Principal and President, Urban Works, Ltd.

The profession will become more and more marginalized if architects do not take a leadership role in society.

Trinity Simon, ASSOCIATE AIA
Vice President (2004–2005), American Institute of Architecture Students

Near the end of the epilogue of their 1996 study of architecture in higher education, *Building Community,* Boyer and Mitgang observe that "the world needs more scholars and practitioners not only educated to prosper in their own careers but also prepared to fulfill social and civic obligations through the genius of design." They note the count-less matters of health, safety, welfare, and happiness in the task of building communities and that "the voices of architects must be heard, and their talents meaningfully employed." Their final appeal is that "architects must unite with all professions and all citizens in common cause." Thus we were given the challenge and the door, I believe, to the future.

Today we are in the early stages of discovery and assessment of a new demand on the dynamic of design for both community architecture and building architecture. The principles of sustainability are challenging the twentieth-century assumptions of the preeminence of consumption and disposability. A gradual realization of the ecological principle that everything is connected to everything else and that humankind is only one component of the myriad natural systems of the planet is working its way into our cognizance. A fifty-year awakening to the fact that humankind's unchecked consumption behavior has brought its survival on Earth into serious doubt is now emerging.

W. Cecil Steward, FAIA
Dean Emeritus, University of Nebraska — Lincoln
President/CEO, Joslyn Castle Institute for Sustainable Communities

Architects must learn that collaboration with a diverse population will drive us into the next hundred years. To create the diversity we all hope for, the profession must continue to strongly reach out to children and young adults and express its own importance. Once the youngest generation begins to understand the role of architects, the more society appreciate the breadth of our work and responsibility.

F. Michael Ayles, AIA
Director of Operations, Antinozzi Associates

The future has never been brighter. Architects find themselves at the intersection of numerous issues that are important to society. Environmental sustainability, emerging building technologies, material science, digital knowledge systems, livable and healthy cities, and affordable housing are exploding with innovation. Creative teams put together from around the world, as for the space program, will replace traditional practice. When a project is concluded, teams will disassemble and reconfigure to solve other problems. However, architects will continue to do what they have always done well: intelligently build communities.

Richard A. Eribes, Ph.D., AIA
Professor and Dean Emeritus, University of Arizona

In the near term, the architectural profession is in for a bumpy ride, in many cases serving as the puppet of design-build team leaders who are not architects. Beyond that, architects must shed their liability fears and take on more responsibility for the total project. Architects can lead design-build teams if they choose. Schools of architecture must look at the profession more broadly and help students understand that not all are destined to become great designers — and then offer an alternate road to a professional degree after instilling the essentials of good design in all students at the beginning of their coursework.

Gaines Hall, FAIA
Vice President, Kirkegaard & Associates

Within the foreseeable future, the traditional architect will always have a place. However, the profession as a whole must respond more quickly and responsibly to the needs of clients, society, environment, and global responsibilities. Architects must assume more responsibility and provide stronger leadership. The profession must invest heavily in life-long learning, expanding and clarifying the role of architecture, and building a greater sense of respect and need for the profession within the public. Individual architects and the profession as a whole must demonstrate leadership and vision to build a better global community.

Clark Llewellyn, AIA
Director, Montana State University

The profession of architecture currently does not reflect the changing dynamics of society, particularly gender and race. The profession must increase the number and visibility of architects who are women and people of color; otherwise, it will become obsolete and irrelevant. It is the responsibility of both the architecture schools and the profession as a whole to promote and assist these underrepresented groups.

Further, the profession has a responsibility to make the role of architects known to society. Society must understand that we are a vibrant, well-trained, intelligent, creative group of individuals who can improve neighborhoods and catalyze change in communities.

Tamara Redburn, ASSOCIATE AIA
Intern Architect, Fanning/Howey Associates, Inc.

Wexner Center, Columbus, Ohio. Architect: Peter Eisenman. Photographer: David Mogensen.

I see a delightful, humane, quality built environment for the "forgotten middle." Right now architecture seems to serve the upper and lower classes of society most. The wealthy have always and will continue to hire architects for architectural solutions to their building needs. To an extent, the poor are often afforded good architecture through social programs. But then there is the forgotten middle, the suburban middle-class sector. This is where I see the greatest architectural mediocrity, particularly in single-family houses, which are often a family's biggest material asset. The New Urbanist and Not-So-Big House movements are excellent efforts that are helping to turn things in a different direction. However, it's a huge ship that must be brought about. It may take generations to restore the middle-class built environment to humaneness.

Edward Shannon, AIA
Assistant Professor, Judson College

The future is already here; the next generation of architects is studying in our schools today. These students are fully engaged with the complex realities of their evolving world, and they understand that a fundamental rethinking of architectural practice is necessary. They are investigating dynamic interpretations that continually adapt and respond to an open-ended and indeterminate future.

Max Underwood, AIA
Professor, Arizona State University
Architect and Principal, Underwood + Crisp

The future of the architecture profession in American culture should be to educate the public to have a critical eye for architecture and to critique, through the making of architecture, the status of our society with a vision of human and cultural progress as its driving force.

Margaret DeLeeuw
Graduate, University of Maryland

The profession will broaden beyond traditional building. More diverse and better-trained architects with the advantages of the technical age will allow the profession to catapult way beyond building.

Chris Gribbs, ASSOCIATE AIA
Senior Director, The American Institute of Architects

Students, faculty, and professionals must keep up with technological and globalization changes as best they can, yet keep lose sight of the fact that their projects must not only

serve but also enhance the lives of the people who use them.

Kathryn Anthony, Ph.D.
Professor, University of Illinois at Urbana-Champaign

Architecture will continue to thrive and have increasing impact on our society and culture. Architects will be the leaders in developing new production approaches, including new building products and the systemization of these products. Architects will increasingly be recognized for the value they bring to the quality of life and economic productivity. Architects are uniquely qualified because of their educational background and the problem-solving skills provided by that background. Architecture captures the integration of theory and application that is crucial to successful implementation of our dreams and goals.

Jack Kremers, AIA
Professor, Judson College

As architects, we must acknowledge our connectivity to others; we must know that what we see is often not the entire truth. We must venture beyond our comfortable boundaries into the reality of others.

Kathryn T. Prigmore, FAIA
Project Manager, HDR Architecture, Inc.

Because we live and work in physically constructed environments, the need for the architectural profession and the services of which architects are capable — often uniquely — of providing is increasing. Throughout their studies and life, students are encouraged to consciously and continuously assess their interests and options and to make decisions that allow them to avail themselves of the wide array of choices, and thus opportunities, the future may present.

Roger Schluntz
Dean and Professor, University of New Mexico

The profession of architecture has changed over its history. Architects were historically involved in every aspect of the design and construction of buildings, but that process has been lost. I believe the idea of the master builder will continue to dissolve, resulting in many specialties in the future. Architecture will comprise thousands of areas of expertise.

Lisa Van Veen, ASSOCIATE AIA
Architectural Designer, Design Forward

As a society, we will always need places to live, work, and convene. We must take steps to safeguard ourselves from the gradual degradation of the public and private realms through poor practices and difficult political hurdles. As engineers and builders are creating stock buildings and housing developments with more and more ease, the architectural profession faces challenges in competing with minimalists. We see the underlying meaning of architecture and its importance to the human psyche; it is essential that we project this knowledge to the public. In light of the increasing awareness of our social ills' inextricable link to the absence of a sense of place, I remain confident in our profession's future.

> **Joe Nickol**
> **Graduate, University of Notre Dame**

As architects, we will be confronted by many problems, but the core issue will be the need to focus and manage change. Our clients need us to expand our definition of *architecture* to include all aspects of project success. Clients and society want architects to lead projects including change management, process design, master planning, strategy, and financing. When architects realize the design of the building is only a small part of the project and take ownership of the entire process, their profession will have reached its higher calling.

> **Roy Abernathy,** AIA, IDSA, LEED AP
> **President, Jova/Daniels/Busby**

I see a diversified profession, one that encourages and fosters the efforts of young women, African Americans, Hispanic Americans, and other minorities to become architects. More important, architecture is a profession rich in diversity of thought. Architects will migrate beyond and above the traditional boundaries defined by the term *architect.*

> **Jacob Day**
> **President (2004–2005), American Institute of Architecture Students**

Architecture will continue to be one of the most exciting and important professions. Architects will collaborate with other design professionals to improve our built and virtual environments. They will become more sensitive to elements of sustainable design as stewards of natural resources. They will create enriching places for our increasingly global community.

> **Dianne Blair Black,** AIA
> **Vice President, RTKL Associates, Inc.**

Architects are becoming increasingly specialized, which is not necessarily good for the profession as a whole.

> **Lynsey Gemmell**
> **Architect II, Holabird & Root**

As the future continues to become more technology-driven, architects will have to constantly learn about new technologies for both design and construction in order to adapt to the changing landscape and to serve their clients' growing needs. Architects will play a larger role in helping solve many of the society's current imperfections. Whether they are helping provide shelter for all, building more earth-friendly structures, or designing more integrated and efficient cities, architects will need to use more of their expertise for the common good.

> **David Groff**
> **Intern Architect, Dalgliesh, Gilpin, and Paxton Architects**

Architects will be active leaders in their communities, active leaders in the environment and on issues of sustainability, and active leaders in evidence-based design. The profession will welcome all of those that pursue it —that is, become increasingly diverse and culturally rich. Architects do more than design

Otaniemi Technical University, Otaniemi, Finland. Architect: Alvar Aalto. Photographer: Ted Shelton, AIA.

buildings; they build communities. The profession will embrace those individuals who pursue alternative careers, who find themselves on the client side of the table, or who seek to represent architects and communities through public pursuits. The profession will evolve as architects retake more responsibility in the building process and as technologies such as BIM emerge.

Shannon Kraus, AIA
Associate Architect, HKS

I see the world shrinking, and more and more of the work we do will be collaborative. We may collaborate with people we know, but more often we may never even see them. We must be comfortable with technology because it will enable us to describe our design ideas digitally and communicate them to the craftsmen. We must be able to work with people from a wide array of backgrounds and languages.

Katherine S. Proctor, FCSI, CDT, AIA
Director of Facilities, Jewelry Television

In the last thirty years, the architect's role has shifted farther from artist and craftsman to manager of the process of project delivery. This new identity will continue to solidify. Clients are seldom individuals anymore but rather committees that must be led through a complex process. Moreover, jurisdictional approvals and public hearings expose our designs to individuals without formal architectural training or a financial investment in the project's success. The traditional phases of schematic design, design development, and contract documents are being blurred into one phase of design/documentation. The advent of digital drafting has put the design and documentation processes in constant flux; drawings have become databases that are constantly altered, updated, revised, refined, and transmitted to a host of groups, including clients, lenders, marketing consultants, municipalities, consultants, and vendors. Architects have become the arbiters of a fast-moving and complex documentation exercise. No matter what changes accrue to their role, however, architects will continue to provide aesthetic oversight, technical experience, and legal knowledge to the building process. They will always serve as the conscience of the built environment.

W. Stephen Saunders, AIA
Principal, Eckenhoff Saunders Architects Inc.

The Resources of an Architect

The following are professional associations, resources, and websites that may be of assistance in your quest to become an architect. In all cases, you should contact them for further information. Many of the associations have state or local chapters that may also be helpful.

COLLATERAL ORGANIZATIONS

These first five associations (AIA, AIAS, ACSA, NAAB, and NCARB) are commonly known as the *collateral organizations* and represent the primary players in the profession — architects, students, educators, the accrediting agency, and the state registration boards.

American Institute of Architects (AIA)
1735 New York Avenue NW
Washington, DC 20006
(202) 626-7300
www.aia.org

Comprising over 58,000 architects in almost 300 local and state chapters, the AIA is the largest association for the architectural profession. Its mission is to promote and advance the profession and the living standards of people through their built environment.

American Institute of Architecture Students (AIAS)
1735 New York Avenue NW
Washington, DC 20006
(202) 626-7472
www.aias.org

The mission of the AIAS is to promote excellence in architectural education, training, and practice; to foster an appreciation of architecture and related disciplines; to enrich communities in a spirit of collaboration; and to organize architecture students and combine their efforts to advance the art and science of architecture.

Association of Collegiate Schools of Architecture (ACSA)
1735 New York Avenue NW
Washington, DC 20006
(202) 785-2324
www.acsa-arch.org

The ACSA is the membership organization representing the over 100 U.S. and Canadian schools offering accredited first professional degree programs in architecture. Its mission is to advance architectural education through support of member schools, their faculty, and students.

The National Architectural Accrediting Board (NAAB)
1735 New York Avenue NW
Washington, DC 20006-5292
(202) 783-2007
www.naab.org

The NAAB is the sole agency authorized to accredit U.S. professional degree programs in architecture. While graduation from a NAAB-accredited program does not assure registration, the accrediting process is intended to verify that each accredited program substantially meets those standards that, as a whole, constitute an appropriate education for an architect.

National Council of Architectural Registration Boards (NCARB)

1801 K Street, Suite 1100K
Washington, DC 20006
(202) 783-6500
www.ncarb.org

The NCARB is the organization of the fifty-five state, territorial, and district registration boards that license architects, and the preparer of the Architect Registration Examination (ARE) and the certification process that facilities reciprocity of individual license between jurisdictions.

ARCHITECTURE-RELATED ASSOCIATIONS

Alpha Rho Chi

www.alpharhochi.org

Alpha Rho Chi (APX) is the national professional coeducational fraternity for students in architecture and the allied arts.

American Architectural Foundation (AAF)

1735 New York Avenue NW
Washington, DC 20006
(202) 626-7500
www.archfoundation.org

An educational organization, the AAF believes that our surroundings affect all of us. Our houses and places of work and the communities in which we live profoundly shape our spiritual and mental well being. Our ability to be productive, our capacity to use our physical and cognitive skills, even our susceptibility to stress are measurably influenced by what we inhabit.

American Indian Council of Architects and Engineers

P.O. Box 15096
Portland, OR 97215
(503) 684-5680
www.aicae.org

The American Indian Council of Architects and Engineers advances the role of American Indian professional engineers, architects, and design professionals in practice. It works to advance their professional skills and encourage their pursuit of careers as professional engineers, architects, and design professionals.

American Society of Architectural Illustrators (ASAI)

5310 E. Main Street #104
Columbus, OH 43213
(614) 552-DRAW (3729)
www.asai.org

The ASAI is a nonprofit international professional organization of architectural illustrators. Its goals are to foster communication among architectural illustrators, to raise the standards of architectural illustration, and to acquaint the public with the importance of such drawing as integral to the practice of architecture.

American Society of Golf Course Architects

125 N. Executive Drive, Suite 106
Brookfield, WI 53005
(262) 786-5960
www.golfdesign.org

The American Society of Golf Course Architects comprises leading golf course designers in the United States and Canada who are actively involved in the design of new courses and the renovation of older courses.

Architects, Designers, and Planners for Social Responsibility (ADPSR)

P.O. Box 18375
Washington, DC 20036-8375
(415) 974-1306
www.adpsr.org

ADPSR works for peace, environmental protection, ecological building, social justice, and the development of healthy communities.

Asian American Architects and Engineers Association
8320 Lincoln Boulevard #108
Los Angeles, CA 90045
(213) 896-9270
www.aaaesc.com

The Asian American Architects and Engineers Association is committed to the empowerment of fessionals in the built environment through personal growth, professional excellence, business development, and community leadership.

Association of University Architects
www.auaweb.net

This special group of architectural professionals focuses on the development and enhancement of university campuses. University architects plan for the future and carefully build and renovate facilities for current needs.

The Association for Computeraided Design in Architecture (ACADIA)
www.acadia.org

The purpose of ACADIA, which was founded in the 1980s, is to facilitate communication and critical thinking about the use of computers in architecture, planning, and building science. A particular focus is education and the software, hardware, and pedagogy involved in education.

Congress for the New Urbanism (CNU)
The Marquette Building
140 S. Dearborn Street, Suite 310
Chicago, IL 60603
(312) 551-7300
www.cnu.org

Founded in 1993, the CNU works with architects, developers, planners, and others involved in the creation of cities and towns, teaching them how to implement the principles of the New Urbanism.

National Organization of Minority Architects (NOMA)
c/o School of Architecture and Design
College of Engineering, Architecture, and Computer Sciences
Howard University
2366 Sixth Street NW, Room 100
Washington, DC 20059
(202) 686-2780
www.noma.net

NOMA's mission is to build a strong national organization, strong chapters, and strong members for the purpose of minimizing the effects of racism in the architectural profession.

Royal Architectural Institute of Canada (RAIC)
55 Murray Street, Suite 330
Ottawa, Ontario K1N 5M3
Canada
(613) 241-3600
www.raic.org

Established in 1907, the RAIC is the voice for architecture and its practice in Canada. It represents more than 3,000 professional architects, faculty, and graduates of accredited Canadian schools of architecture from every region of the country.

Society of American Registered Architects (SARA)
303 South Broadway
Tarrytown, NY 10591
(914) 631-3600
www.sara-national.org

SARA was founded in 1956 as a professional society for all architects regardless of their role in the architectural community. SARA follows the Golden Rule and supports the concept of profitable professionalism for its members.

Tau Sigma Delta
www.tausigmadelta.org

Tau Sigma Delta is a national collegiate honor society open to students of all American colleges and universities wherein an accredited program of architecture, landscape architecture, or allied arts is established. The society derives its Greek name from the first letter of each of the words of its motto, "Technitai sophoikai dexioti"—tau, sigma, and delta. The motto means "Craftsmen, skilled and trained."

Union of International Architects (UIA)
51, Rue Raynouard
Paris 75016
France
33 (1) 45 24 36 88
www.uia-architectes.org/

The UIA is an international non-governmental organization founded in Lausanne, Switzerland, in 1948 to unite architects from all nations regardless of nationality, race, religion, or architectural school of thought, within the federations of their national associations. The union represents over one million architects through national architectural associations that form the ninety-two UIA Member Sections.

ASSOCIATIONS— RELATED CAREERS

Architectural History

Society of Architectural Historians
1365 N. Astor Street
Chicago, IL 60610-2144
(312) 573-1365
www.upenn.edu/sah

Founded in 1940, the Society of Architectural Historians encourages scholarly research in the field and promotes the preservation of significant architectural monuments that are an integral part of our worldwide historical and cultural heritage.

Construction

American Council for Construction Education (ACCE)
1717 North Loop 1604 East, Suite 320
San Antonio, TX 78232-1570
(210) 495-6161
www.acce-hq.org

The mission of the ACCE is to be a leading global advocate of high-quality construction education programs and to promote, support, and accredit them.

Associated Schools of Construction
Colorado State University
Manufacturing Technology and Construction Management
102 Guggenheim
Fort Collins, CO 80523
www.ascweb.org

The Associated Schools of Constructions is a professional association that supports the development and advancement of construction education, where the sharing of ideas and knowledge inspires, guides, and promotes excellence in curriculum, teaching, research, and service.

Construction Management Association of America (CMAA)
7918 Jones Branch Drive, Suite 540
McLean, VA 22102
(703) 356-2622
www.cmaanet.org

The mission of the CMAA is to promote professionalism and excellence in the management of the construction process. CMAA is leading the growth and acceptance of construction management as a professional discipline that can add significant value to the entire construction process, from conception to ongoing operation.

Construction Specifications Institute (CSI)
601 Madison Street
Alexandria, VA 22314-1791
(800) 689-2900
www.csinet.org

The mission of CSI is to continuously improve the process of creating and sustaining the built environment. The organization does this by facilitating communication among all those involved in that process.

National Association of Women in Construction (NAWIC)
327 S. Adams Street
Fort Worth, TX 76104
(800) 552-3506
www.nawic.org

Founded in Fort Worth, Texas, in 1955, NAWIC advances the causes of all women in construction, whose careers range from business ownership to the skilled trades.

Design — Graphic, Industrial, Furniture, Lighting

American Design Council
107 South Street, Suite 502
Boston, MA 02111
(617) 338-7210
www.americandesigncouncil.com

The American Design Council is an alliance of professional associations interested in advancing a shared agenda to promote effective design. The council enables a unified message on the value of the design process and the contribution designers make to corporate objectives; a comprehensive program for communicating this message to business; and a plan for individual and collective pursuit of these objectives.

American Institute of Graphic Arts (AIGA)
64 Fifth Avenue
New York, NY 10010
(212) 807-1990
www.aiga.org

The purpose of AIGA is to further excellence in design as a broadly defined discipline, strategic tool for business, and cultural force. AIGA is a professional association committed to stimulating thinking about design through the exchange of ideas and information, the encouragement of critical analysis and research, and the advancement of education and ethical practice."

American Society of Furniture Designers (ASFD)
144 Woodland Drive
New London, NC 28127
(910) 576-1273
www.asfd.com

Founded in 1981, ASFD is the only international nonprofit professional organization dedicated to advancing, improving, and supporting the profession of furniture design and its positive impact in the marketplace.

Industrial Designers Society of America (IDSA)
1142 E. Walker Road
Great Falls, VA 22066

(703) 759-0100
www.idsa.org

As the voice of the profession, IDSA advances the quality and positive impact of design.

International Association of Lighting Designers (IALD)
Merchandise Mart, Suite 9-104
200 World Trade Center
Chicago, IL 60654
(312) 527-3677
www.iald.org

Founded in 1969 and based in Chicago, the IALD is an internationally recognized organization dedicated solely to the concerns of independent professional lighting designers.

Organization of Black Designers (OBD)
300 M Street SW, Suite N110
Washington, DC 20024-4019
(202) 659-3918
www.core77.com/OBD

The OBD is a nonprofit national professional association dedicated to promoting the visibility, education, empowerment, and interaction of its membership and the understanding and value that diverse design perspectives contribute to world culture and commerce.

Society for Environmental Graphic Design (SEGD)
1000 Vermont Avenue, Suite 400
Washington, DC 20005
(202) 638-5555
www.segd.org

SEGD is an international nonprofit educational organization providing resources for design specialists in the field of environmental graphic design, architecture, and landscape, interior, and industrial design.

Planning/Landscape Architecture

American Planning Association (APA)
1776 Massachusetts Avenue NW
Washington, DC 20036-1904
(202) 872-0611
www.planning.org

The APA brings together thousands of people — practicing planners, citizens, elected officials — committed to making great communities happen. APA is a nonprofit public interest and research organization committed to urban, suburban, regional, and rural planning. APA and its professional institute, the American Institute of Certified Planners, advance the art and science of planning to meet the needs of people and society.

Association of Collegiate Schools of Planning (ACSP)
University of Wisconsin — Madison
925 Bascom Mall, Music Hall
Madison, WI 53706
www.acsp.org

The ACSP is a consortium of university-based programs offering credentials in urban and regional planning. Acting together, ACSP members are able to express their shared commitment to understanding the dynamics of urban and regional development, enhancing planning practices, and improving the education of both novice and experienced planners.

American Society of Landscape Architects (ASLA)
636 Eye Street NW
Washington, DC 20001-3736
(202) 898-2444
www.asla.org/asla

Founded in 1899, ASLA is the national professional association representing landscape architects. The society promotes the landscape architecture profession and advances its practice through advocacy, education, communication, and fellowship.

Council of Landscape Architectural Registration Boards (CLARB)
144 Church Street NW, Suite 201
Vienna, VA 22180

(703) 319-8380
www.clarb.org

CLARB is dedicated to ensuring that all individuals who affect the natural and built environment through the practice of landscape architecture are sufficiently qualified to do so.

Technical/ Engineering

Acoustical Society of America (ASA)
335 East Forty-fifth Street
New York, NY 10017
(202) 661-9404
asa.aip.org

The ASA is the premier international scientific society in acoustics, dedicated to increasing and diffusing knowledge of acoustics and its practical applications.

American Association of Engineering Societies (AAES)
1828 L Street NW, Suite 906
Washington, DC 20036
(202) 296-2237
(202) 296-1151 (fax)
www.aaes.org

The AAES is a multidisciplinary organization of engineering societies dedicated to advancing the knowledge, understanding, and practice of engineering. Member societies represent the mainstream of U.S. engineering with more than one million engineers in industry, government, and academia.

Architectural Engineering Institute (AEI)

1801 Alexander Bell Drive, 1st Floor
Reston, VA 20191-4400
(703) 295-6370
www.aeinstitute.org

A division of ASCE, the mission of the AEI is to provide a multidisciplinary forum in which building industry professionals engaged in the planning, design, construction, and operation of buildings can examine technical and professional issues of common interest.

American Society of Civil Engineers (ASCE)

1801 Alexander Bell Drive
Reston, VA 20191-4400
(800) 548-2723
www.asce.org

The mission of the ASCE is to provide essential value to members, their careers, its partners, and the public by developing leadership, advancing technology, advocating lifelong learning, and promoting the profession of civil engineering.

Accreditation Board for Engineering and Technology, Inc. (ABET)

111 Market Place, Suite 1050
Baltimore, MD 21202-4012
(410) 347-7700
www.abet.org

ABET provides world leadership in assuring quality and stimulating innovation in applied science, computing, engineering, and technology education. ABET serves the public through the promotion and advancement of education in applied science, computing, engineering, and technology.

National Society of Professional Engineers (NSPE)

2029 K Street NW
Washington, DC 20006
(202) 463-2300
www.nspe.org

The NSPE is the only engineering society that represents individual engineering professionals and licensed engineers (PEs) across all disciplines. Founded in 1934, NSPE strengthens the engineering profession by promoting engineering licensure and ethics, enhancing the engineer image, and protecting PEs' legal rights at the national and state levels.

Society of Building Science Educators

www.sbse.org

The Society of Building Science Educators is an association of university educators in architecture who support excellence in the teaching of environmental science and building technologies.

Interior Design

American Society of Interior Designers (ASID)

608 Massachusetts Avenue NE
Washington, DC 20002-6006
(202) 546-3480
www.asid.org

ASID is a nonprofit professional society representing the interests of interior designers and the interior design community.

International Interior Design Association (IIDA)

13-500 Merchandise Mart
Chicago, IL 60654-1104
(888) 799-IIDA
www.iida.com

The IIDA is committed to enhancing quality of life through excellence in interior design and to advancing interior design through knowledge.

Foundation for Interior Design Education Research (FIDER)

146 Monroe Center NW, Suite 1318
Grand Rapids, MI 49503-2822
(616) 458-0400
www.fider.org

FIDER provides the foundation for excellence in the interior design profession by setting standards for education and accrediting academic programs that meet those standards.

Historic Preservation

National Trust for Historic Preservation

1785 Massachusetts Avenue NW
Washington, DC 20036
(202) 673-4064
www.nationaltrust.org

The National Trust is a privately funded nonprofit organization that provides leadership, education, and advocacy to save America's diverse historic places and revitalize communities.

National Council for Preservation Education (NCPE)

www.ncpe.us

The NCPE encourages and assists in the development and improvement of historic preservation education programs and endeavors in the United States and elsewhere.

Historic American Buildings Survey

HAER/HALS Division
National Park Service
Department of the Interior
1849 C Street NW, 2270
Washington, DC 20240
(202) 354-2135/2136
www.cr.nps.gov/habshaer

The Historic American Buildings Survey/Historic American Engineering Record (HABS/HAER) is an integral component of the federal government's commitment to historic preservation. The program documents important architectural, engineering, and industrial sites throughout the United States and its territories.

INSTITUTIONS DEDICATED TO ARCHITECTURE

National Building Museum

401 F Street NW
Washington, DC 20001
(202) 272-2448
www.nbm.org

Created by an act of Congress, the National Building Museum is the only institution uniquely dedicated to exploring the what, who, how, and why of American building. It is a focal point for all those who want to learn about American architecture. The National Building Museum seeks to broaden public understanding and appreciation of the American building heritage by providing people with the skills needed to understand and shape the built environment.

Chicago Architecture Foundation (CAF)

224 S. Michigan Avenue
Chicago, IL 60604
(312) 922-3432
www.architecture.org

The CAF is dedicated to advancing public interest and education in architecture and related design. Because no art other than architecture so vividly expresses what Chicago is and where it is going, CAF educates the public to expect the highest standards from Chicago's built environment.

Architecture in Education

Foundation for Architecture
1737 Chestnut Street, 2nd Floor
Philadelphia, PA 19103
(215) 569-3187
www.aiaphila.org/aie

Architecture in Education brings architects, landscape architects, and other design professionals into classrooms to help young people understand what it takes to make buildings and communities work for the people who live in them.

Built Environment Education Program (BEEP)

c/o AIA California Council
1303 J Street, Suite 200
Sacramento, CA 95814
(916) 448-9082
www.aiacc.org

BEEP involves the introduction of built environment issues to the classroom, particularly at the elementary-age level. Teachers and architects or intern architects working together through a variety of media (slides, lectures, participatory activities) help make schoolchildren aware of the built environment in which they live.

Center for Understanding the Built Environment (CUBE)

5328 W. Sixty-seventh Street
Prairie Village, KS 66208-1408
(913) 262-0691
www.cubekc.org

CUBE brings together educators with community partners to effect change that will lead to a high-quality built and natural environment.

Learning by Design in Massachusetts

c/o The Boston Society of Architects
52 Broad Street
Boston, MA 02019
www.architects/org/LBD

A core element of the Boston Society of Architects' K–12 design education and design awareness program, Learning by Design gives children the opportunity to express their ideas about their built and natural environments.

Graham Foundation for Advanced Studies in the Fine Arts

4 W. Burton Place
Chicago, IL 60610-1416
(312) 787-4071
www.grahamfoundation.org

The mission of the Graham Foundation is to nurture and enrich an informed and creative public dialog about architecture and the built environment.

ACE Mentor Program of America

c/o National Institute of Building Sciences
1090 Vermont Avenue NW
Washington, DC 20005
(202) 289-7800
www.acementor.org

The ACE (Architecture, Construction, Engineering) Mentor Program was founded by the principals of leading design and construction firms to introduce high school students to career opportunities in the industry.

COMMUNITY SERVICE

AmeriCorps

1201 New York Avenue NW
Washington, DC 20525
(202) 606-5000
www.americorps.org

AmeriCorps is a network of national service programs that engage more than 50,000 Americans each year in intensive service to meet critical needs in education, public safety, health, and the environment.

Architecture for Humanity

www.architectureforhumanity.org

Architecture for Humanity promotes architectural and design solutions to global, social, and humanitarian crises. Through competitions, workshops, educational forums, partnerships with aid organizations, and other activities, the organization creates opportunities for architects and designers from around the world to help communities in need.

Design Corps

302 Jefferson Street #250
Raleigh, NC 27605
(919) 828-0048
www.designcorps.org

Design Corps is a private nonprofit organization founded in 1991 to coordinate design services that help create responsive affordable housing. Respect for those housed, the local communities, and the cultures involved is encouraged.

Habitat for Humanity International

121 Habitat Street
Americus, GA 31709-3498
(229) 924-6935
www.habitat.org

Habitat for Humanity is a nonprofit Christian housing ministry that works to build or renovate homes for the inadequately sheltered in the United States and twenty countries around the world.

The Mad Housers, Inc.
534 Permalume Place
Atlanta, GA 30318
(404) 806-6233
www.madhousers.org

Mad Housers is an Atlanta-based nonprofit corporation engaged in charitable work, research, and education. Their primary endeavor is building temporary emergency shelters for homeless individuals and families regardless of race, creed, national origin, gender, religion, age, family status, sexual orientation, etc.

Peace Corps
Paul D. Coverdell Peace Corps Headquarters
1111 Twentieth Street NW
Washington, DC 20526
(800) 424-8580
www.peacecorps.gov

Established in 1961 by President John F. Kennedy, the Peace Corps has shared with the world America's most precious resource — its people. Peace Corps Volunteers serve in seventy-two countries in Africa, Asia, the Caribbean, Central and South America, Europe, and the Middle East. Collaborating with local community members, volunteers work in areas such as education, youth outreach and community development, the environment, and information technology.

Public Architecture
1126 Folsom Street #3
San Francisco, CA 94102-1397
(415) 861-8200
www.publicarchitecture.org

Established in 2002, Public Architecture is a nonprofit organization that identifies and solves practical problems of human interaction in the built environment. It acts as a catalyst for public discourse through education, advocacy, and the design of public spaces and amenities.

RECOMMENDED READING

Lewis, R.K. (1998). *Architect? A candid guide to the profession.* Boston: MIT Press. ISBN 0-262-12110-7

In three sections — "To Be or Not To Be...an Architect," "Becoming an Architect," and "Being an Architect" — the author provides an inside look at the profession, its educational process, and weighing the pros and cons of becoming an architect. Written by Roger Lewis, a professor of architecture at the University of Maryland, the book is excellent reading for an aspiring architect.

ACSA. (Ed.). (2003). *Guide to architecture schools* (6th ed.). Washington, D.C.: Association of

Collegiate Schools of Architecture. ISBN 0-935502-06-8

Compiled approximately every five years by the Association of Collegiate Schools of Architecture (ACSA), *Guide to Architecture Schools* is a valuable resource for individuals seeking to pursue an architectural education. Its primary content is a compilation of two-page descriptions of the over 100 universities offering accredited degree programs in architecture. In addition, the resource contains an introduction outlining the history of architectural education, high school preparation, selecting a school, architectural practice, and accreditation.

Piper, R. (1993). *Opportunities in architectural careers.* Lincolnwood, IL: VGM Career Horizons. ISBN 0-8442-4039-7

Part of the extensive "Opportunities In" series by VGM Career Horizons, *Opportunities in Architectural Careers* aims to inform readers about the purpose of architecture in today's environment, help them understand what an architect does, and grasp the many career opportunities in architecture. The book accomplishes its purpose through five chapters: "Our Physical Environment," "The Professional Architect," "The Architect's Practice," "Education for

Architecture," and "Architectural Resources." Targeted at high school students, the book provides a good picture of the architecture profession and the tasks of an architect.

Camenson, Blythe. (2002). *Careers in architecture.* New York: McGraw-Hill. ISBN 0-658-00460-3

Part of the VGM Career Books series, *Careers in Architecture* provides insight on the variety of positions within the architecture field — residential, commercial, and institutional architecture; historic preservation; landscape architecture; engineering; urban and regional planning; and more.

Kim, Grace. (2006). *The survival guide to architectural internship and career development.* Hoboken, NJ: John Wiley and Sons. ISBN 0-471-69263-8.

This book offers a concise guide to the process from architectural education to licensure. It also covers issues related to obtaining a first professional job upon graduating, and the various questions and issues involved in going from education to practice. Profiles of interns and young architects enliven the text, and contributions have been written by experts on firm human resources and career counseling.

Pressman, Andy. (1993). *Architecture 101: A guide to the design studio.* New York: John Wiley and Sons. ISBN 0-471-57318-3

This book introduces students to the design studio and helps them develop a process by which they can complete design projects. Covering every practical element of this central experience, from setting up on the first day to landing the first job, this important work features contributions from some of the most distinguished names in architecture.

O'Gorman, James F. (1998). *ABC of architecture.* Philadelphia: University of Pennsylvania Press. ISBN 0-8122-1631-8

ABC of Architecture is an accessible, nontechnical text on the first steps to understanding architectural structure, history, and criticism. Author James O'Gorman moves seamlessly from a discussion of the most basic inspiration for architecture (the need for shelter from the elements) to an exploration of space, system, and material, and, finally, to an examination of the language and history of architecture.

Anthony, Kathryn. (2001). *Designing for diversity: Gender, race, and ethnicity in the architectural profession.* Champaign: University of Illinois Press. ISBN 0-252-02641-1

This landmark book offers insight into the issue of diversity as it relates to the profession of architecture. As one reviewer stated, "a must-read."

Anthony, Kathryn. (1991). *Design juries on trial: The renaissance of the design studio.* New York: Van Nostrand Reinhold. ISBN 0-442-00235-1

Design Juries on Trial unlocks the door to the mysterious design jury system, exposing its hidden agendas and helping you overcome intimidation, confrontation, and frustration. It explains how to improve the success rate of submissions to juries, whether in academic settings, for competitions and awards programs, or for professional accounts.

NAAB. (1998). *Guide to Student Performance Criteria.* Washington, D.C.: NAAB.

Written for faculty and students of professional degree programs in architecture, this guide informs the reader about one of the twelve conditions — student performance criteria — required for a program to maintain accreditation. These are the areas every student who graduates from an accredited architecture program must demonstrate. The criteria define the minimum requirements for a professional education in architecture.

American Institute of Architecture Students. (2002). *The redesign of the studio culture.* Washington, D.C.: American Institute of Architecture Students.

The result of an AIAS task force, this report examines the issue of studio culture and lists goals to embrace in creating change for architectural education.

Slafer, Anna, and Cahill, Kevin. (1995). *Why design? Activities and projects from the National Building Museum.* Washington, D.C.: National Building Museum. ISBN 1-55652-249-5

Projects cover a range of design themes: buildings, landscapes, nature, products, and communications. Grades 6–12.

Thorne-Thomsen, Kathleen. (1994). *Frank Lloyd Wright for kids: His life and ideas: 21 activities.* Chicago: Chicago Review Press. ISBN 1-55652-207

Both a biography and an activity book, Frank Lloyd Wright for Kids is about a boy growing up on an American farm, a boy who works hard and sees structures and harmonies in the landscape around him. It is the story of a young man becoming a great architect as he uses his love of nature's colors and shapes in his unique designs. Delightful activities enable kids to understand and appreciate the ideas presented in his biography. Grades 4–8.

Cuff, Dana. (1991). *Architecture: The story of practice.* Boston: MIT Press. ISBN 0-262-53112-7

Cuff delves into the architect's everyday work world to uncover an intricate social art of design. The result is a new portrait of the profession that sheds light on what it means to be an architect, how design problems are construed and resolved, how clients and architects negotiate, and how design excellence is achieved.

Crowe, Norman, and Laseau, Paul. (1984). *Visual notes for architects and designers.* New York: Van Nostrand Reinhold. ISBN 0-442-29334-8

The authors examine the relationship between note-taking, visualization, and creativity. They provide practical guidance on visual acuity, visual literacy, and graphic analysis

Kostof, Spiro. (Ed.). (1977). *The architect.* New York: Oxford University Press. ISBN 0-19-504044-9

A collection of essays by historians and architects, *The Architect* explores and surveys the profession of architecture from its beginnings in ancient Egypt to the modern day.

Rasmussen, Steen Eiler. (1959). *Experiencing architecture.* Cambridge: MIT Press. ISBN 0-262-68002-5

Profusely illustrated with fine examples of architectural experimentation through the centuries, this classic conveys the intellectual excitement of superb design.

Boyer, Ernest L., and Mitgang, Lee D. (1996). *Building community: A new future for architecture education and practice.* Princeton, NJ: Carnegie Foundation for the Advancement of Teaching. ISBN 0-931050-59-6

Published in May of 1996 by the Carnegie Foundation for the Advancement of Teaching, this study takes an in-depth look at the education and practice of architects. Boyer and Mitgang surveyed educators, students, and practitioners to decipher what issues separate education and practice, and more importantly, what can bring them together.

Ginsberg, Beth (2004). *The ECO guide to careers that make a difference: Environmental work for a sustainable world.* Washington, D.C.: Island Press. ISBN 1-55963-967-9

This publication provides an overview of career choices and opportunities and identifies development employment trends as the environmental community looks forward to the pressing needs of the twenty-first century.

Linton, Harold (2003). *Portfolio design.* New York: W.W. Norton. ISBN 0-393-73095-6

More than any other, this book provides critical information on creating, preparing, and producing a portfolio, an element necessary for architecture students applying to graduate programs or seeking employment.

WEBSITES

These websites are directly related to the topic of this book and are current at the time of publication. You can explore the many other architecture-related websites as well.

**ARCHVoices —
www.archvoices.org**
ARCHVoices is an independent, nonprofit organization and think tank on architectural education, internship, and licensure. It fosters a culture of communication through the collection and dissemination of information and research.

**ARCHCareers.org —
www.archcareers.org**
ARCHCareers.org is an interactive guide to careers in architecture designed to help people become architects. It helps the user learn about and understand the process of becoming an architect: education, experience, and exam.

**Design Careers and
Education Guide —
ucda.com/careers.lasso**
Thinking about an education or career in design? Browse this guide to help you decide which specialties you are most interested in pursuing. Each specialty is presented with a general description and education and career perspectives.

**InsideArch —
www.insidearch.org**
The primary goal of InsideArch is to gather quantitative and qualitative information about the work, culture, and employee experience at architecture firms and to synthesize and present that information in a meaningful, valuable format so as to empower interns and architects to make career decisions more beneficial to themselves and the profession as a whole.

**International Archive of
Women in Architecture —
spec.lib.vt.edu/IAWA**
The purpose of the International Archive of Women in Architecture is to document the history of women's involvement in architecture by collecting, preserving, storing, and making available to researchers the professional papers of women architects, landscape architects, designers, architectural historians and critics, and urban planners, as well as the records of women's architectural organizations from around the world.

**ArchNewsNow.com —
www.archnewsnow.com**
ArchNewsNow.com delivers the most comprehensive coverage of national and international news, projects, products, and events in the world of architecture and design.

**Archinect —
www.archinect.com**
The goals of Archinect are to make architecture more connected and open-minded and to bring together designers from around the world to introduce new ideas from all disciplines.

**Architectural Record —
archrecord.construction.com**
Architecturalrecord.com supplements the monthly *Architectural Record* magazine with expanded multimedia project stories, in-depth interviews with giants of architecture, daily news updates, weekly book reviews, green architecture stories, and archival material as well as links to people and products and access to online continuing education credit registration.

**Portfolio Design —
www.portfoliodesign.com**
A companion to the ever-popular publication by the same name, *Portfolio Design*, the website includes essential information on the digital and multimedia direction of portfolios today. Portfolio Design shows you how to assemble a portfolio that will display your talents and qualifications to the best advantage.

**DesignIntelligence —
www.di.net**
DesignIntelligence contains a wealth of timely articles, original research, and essential industry news.

**Emerging Professional's
Companion —
www.epcompanion.org**
Launched in 2004, this site helps interns better understand and complete the training areas of IDP concurrent with their internship.

**Mentorship: A Journey in
Collaborative Learning
www.aia.org/static/majicl/**
Developed by the AIA national website, this resource provides insight into mentoring in the profession of architecture. It is for aspiring architects, educators, and the practitioners of all experience levels who wish to discover the possibilities in a mentoring relationship.

**Design Disciplines — Whole
Building Design Guide
www.wbdg.org/design/design_
disciplines.php**
A branch of the Whole Building Design Guide, Design Discipline assists in understanding how building design disciplines are organized and practiced. Disciplines included: Architecture, Architectural Programming, Fire Protection Engineering, Interior Design, Landscape Architecture, Planning, and Structural Engineering.

NAAB/CACB-Accredited Architecture Programs in the United States and Canada

This list is current as of the publication date. For an up-to-date list, contact NAAB at www.naab.org.

ALABAMA

Auburn University
College of Architecture, Design, and Construction
School of Architecture
Auburn University
www.arch.auburn.edu

Tuskegee University
College of Engineering, Architecture, and Physical Sciences
Department of Architecture
Tuskegee
www.tuskegee.edu

ALASKA

None

ARIZONA

Arizona State University
College of Architecture and Environmental Design
School of Architecture and Landscape Architecture
Tempe
www.asu.edu/caed

Arizona, University of
College of Architecture, Planning, and Landscape Architecture
School of Architecture
Tuscon
www.architecture.arizona.edu

Frank Lloyd Wright School of Architecture

Scottsdale
www.taliesin.edu

ARKANSAS

Arkansas, University of
School of Architecture
Fayetteville
www.uark.edu/~archsite

CALIFORNIA

California, Berkeley, University of
College of Environmental Design
Department of Architecture
Berkeley
arch.ced.berkeley.edu

California, Los Angeles, University of
Department of Architecture and Urban Design
Los Angeles
www.aud.ucla.edu

California College of the Arts
School of Architectural Studies
San Francisco
www.ccac-art.edu

California Polytechnic State
University—San Luis Obispo
College of Architecture and
Environmental Design
Architecture Department
San Luis Obispo
www.arch.calpoly.edu

California State Polytechnic
University—Pomona
College of Environmental Design
Pomona
www.csupomona.edu/~arc

NewSchool of Architecture and
Design
Architecture
San Diego
www.newschoolarch.edu

Southern California Institute of
Architecture (SCI-ARC)
Los Angeles
www.sciarc.edu

Southern California,
University of
School of Architecture
Los Angeles
www.usc.edu/dept/architecture

Woodbury University
School of Architecture and
Design
Burbank
www.woodbury.edu
Colorado

Colorado at Denver,
University of
College of Architecture and
Planning
Denver
www.cudenver.edu/aandp

CONNECTICUT

Yale University
School of Architecture
New Haven
www.architecture.yale.edu

DELAWARE

None

DISTRICT OF COLUMBIA

Catholic University of America
School of Architecture and
Planning
architecture.cua.edu

Howard University
College of Engineering,
Architecture, and Computer
Science
School of Architecture and
Planning
www.howard.edu/ceacs

FLORIDA

Florida A&M University
School of Architecture
Tallahassee
www.famusoa.net

Florida Atlantic University
College of Architecture and
Urban and Public Affairs

School of Architecture
Fort Lauderdale
www.fau.edu/arch

Florida International University
School of Architecture
Miami
www.fiu.edu/~soa

Florida, University of
Department of Architecture
Gainesville
www.arch.ufl.edu

Miami, University of
School of Architecture
Coral Gables
www.arc.miami.edu

South Florida, University of
School of Architecture and
Community Design
Tampa
www.arch.usf.edu

GEORGIA

Georgia Institute of
Technology
College of Architecture
Architecture Program
Atlanta
www.arch.gatech.edu

Savannah College of Arts and
Design
Department of Architecture
Savannah
www.scad.edu

Southern Polytechnic State
University
College of Architecture, Civil
Engineering Technology, and
Construction
School of Architecture
Marietta
architecture.spsu.edu

HAWAII

Hawaii at Manoa, University of
School of Architecture
Honolulu
www.arch.hawaii.edu

IDAHO

Idaho, University of
College of Letters, Arts, and
Social Sciences
Department of Architecture
Moscow
www.aa.uidaho.edu/arch

ILLINOIS

Illinois Institute of Technology
College of Architecture
Chicago
www.arch.iit.edu

Illinois at Chicago, University of
College of Architecture and the
Arts
School of Architecture
Chicago
www.uic.edu/depts/arch/

Illinois at Urbana-Champaign,
University of
School of Architecture
Champaign
www.arch.uiuc.edu/

Judson College
Art, Design, and Architecture
Division
Department of Architecture
Elgin
www.judson-il.edu

INDIANA

Ball State University
College of Architecture and
Planning
Muncie
www.bsu.edu/architecture

Notre Dame, University of
School of Architecture
Notre Dame
www.architecture.nd.edu

IOWA

Iowa State University
College of Design
Department of Architecture
Ames
www.arch.iastate.edu

KANSAS

Kansas State University
College of Architecture,
Planning, and Design
Department of Architecture
Manhattan
aalto.arch.ksu.edu/arch

Kansas, University of
School of Architecture and
Urban Design
Lawrence
www.saud.ku.edu

KENTUCKY

Kentucky, University of
College of Design
Lexington
www.uky.edu/Design

LOUISIANA

Louisiana at Lafayette,
University of
School of Architecture and
Design
Lafayette
arts.louisiana.edu/degree/arch

Louisiana State University
College of Art and Design
School of Architecture
Baton Rouge
www.arch.lsu.edu

Louisiana Tech University
College of Liberal Arts
School of Architecture
Ruston
www.latech.edu/tech/
liberal-arts/architecture

Southern University and A&M
College
School of Architecture
Baton Rouge
www.susa.subr.edu

Tulane University
School of Architecture
New Orleans
www.tulane.edu

MAINE

None

MARYLAND

Maryland, University of
School of Architecture,
Planning, and Preservation
College Park
www.arch.umd.edu

Morgan State University
Institute of Architecture and
Planning
Baltimore
www.morgan.edu/academics/
IAP/index.html

MASSACHUSETTS

Boston Architectural Center
College of Architecture
Boston
www.the-bac.edu

Harvard University
Graduate School of Design
Cambridge
www.gsd.harvard.edu

Massachusetts Institute of
Technology
School of Architecture and
Planning
Department of Architecture
Cambridge
sap.mit.edu

Northeastern University
College of Arts and Sciences
Department of Architecture
Boston
www.architecture.neu.edu

Wentworth Institute of
Technology
Department of Architecture
Boston
www.wit.edu

MICHIGAN

Andrews University
Division of Architecture
Berrien Springs
www.arch.andrews.edu

Detroit — Mercy, University of
School of Architecture
Detroit
www.arch.udmercy.edu

Lawrence Technological
University
College of Architecture and
Design
Southfield
ltu.edu/architecture_and_
design

Michigan, University of
Taubman College of Architecture
and Urban Planning
Ann Arbor
www.tcaup.umich.edu

MINNESOTA

Minnesota, University of
College of Architecture and
Landscape Architecture
Department of Architecture
Minneapolis
www.cala.umn.edu

MISSISSIPPI

Mississippi State University
College of Architecture, Art, and
Design
School of Architecture
Mississippi State
www.sarc.msstate.edu

MISSOURI

Drury College
Hammons School of
Architecture
Springfield
www.drury.edu

Washington University
School of Architecture
St. Louis
www.arch.wustl.edu

MONTANA

Montana State University
College of Arts and Architecture
School of Architecture
Bozeman
www.montana.edu/wwwdt

NEBRASKA

Nebraska — Lincoln,
University of
College of Architecture
Department of Architecture
Lincoln
archweb.unl.edu

NEVADA

Nevada—Las Vegas,
University of
College of Fine Arts
School of Architecture
Las Vegas
architecture.unlv.edu

NEW HAMPSHIRE

None

NEW JERSEY

New Jersey Institute of
Technology
School of Architecture
Newark
architecture.njit.edu

Princeton University
School of Architecture
Princeton
www.princeton.edu/~soa

NEW MEXICO

New Mexico, University of
School of Architecture and
Planning
Albuquerque
saap.unm.edu

NEW YORK

City College of The City
University of New York
School of Architecture, Urban
Design, and Landscape
Architecture
New York
www.ccny.cuny.edu/architecture/
archprog/intropage.htm

Columbia University
Graduate School of
Architecture, Planning,
and Preservation
New York
www.columbia.edu

Cooper Union
Irwin S. Chanin School of Architecture
New York
www.cooper.edu/architecture

Cornell University
Department of Architecture
Ithaca
www.architecture.cornell.edu

New York Institute of
Technology
School of Architecture and
Design
Old Westbury
iris.nyit.edu/architecture

Parsons School of Design
Department of Architecture,
Interior Design, and Lighting
New York
www2.parsons.edu/architecture

Pratt Institute
School of Architecture
Brooklyn
www.pratt.edu/arch

Rensselaer Polytechnic Institute
School of Architecture
Troy
www.arch.rpi.edu

State University of New York at
Buffalo
School of Architecture and
Planning
Department of Architecture
Buffalo
www.ap.buffalo.edu

Syracuse University
School of Architecture
Syracuse
soa.syr.edu

NORTH CAROLINA

North Carolina at Charlotte, University of
College of Architecture
Charlotte
www.coa.uncc.edu

North Carolina State University
College of Design
School of Architecture
Raleigh
www.design.ncsu.edu

NORTH DAKOTA

North Dakota State University
College of Engineering and
Architecture
Department of Architecture and
Landscape Architecture
Fargo
www.ndsu.nodak.edu/arch

OHIO

Cincinnati, University of
College of Design, Architecture,
Art, and Planning

School of Architecture and Interior Design
Cincinnati
www.daap.uc.edu

Kent State University
College of Architecture and Environmental Design
Kent
www.saed.kent.edu

Miami University
Department of Architecture and Interior Design
Oxford
www.muohio.edu/architecture

Ohio State University
Knowlton School of Architecture
Columbus
knowlton.osu.edu

OKLAHOMA

Oklahoma State University
College of Engineering, Architecture, and Technology
School of Architecture
Stillwater
architecture.ceat.okstate.edu

Oklahoma, University of
Division of Architecture
Norman
www.ou.edu/architecture

OREGON

Oregon, University of
School of Architecture and Allied Arts
Department of Architecture
Eugene
aaa.uoregon.edu

PENNSYLVANIA

Carnegie Mellon University
School of Architecture
Pittsburgh
www.arc.cmu.edu

Drexel University
College Media Arts and Design
Department of Architecture
Philadelphia
www.drexel.edu/academics/comad

Pennsylvania State University
College of Arts and Architecture
School of Architecture and Landscape Architecture
University Park
www.arch.psu.edu

Pennsylvania, University of
Department of Architecture
Philadelphia
www.upenn.edu/gsfa/arch

Philadelphia University
School of Architecture
Philadelphia
www.philau.edu/schools/add

Temple University
Tyler School of Art
Architecture Program
Philadelphia
www.temple.edu/architecture

PUERTO RICO

Puerto Rico, Polytechnic University of
Architecture Program
San Juan
www.pupr.edu/arqpoli

Puerto Rico, Universidad de
Escuela De Arquitectura
San Juan
www.uprrp.edu/archweb

RHODE ISLAND

Rhode Island School of Design
Department of Architecture
Providence
www.risd.edu

Roger Williams University
School of Architecture, Art, and Historic Preservation
Bristol
arch.rwu.edu

SOUTH CAROLINA

Clemson University
College of Architecture, Arts, and Humanities
School of Architecture
Clemson
www.clemson.edu/caah

SOUTH DAKOTA

None

TENNESSEE

Tennessee—Knoxville,
University of
College of Architecture and
Design
Knoxville
www.arch.utk.edu

TEXAS

Houston, University of
Gerald D. Hines College of
Architecture
Houston
www.arch.uh.edu

Prairie View A&M University
School of Architecture
Prairie View
www.pvamu.edu/gridold/
architect/soa/

Rice University
School of Architecture
Houston
www.arch.rice.edu

Texas A&M University
College of Architecture
College Station
archone.tamu.edu

Texas at Arlington, University of
Architecture Program
Arlington
www.uta.edu/architecture

Texas at Austin, University of
School of Architecture
Austin
www.ar.utexas.edu

Texas at San Antonio,
University of
School of Architecture
San Antonio
www.utsa.edu/architecture

Texas Tech University
College of Architecture
Lubbock
www.arch.ttu.edu/architecture

UTAH

Utah, University of
Graduate School of Architecture
Salt Lake City
www.arch.utah.edu

VERMONT

Norwich University
Division of Architecture and Art
Northfield
www.norwich.edu

VIRGINIA

Hampton University
School of Engineering and
Technology
Architecture
Hampton
www.hamptonu.edu/academics/
schools/engineering

Virginia Polytechnic Institute
and State University
College of Architecture and
Urban Studies
School of Architecture and
Design
Blacksburg
www.arch.vt.edu

Virginia, University of
School of Architecture
Charlottesville
www.virginia.edu/arch

WASHINGTON

Washington, University of
College of Architecture and
Urban Planning
Department of Architecture
Seattle
www.arch.washington.edu

Washington State University
School of Architecture and
Construction Management
Pullman
www.arch.wsu.edu

WEST VIRGINIA

None

WISCONSIN

Wisconsin — Milwaukee,
University of
School of Architecture and
Urban Planning
Milwaukee
www.uwm.edu/sarup

None

NAAB CANDIDATE PROGRAMS

Academy of Art University
University of Hartford
Ward School of Technology
Department of Architecture
uhaweb.hartford.edu/
wardweb/descaet.htm

University of Massachusetts
Department of Art and
Art History
www.massart.edu/at_massart/
academic_prgms/environmental

CANADA

For an up-to-date list, contact
CACB at www.CACB.ca.

British Columbia, University of
School of Architecture
Vancouver, British Columbia
www.arch.ubc.ca

Calgary, University of
Environmental Design
Calgary, Alberta
www.ucalgary.ca/evds

Carleton University
School of Architecture
Ottawa, Ontario
www.arch.carleton.ca

Dalhousie University
Faculty of Architecture and
Planning
Halifax, Nova Scotia
www.dal.ca/architecture

Manitoba, University of
Department of Architecture
Winnipeg, Manitoba
umanitoba.ca/faculties/
architecture

Toronto, University of
Faculty of Architecture,

Landscape, and Design
Toronto, Ontario
www.ald.utoronto.ca

McGill University
School of Architecture
Montreal, Quebec
www.mcgill.ca/arch

Montreal, Université de
School of Architecture
Montreal, Quebec
www.arc.umontreal.ca

Université Laval
School of Architecture
Quebec City, Quebec
www.arc.ulaval.ca

Waterloo, University of
School of Architecture
Waterloo, Ontario
www.architecture.uwaterloo.ca/

Career Profiles

Roy Abernathy, AIA, IDSA, LEED AP
President
Jova/Daniels/Busby
Atlanta, Georgia

Kathyrn Anthony, Ph.D.
Professor
School of Architecture
Department of Landscape
Architecture
Gender and Women's Studies
Program
University of Illinois at Urbana-
Champaign
Champaign, Illinois

F. Michael Ayles, AIA
Director of Operations
Antinozzi Associates
Stratford, Connecticut

Robert Beckley, FAIA
Professor and Dean Emeritus
Taubman College of Architecture
and Urban Planning
University of Michigan
Ann Arbor, Michigan

Joseph Bilello, Ph.D., AIA
Dean
College of Architecture and
Planning
Ball State University
Muncie, Indiana

Dianne Blair Black, AIA
Vice President
RTKL Associates Inc.
Baltimore

H. Alan Brangman, AIA
University Architect
Georgetown University
Washington, D.C.

William Carpenter, Ph.D., FAIA
Associate Professor
School of Architecture, Civil
Engineering Technology and
Construction
Southern Polytechnic State
University
Marietta, Georgia

President
Lightroom
Decatur, Georgia

Barbara Crisp
Principal
Underwood + Crisp
Tempe, Arizona

Jacob R. Day
President (2004–2005)
American Institute of
Architecture Students
Washington, D.C.

Margaret DeLeeuw
Graduate, B.S. in Architecture
University of Maryland
Chester, Connecticut

Richard A. Eribes, Ph.D., AIA
Professor and Dean Emeritus
College of Architecture,
Planning, and Landscape
Architecture
University of Arizona
Tuscon, Arizona

Thomas Fowler IV
Associate Professor and
Associate Head
College of Architecture and
Environmental Design
California Polytechnic State
University — San Luis Obispo
San Luis Obispo, California

Douglas Garofalo, FAIA
Professor
School of Architecture
University of Illinois—Chicago
Chicago

President, Garofalo
Architects, Inc.
Chicago

Lynsey Gemmell
Architect II
Holabird & Root
Chicago

Chris Glapinski
Student
University of Miami
Oconomowoc, Wisconsin

Christopher J. Gribbs,
ASSOCIATE AIA
Senior Director, Convention
The American Institute of
Architects
Washington, D.C.

David R. Groff
Intern Architect
Dalgliesh, Gilpin and Paxton
Architects
Charlottesville, Virginia

Gaines Hall, FAIA
Vice President
Kirkegaard & Associates
Chicago

Michelle Hunter
Lead Designer
Garage Takeover — Discovery
Channel
Washington, D.C.

Ahkilah Z. Johnson
Senior Analyst
Cherokee Northeast, LLC
East Rutherford, New Jersey

Carolyn G. Jones, AIA
Associate Principal
Callison Architecture, Inc.
Seattle, Washington

Elizabeth Kalin
Architectural Intern
Studio Gang Architects
Chicago

Grace H. Kim, AIA
Principal and Co-founder
Schemata Workshop, Inc.
Seattle, Washington

Nathan Kipnis, AIA
Principal
Nathan Kipnis Architects, Inc.
Evanston, Illinois

Shannon Kraus, AIA
Associate Architect
HKS Architects
Dallas, Texas

Jack Kremers, AIA
Professor
Department of Architecture
Judson College
Elgin, Illinois

Clark E. Llewellyn, AIA
Director
School of Architecture
Montana State University
Bozeman, Montana

Patricia Saldana Natke, AIA
Principal and President
Urban Works Ltd.
Chicago

Joseph J. Nickol
Graduate, Bachelor of
Architecture
University of Notre Dame
Coeur D'Alene, Idaho

Monica Pascatore, LEED
Freelance Designer
P Inc.
Baltimore

Casius Pealer, J.D.
Associate
Reno & Cavanaugh, PLLC
Washington, D.C.

Co-founder
ARCHVoices

Andy Pressman, FAIA
Professor
University of New Mexico
Albuquerque, New Mexico

Editor-in-Chief, *Graphic
Standards*
The American Institute of
Architects
Washington, D.C.

Kathryn T. Prigmore, FAIA
Project Manager
HDR Architecture
Alexandria, Virginia

Katherine S. Proctor, FCSI, CDT,
AIA
Director of Facilities
Jewelry Television
Knoxville, Tennessee

Tamara Redburn, ASSOCIATE AIA
Intern Architect
Fanning/Howey Associates, Inc.
Novi, Michigan

Carol Ross Barney, FAIA
Founder and President
Ross Barney + Jankowski, Inc.
Chicago

W. Stephen Saunders, AIA
Principal
Eckenhoff Saunders Architects,
Inc.
Chicago

Roger Schluntz, FAIA
Dean and Professor
School of Architecture and
Planning
University of New Mexico
Albuquerque, New Mexico

Ed Shannon, AIA
Assistant Professor
Department of Architecture
Judson College
Elgin, Illinois

Trinity Simons, ASSOCIATE AIA
Vice President (2004–2005)
American Institute of
Architecture Students
Washington, D.C.

W. Cecil Steward, FAIA
Dean Emeritus
College of Architecture
University of Nebraska—
Lincoln

President/CEO
Joslyn Castle Institute for
Sustainable Communities
Omaha and Lincoln, Nebraska

Eric Taylor, ASSOCIATE AIA
Photographer
Taylor Design & Photography,
Inc.
Fairfax Station, Virginia

Randall J. Tharp, RA
Senior Vice President
A. Epstein and Sons
International, Inc.
Chicago

Lois Thibault, RA
Coordinator of Research
U.S. Architectural and
Transportation Barriers
Compliance Board (Access
Board)
Washington, D.C.

Max Underwood, AIA
Professor
School of Architecture and
Landscape Architecture
College of Design and
Environmental Design
Arizona State University
Tempe, Arizona

Architect and Principal
Underwood + Crisp
Tempe, Arizona

Lisa Van Veen, ASSOCIATE AIA
Architectural Designer
Design Forward
Pasadena, California

Scott Windley
Accessibility Specialist
U.S. Architectural and Trans-
portation Barriers Compliance
Board (Access Board)
Washington, D.C.

Brad Zuger
Student
University of Nebraska—
Lincoln
Springfield, Nebraska

Index

A

Abernathy, Roy, 9, 33, 50-53, 79, 164, 268

Accreditation, 120

ACSA, *see* Association of Collegiate Schools of Architecture

Action plan, 230

ADA, *see* American with Disabilities Act

Advanced placement, 72

AIA, *see* American Institute of Architects

AIAS, *see* American Institute of Architecture
    Students

American with Disabilities Act, 30

American Institute of Architects (AIA), 74, 194, 271

American Institute of Architecture Students (AIAS), 126, 271

Anthony, Kathyrn, 6, 32-33, 45-46, 78, 267

Application process, 104-106
   application, 104
   personal statement, 104
   portfolio, 106
   recommendations, 10
   test scores, 105
   transcripts, 105

Architect:
   careers of, 223-232
   definition of, 1-4,
   education of, 69-75, 94-106, 117-127
   employment projection, 31
   employment statistics, 31
   experience of, 157-161, 190-197
   profile of, 31-32
   tasks, 2

Architect Registration Examination (ARE), 96, 161, 196

Architectural photography, 134

Architecture
    definition, 5-10
    future of, 261-270
Architecture in education, 71
Arquitectos, 127
Association of Collegiate Schools of Architecture (ACSA), 271
Ayles, F. Michael, 9, 33, 83, 164, 208-211, 265

B

Beckley, Robert, 6, 34, 76, 128-131, 163, 262
BEEP, *see* Built Environment Education Program
Bilello, Joseph, 7, 34, 82, 219-221
Black, Dianne Blair, 5, 33, 76, 146-148, 268
Boy Scouts of America Explorer Post, 75
Brangman, H. Alan, 7, 33, 76, 237-239, 262
Built Environment Education Program (BEEP), 71, 278

C

CACB, *see* Canadian Architectural Certification Board
Canadian Architectural Certification Board, 96-97
Career designing, 224-230
    assessing, 224
    exploring, 226
    decision-making, 227
    planning, 229
Career paths:
    nontraditional, 230-231
    traditional, 230
Career profiles, 293-295
Carpenter, William, 5, 21-22, 34, 79, 163
Center for the Understanding of the Built Environment (CUBE), 71, 278
Certificate program, *see* Programs, certificate
Certificate, NCARB, 95, 197
Chicago Architecture Foundation, 71, 75, 278
Community college, 95, 98
Community service, 48, 126
Construction Specification Institute, 206
Cooperative education, 101, 159
Coursework:
    art, 73
    CAD, 73
    construction materials and methods, 122
    design, 73, 121

drawing, 73, 97
electives, 121
    architectural, 97, 123
English, 72
history and theory, 97, 121–122
humanities, 121
mathematics, 72, 121
physics, 72
professional practice, 97, 121–122, 150
social sciences, 121
studio, 97, 121
technology, 97, 121–122
Cover letters, *see* Job searching
Crisp, Barbara, 8, 34, 78, 163, 216–218
Criteria, selecting a program, 97–104
    academic structure, 98
    budget, 98
    career programs, 101
    closeness to home, 98
    cost, 99
    degree, 99
    enrollment, 100
    faculty, 100
    financial aid, 99
    institution size, 98
    level of confidence, 97
    locale, 98
    personality type, 98
    philosophy/approach, 100
    postgraduate plans, 101
    public *vs.* private, 99
    reputation/tradition, 100
    resources, academic, 100
    school type, 98
    special programs, 100
    student body, 101
Critical thinking, 122
Criticism, 122
CUBE, *see* Center for the Understanding of the Built Environment

D

Day, Jacob, 35, 82, 107–110, 268
Degrees:
    Accredited Professional, 94

Bachelor of Architectural Studies, 95
Bachelor of Architecture, 94, 97
Bachelor of Environmental Design, 95
Bachelor of Science, Pre-professional, 94
Bachelor of Science in Architectural Studies, 95
Bachelor of Science in Architecture, 94
Doctor of Architecture, 94, 96
Doctor of Philosophy, 96
Dual, 124
Post-professional, 96
Master of Architecture, 94–95, 97
Master of Architecture/Master of Business Administration, 18, 124
Deleeuw, Margaret, 5, 35, 73–74, 76, 111–113, 267
Design-build, 235
Design Competitions, 59
DesignIntelligence, 104, 284
Disability, 30
Diversity, 32, 48
Double Major, 124

E

Ecole des Beaux-Arts, 11
Electives, *see* also Coursework
Emerging Professional Companion, 194, 221, 284
Erector Set, 70
Eribes, Richard, 9, 35, 79, 163, 202–204, 265
Experience, 96, 158
    career-related, 161
    definition of, 158
Externship, 159

F

Fowler, IV, Thomas, 10, 27–29, 33, 80, 165, 263
Froebel Blocks, 70
Froebel, Friedrich, 70

G

Garofalo, Douglas, 5, 35, 42–44, 76, 164, 262
Gemmell, Lynsey, 6, 35, 80, 185–186, 268
Glapinski, Chris, 35, 87–90
Gribbs, Christopher, 7, 35, 82, 255–258, 267
Groff, David, 9, 35, 77, 173–176, 268

H

HABS, *see* Historic American Building Survey
Hall, Gaines, 9, 35, 83, 139-140, 163, 265
Historic American Building Survey (HABS), 174-175, 256, 278
Hunter, Michelle, 7, 35, 181-184

I

IDP, *see* Intern Development Program
Independent Study, 124
Information Interviewing, 227
Intern Development Program (IDP), 157, 194
    training areas, 195
Internship, 101, 159
    summer, 75

J

Job searching, 190-193
    assessment, 190
    commitment, 192
    connections, 190
    experience, 192
    help, 190
    interim positions, 191
    portfolio, 191
    research, 190
    resumes/cover letters, 191
    transition, 192
Johnson, Ahkilah, 7, 36, 248-252
Jones, Carolyn, 6, 36, 54-56, 78, 165
Jury, 121

K

Kalin, Elizabeth, 6, 36, 77, 169-172
Kelly, Brian, 121-122, 127
Kim, Grace, 5, 37, 79, 156, 165, 198-201, 262
Kipnis, Nathan, 5, 37, 141-145, 262
Kraus, Shannon, 10, 15-20, 37, 83, 269
Kremers, Jack, 5, 38, 64-67, 81, 163, 267

L

Leadership in Energy and Environmental Design, 168
Learning by design, 71–72
Lecture series, 75, 126
LEED, *see* Leadership in Energy and Environmental Design
Legos, 72, 169
Lincoln Logs, 70
Linton, Harold, 192
Llewellyn, Clark, 38, 81, 152–155, 265

M

Masonry camp, 201
Mentoring, 126, 155, 200, 284
Minors, 124
Mission statement, 230

N

NAAB, *see* National Architectural Accrediting Board
Natke, Patricia Saldana, 6, 39, 47–49, 79, 165, 264
National Architectural Accrediting Board (NAAB), 31, 94, 96, 103, 117, 271
    Accreditation Program Report (APR), 103
    Accredited Programs, 285–292
    Student Performance Criteria, 117
    Visiting Team Report (VTR), 103
National Building Museum, 70, 278
National Council of Architectural Registration Boards, 31, 194, 272
National Organization of Minority Architects, 126, 273
NCARB, *see* National Council of Architectural Registration Boards, 31
Newhouse Program and Architecture Competition, 75
Nickol, Joe, 9, 38, 80, 114–116, 268
NOMA, see National Organization of Minority Architects

O

Off-campus programs, 125
Odyssey of the Mind, 75

P

Pascatore, Monica, 7, 38, 78, 166–168, 264
Pealer, Casius, 9, 38, 82, 244–247, 263
Peace Corps, 26, 245, 280
Perzynski, Dana, 75

Portfolio, *see* Application process *or* Job searching
Positions, 161
  full-time, 161
  interim, 191
  part-time, 161
  summer, 89, 161, 171
Pressman, Andy, 149–151
Prigmore, Kathryn, 9, 38, 77, 135–138, 164, 267
Proctor, Kathy, 7, 39, 164, 205–207, 231, 269
Programs
  after-school, 73, 75
  certificate, 124
  high school summer, 73–74, 89
  selection of, 96–104

R

Ranking of architecture programs, 103
Raskin, Eugene, 4
Real estate development, 250
Reciprocity, 197
Redburn, Tamara, 38, 77, 177–180, 265
Research:
  architectural, 221
  with faculty, 158
Resources, preparation: Pre-high school, 71
Resources, selecting a program, 102–104
  Accreditation Program Report (APR), 103
  admissions counselor, 103
  campus visits, 102
  Guide to Architecture Schools, 102
  New England Career Day in Architecture, 102
  promotional materials, 102
  ranking of architecture programs, 103
  Students, Faculty, Alumni, and Architects, 103
  Visiting Team Report (VTR), 103
Resumes, *see* Job searching
Retail Design, 54
Review, 121
Ross Barney, Carol, 5, 23–26, 33, 49, 76, 262

S

Salaries, 31
Saunders, W. Stephen, 5, 39, 82, 132–34, 165, 270
Schluntz, Roger, 40, 57–60, 76, 267
Shadowing an architect, 75, 158

Shannon, Edward, 7, 80, 212-215, 266
Simons, Trinity, 78, 84-86, 264
Sketch, 73-74
Skills, most important, 33-41
Steward, W. Cecil, 5, 11-14, 40, 80, 264
Students for Congress for New Urbanism, 127
Student organizations, 126
Studio, 121
Studio culture, 108
Study abroad, 112, 125, 127

T

Taylor, Eric, 7, 40, 80, 240-243
Tharp, Randall, 5, 41, 76, 165, 233-236, 263
Thibault, Lois, 7, 80, 253-254
Tinkertoys, 70
Transition, 192-193

U

Underwood, Max, 7, 41, 61-63, 78, 165, 267
Urban Planning, 130-131

V

Van Veen, Associate AIA, Lisa, 5, 41, 81, 187-189, 267
Volunteer, 158

W

Waldrep, Lee W., 99
Windley, Scott, 30
Wright, Eric Lloyd, 70
Wright, Frank Lloyd, 70
Women in the profession, 32
Work program, 94

Y

Young Architects Forum, 210

Z

Zuger, Brad, 6, 41, 77, 91-93, 120